Glimpses into the Life of an Ordinary Guy, Volume II

Glimpses into the Life of an Ordinary Guy, Volume II

Letters 1938-1946

Bill

William Rourke Sisson, M.D

To order additional copies of this book, contact:
Xlibris Corporation
1-888-795-4274
www.Xlibris.com
Orders@Xlibris.com
28680

CONTENTS

A big thank you to my family for giving me the time to work on this with Dad and to Bob and his family for all of their hospitality when I came to Albuquerque to work on it. Also thank you to Bob Inman and everyone else who has given their encouragement. A million thanks to my mother for fixing meals, getting healthy, and allowing Dad and me to have time to work on this plus all of her hours of researching, finding photos, and proofing.

Thank you, Dad, for your dedication to the project. And thanks for sharing.

Teresa Sisson Rijks

The Pacific—
end of World War II

April, 1945 – August, 1945

Letter No. 62

Thursday April 19,1945

Dear Tom and Bill:

I got scolded last night when Dad came home and found that I had not put the slip that Mr. Richert gave him for it had where Milton lives and all on the back of it but I had not looked on the back so did not know that so will send it to you tonight and sort of exonerate myself, perhaps.

My! what a day this has been as far as weather has been concerned. Bright and pretty and just right for temperature. I washed the bedspread, rugs etc and they have dried so well.

As I was out setting the hose Lucile Klinker (Houghton) came by on her way to the hospital. Their baby has been in the hospital for three weeks and most of that time running a high fever but the doctors or at least Dr. Davis who is taking care of him, could not find out what was the trouble. They have given him all kinds of tests, but still did not know. Last night his ears began to show signs of trouble so they lanced them and he is much better today so guess it was there the trouble was all the while.

Tom, at last I think that I am really getting to know your little tricks and now know why you thought Judy was six months old, and Bobby's age too.

Bob Green is home after finishing his 30 missions as a gunner and will go, after a little time here to Santa Ana for reassignment.

Mrs. Guthrie called me just after dinner today asking me to go with her to Rocky Ford for plants. It was a temptation since the day was so grand but when I got busy washing this morning I did not do the dishes and had not gotten to them when she called so thought I had better stay home and do them so Dad would not have to help when he got home.

Dad and Mac did not go to the Springs today but will go Saturday instead. Hope it is as nice then as it was today.

We got the enlargement of you and Bob this morning, Bill and thank you very much for it. It is very good and Dad is going to have it framed. We also get a lovely picture of Johnny Lee. He is really a fine looking boy.

In over the fence last night it told about Walter and Don's discovery that their folks had known each other in the way back when, and I will send it to you Tom so Walter and Don can see their names in the Daily paper. I will send the paper in a box which I will send tomorrow or next day so when you see that little cut out space you will know what it was.

I think that it is a little strange that you have not yet gotten a package form me but surely they will start and then you should get one about once a week for that is about the way I have been sending them to you.

Bill, you say that you will not be playing golf and so wont need the balls but they are already on their way so maybe if you have left (that was one of the reasons that I thought you are due for a change) Bob can use them. I hope you dont leave before the angel food arrives and that you can eat it. Maybe it will be hard as a rock.

Tom do you get a letter every day or do they pile up and come several at a time and then none for a while like Buds do.

Our new water softener and new hot water heater are doing just fine. The water is nice and soft and hot. We do not any longer have to have a hose in the basement for it is piped so we can just run it off right into the drain and too we put 100 lbs into a brine tank and that does for three softenings and the process of softening is much simpler for all one has to do is just turn one lever. The basement is such a mess after all the plumbing work being done down there I wonder if I will ever get it clean again.

I am sitting here in my bath robe having had my bath in preparation for the party so now better go and finish the job or Mr. Sisson will beat me ready.

*   *   *

Letter No. 63

Friday April 20,1945

Dear Bill and Tom:

Last night after I had the letters all sealed up I saw that I had not put in the slip of paper with the information about Milton so now I will try very hard to get it in tonight.

I did a lot of talking over the phone this morning so did not get any work done and this afternoon I went out to the hospital and was well repaid for the director gave me a package of marshmallows for you, Tom so next week I can send them, I have already sent a box this week. Dad mailed it at noon. I put in some cheese and raisins, some little crackers and a couple of candy bars with the Democrats and funnies for packing.

Mrs. McKellar just called a little while ago and we had quite a visit. Blossom Day is a week from Sunday so she thought that would be a good time for us to come up so no doubt we will. If you are not still with Klegg she does not know it either but Mrs. Bond said it was too bad that you were separated from the rest. How about it? She says that he has the purple heart and seemed to know all about it altho she said that Klegg did not tell her. She said that it was written up in Mar.2, Time and Life but we can not find anything so must be the wrong issue.

Dad saw Vernon Konkel down town this morning. He is here after just having gotten his Navy wings and is to go to Florida from here.

Bill I was worrying about your not having any light dress clothes for the occasions like the dance Bobs unit had so asked John about it and he told me that "We dont dress in formal clothes out there ever" so guess you are glad that you did not spend much on things like that.

Was talking to Eleanor at noon and she has a nibble on an apartment which is to be made in a house over in the 400 block on Raton, and she actually said that if the rent was a good deal she could get a job to help pay for it. I surely hope she does for it is terrible to just sit around like she does.

Dad was having swell luck last night staying at the head table where he began with Mrs. McCartney when he pulled some sort of a boner and that upset him so he immediately went down and his luck left him. I guess the boner was not any worse than lots of the rest of us were doing but it just got under his hide. We are going to have the club the next time, which this time will be next week. I will have both clubs in the one week but that will be fine for then I will only have to clean the house once.

The rotary club here is to have their silver jubilee on the 2nd of May and are planning a big dinner party for the occasion. I am to be one committee for the decorations another little job but with the two clubs out of the way, the house cleaning done I wont mind. We have a Mission at the church that week too so I will be a little busy I guess. Paper is full so will stop now.

*   *   *

4/21/45

Dear Mother and Dad,

Today was quite an enjoyable day. This morning we went to the wedding of Carl Kaeser, a friend of Bobs. We had a lot of fun fixing up his car after it. We met several nurses. The couple are both Catholic and the ceremony was in the Catholic chapel.

The most phenomenal event of the day was that we met a nurse by the name of Eileen Sisson. As a matter of fact her name lead to our meeting. I met a chaplain the other day who told me of this girl and where she is stationed. This morning several of the nurses present were from the same place and also remarked on the similarity of our names. Inman & I decided the only thing to do was to meet this girl and see if she were worthy of the name and she turned out to be quite worthy of it—at least in appearance. I hope to get to see her again.

Following this short meeting we went to see the nurses we had a picnic with last week who are on a hospital ship. They showed is all around the ship and had us for dinner. So you see we saw quite a few women today.

I really appreciated the cartoon of the doctor and his lady patient. That is surely true and would fit exactly here if the woman were a coon instead.

Have not much news for the present so shall close

Love, Bill

*   *   *

April 23, 1945

Dear Mother & Dad,

Yesterday after Mass and a swell Sunday dinner of steak I went down to see Bill Davidson who has been here for a few days. I just barely did get to see him, and had quite a little difficulty in doing it. I then went over and spent the rest of the day with Bob. He is working pretty hard these days. We went to a movie last night, and then I returned to the Base here.

It has rained all day here which interfered with a golf game I had in mind and also a spear fishing outing. So I've been sitting around the barracks all day reading a mystery story and a bunch of new magazines they got in at the ship's store. We aren't working at all anymore except being on call one night a week. We are just sort of waiting.

Thanks for the clipping of the engagement of Houston Alexander. I remember when I saw his mother and him in San Francisco—She thought he and I were quite intelligent not getting married. Well—if I had a good chance I'd get married, too.

One day last week I went over and saw Woodruff and Mayhew. Everything seems to be going along very well with them. I also saw Brown and Inman that afternoon; so had quite a bit of La

Junta that afternoon. Did I tell you that Bob & I had dinner one evening with the Browns at the Moana. Some of the fellows in Floyds office took care of Robert K. while we had dinner.
I think that is all the news I have for the present.

Love, Bill

PS: You are psychic, Mother.

*   *   *

Letter No. 64

April 23, 1945

Dear Tom and Bill:
Weather report first. Cloudy with some rain today and somewhat colder. If it keeps up Aunt Fan may not come in as she planned on Wednesday so Dad and Mac may not go to the springs tomorrow as they planned either. It wont make a bit of difference in the ladies playing bridge so I will have that in spite of the weather.
There were two letters from you Tom this morning one written the 12th and one the 14th, this last you see came in about nine days which is fine. No doubt the other one was in the office yesterday.
Yes, we do like things by the Dozen, Tom, and are glad that you spoke of it.
I was glad that your letters were so full of Klegg for now I can tell his mother that you are still together for some one has kept telling her that you had been separated and Don's mother thought so too, I wonder how that got started. We know that he was not flying for a while but I still cant find about it in Time but maybe next week when we go up she can make us straight on it.
The Strains still have not had any further word of Dean other than that he is missing. It would be wonderful if you do find out something about him. They have sort of lost hope, for it has been so long since they got that word.

I see now why you wanted Bud's Belgium address and too bad he moved before you got there. We still wonder what and how Etc you got there and why but suppose that will all wait till you come home. Before you get this Berlin will be in Allied hands for it is almost there right now. I just cant see why sane people would not give up and save some of their people and towns. I guess they are just like a crazy bull dog that gets hold and wont let go.

I saw Mr. Black in the store the other day and asked him how Roy liked B-29s by this time and he said "Oh better but still he would like to be doing the flying himself. You know how that is."

Joan just came over to try out a couple of popular pieces and is struggling away about like I would have to do, picking them out with one finger.

Last night Dad and I went to the Davis party and when the playing was over and she made the husbands and wives add their scores together for the prize and Dad and I got the booby but were we glad for it was a box of Russel Stover's candy and I bet you can guess where it will go. Yes to England. Everyone asked us to which one we would send it but since Bill gets candy and Tom doesn't it is not hard to decide we told them. The first prize was a set of four bottles of nail polish and as Dad cant use that and I hardly ever do it was good to be low instead of high, for once.

Your letter of the 17th, Bill came and I guess I have told you that the angel food is on the way even if you do think it best not to try to send it.

Yes Julia Winchell is still at C.C.

What you said about Floyds wife is the same idea every one has who has seen her, that she is like Gregg. I am glad however that you think she has a better personality and I do hope she is nicer to his mother than poor Gregg was. Guess I told you that we got the enlargement and Tom too will have it to look at and now since he has a whole dresser to him self can sit it up there and gaze at it all the time.

Poor Dad had an inning with the furnace at the apartments again this morning. The first thing he knew the ladies down there were cold and there wasnot a bit of heat in the furnace so he had to go look up the janitor to find that the furnace was clogged up some way or other. I guess they got it straightened out for the time being at least.

If I think that I can spare the time from my cleaning etc in preparation for the clubs Dad and I may go to the show tonight for everyone says that it is good, Old St. Louis, I believe the name is.

This morning is all my effort to be shining for the clubs I cleaned the floor of our closet and then varnished it and at noon when I started to go down town with Dad I found that I had isolated myself from all my clothes even my coat so have had to go in my house dress all afternoon and a coat of Aunt Fan's. Your mother is a very bright woman?

Dad is quite disgusted with my too now for when he got out of the car as we came from town I said I would go to the store in the car and get some cokes which I wanted to serve the ladies tomorrow afternoon but as I turned around I killed the engine and the darned thing would not start for me. I left it a while and came in the house but when I went out again it still would not go so he has gone now to coax it a little. I bet it starts too, and then he has the laugh on me.

Now I will stop for I have run out of stuff etc.

*   *   *

Letter No. 65

Tuesday April 24,1945

Dear Bill and Tom:

Have just finished our bite so will write you a little before we have another meeting here. This one is for the purpose of planning the decorations for the Rotary party and I hope will not be long for Dad and I are both a little weary tonight. I, because the bridge club met here this afternoon and Dad because had had a big day at the office, several deals which had to be closed up today. Then when he got home he cut the lawn in the back and it does look nice. I think that the vigero which we put on it has done it a lot of good for it is such a dark green and seems so thick.

Aunt Betty took home the dollar for high score this afternoon. There were just eight of us playing today. Mrs. Morse came, the first time that she has been to the club for a long long while. She says that the doctor in Pueblo thinks that Bet should have another operation but that he wants them to go to Dr. Packard or Mayos before he would do anything. I wish they would go to Mayos but they think they will go to Dr. Packard. It would be better for Bet to be away back there for then she would have to stay down as long as the doctors say she should. In Denver she will be going to her sisters and when she does that she wont stay in bed or do much of any thing that they tell her to do and consequently undoes all the operation has accomplished or is supposed to accomplish.

Had a letter from Shirley today telling me that Ed has arrived in Belgium and also that she will be down this week. Her plans were not fully made for if the Gardners have room, no company, then Nancy wants her to stay there but if they dont have then she and Eddie will be with us. I hope she does not come at the same time that Bill W. does. It will be fine if Aunt Fan is at ranch but if all are here at the same time guess some one will have to go to the basement.

I served the ladies date bars and cokes this afternoon and there were three of them did not drink the coke so guess I did not choose so well for them but it was easy anyway. I am going to wash in the morning, the first time in about three weeks.

Aunt Fan is coming in in the morning and will bring sweet cream as well as a jar full to churn but I may have to wait till Friday to churn if we have the other club Thursday night. We may put it off as Clyde Davis' mother is very low. So they and the Hays (Mildred Hays is Clyde's sister) will probably not want to come.

They say that Chris Hayes (no relation) husband is going back over seas. Dont know whether he has asked for it or what the deal is and I dont think that he finished his missions when he was over there. He got sick or something. Will go now and write more tomorrow.

*   *   *

Letter No. 66

Wednesday April 25,1945

Dear Tom and Bill:

The laundry for this week and the past two weeks is all done tonight and I am very glad it is over. Now tomorrow I can iron them for we are not going to have the club tomorrow night since there would be so many who could not come. Will have it in two weeks for I dont want it next week as it would follow the Rotary party and I dont think that the men especially like two nights in a row. I know my man doesn't and I am not too keen about it either.

Aunt Fan came in today and over the bombing range for the sergeant who looks after the range out there told them that there is not much bombing going on just now and that it would be all right for them to go through. She brought us milk, cream and eggs and a jar of cream to churn. The cream that we get at the store seems very much like milk now that we are used to our own but ofcourse it is not quite so fattening either.

It rained a little here last night but there was not any at the ranch but sort of streaky between here and there.

Mrs. Davis is much better today. The doctor gave her penicillin and she got a good reaction but she is 84 so one can expect any thing in her case I guess. She had a fever of 104 1/2 at noon yesterday when the doctor took her to the hospital. Today she does not remember anything about going up there.

Our yard looks nice and green now since the snow and rain and the dandelions! Whew! But since my cleaning is done and the partys over I will get out and make a cleaning on those in a hurry.

Dean Kendall razed us women so much about not doing our duty in not answering the Rotary invitation and kept saying that there were not going to be but such a few at it that some of us decided if he liked to get these answers so much we would give him a dose of it so we sent him a few like this using crazy names.

Mr. and Mrs. Med. O. Lark
accept with pleasure etc

Mrs. and Mrs. Wee Wren will be pleased to accept etc.

So far I think he does not know who is doing it and hope we can keep him from finding out.

Must go now and get ready for church. Next week it will be church every night, during the Mission.

*　　*　　*

4/26/45

Dear Mother & Dad,

I am afraid this will be a short note though I would like to make it a long one.

Tuesday night Bob & I had dates and we went to the officers Club where Bob is stationed. I had a date with Eileen Sisson and we really had a grand time. She was a good date and would really like to see more of her—but she left her rain coat in the car—so Bob will have to return it for me.

Last night we had more dates with army nurses. As a matter of fact we almost had two dates apiece. When it rains it pours. There was a little mix up somewhere and we had two extra girls. Fortunately we ran into some friends of Bob's who did not have dates and they showed them a good time.

In addition to our date troubles neither Bob or I had any money, but fortunately before the meal ended we ran into another friend of Bob's who helped us out.

I did not have a place to put your delicious jelly so I gave it to Dr. Carter.

You can now write to me at the following address:

G-10 COMP62
c/o Commandant NOB Navy # 3256
c/o FPO San Francisco, Calif.

I think that is all the news I have for the present. Till Later

Love, Bill

PS: Am enclosing some pictures Bob and I took at the Mormon Temple.

*   *   *

Letter No. 67

Thursday April 26,1945

Dear Bill and Tom:

Dad and Aunt Fan are attending a bank meeting this eve so will be a little late for their supper and I will write you before they get here.

The plumber just left. Glad that he got here this afternoon for the toilet in the big bath room clogged up today and it makes it quite inconvenient for aunt Fan when she gets up in the night to come clear out to this one. Think that they will start next week to put in new pipe clear out to the alley. That is the only way we will have any peace from this for the plumber says that those roots are all along and just to get some of them out only helps till stuff catches in another bunch of them.

Aunt Betty had a letter from Justine today and Johnny is reassigned to San Angelo and she is sort of glad for there are so many worse places that might have gone to and then she does not have to go through the seige of hunting a place to live, which is always a battle when she goes to a new station.

When I was at the store this morning Margurete told me that Harold is on his way across, has been gone from Frisco about a week and perhaps will land in Hawaii at least for a while so I gave her your address, Bill and also your phone number so you might be hearing from him sometime. I also got his address and will put it in your letter.

We read all sort of guesses of what the boys in Europe will be doing when V-E day arrives and today one reporter stated that the pilots of the B-24s and B-17s will be brought here for training on these new ships and the B-29s. There is a fellow here now, Robert Portman who was Sanitation engineer here, who has been in Italy for a long while. He is on leave in the states for three weeks and then heads for the Pacific and he thinks that a lot of the boys from that area will be doing the same thing. wonder if Ed will be in the army occupation.

Seems like the less I have to do the less I do do so today has just fittered away and all the things I should have done remain for to-morrow. I just went in to turn the radio on for the news but all one gets today is the conference. I heard Edward Stettenius and then the China delegate began so I stopped and will now continue my note to you boys.

Had a letter from Virginia Winchell this morning telling me that Bill is on a meatless diet so will have to hunt up some chickens or fish for him. He comes next Monday night but will only tarry till Wednesday. We will have to talk fast to get in all the gossip etc.

Bill, I added a note to Tom's letter last night which I did not put on yours concerning Gene Rourke. We had a letter from Uncle John in which he stated that his and Hatties guess is that Gene is, or rather the Benson is in the English channel. If so it might be that he would have a chance to get to see Tom for I think he get several days shore leave once in a while. Hope he has your correct address but I believe he has all right.

There is some talk now that the B-17s cant be used at this base for they tear up the runways but I still see them flying overhead so guess the change has not been made yet if it is to be. My! how do all the rumors get around anyway.

Shirley has not shown up nor have I heard any thing further from her so maybe she meant next week that she and the baby are coming down.

Tom was your trip to Belgium a military secret? If not how did you happen to go there. Evidently not on a mission for I know you had been sort of thinking about it for some time when you asked for the Belgium address of Bud. Too bad he had to be moved for it would have been a thrill for both of you to have seen each other.

Will stop now and go get the bite ready for the folks when they get here. Aunt Fans hearing has been very much better lately and today she has gone to the bank meeting without the aid. She has not been wearing it for a few weeks and really hears quite well. She wonders if Dr. Lassens treatments are just now doing the good expected of them or what has made the change. It almost seemed that it started to improve when she began to wear the aid.

Clyde Davis mother is very much better today. She is a marvel at her 84 years.

*   *   *

27 April 1945

Dear Mrs. Sisson:

Just a note. but thought you would like news of Bill and also of the good jelly you sent him. He had an unopened jar and when he left he gave it to me - the "raspberry apple 1944". It was superb and all the officers here enjoyed it on toast this morning. Made me a little homesick in fact - just like our mothers' good jellies!

Bill & I had fun while he was here - spear fishing, swimming, etc. Was sorry to see him go, but glad at least that his destination is now a relatively safe one. Am sure you would be glad to hear that also. He is with a good outfit and I am sure, will have an interesting and useful time. You can be ever so thankful that he is neither "sea-going" nor in a land combat outfit.

Perhaps one day, Bill can have jelly w/ us in Boston or even in Oregon, since I call both places "home" now. Wherever we have it, it can be no better than yours.

My best to you all,
Sincerely, Max G. Carter
M.G. Carter Lt. MC US NR
ABPD Navy 128, FPO, San Francisco

*   *   *

Letter 68

Friday April 27 1945

Dear Tom and Bill:

Before I go to the USO for a meeting I will get a short letter off to you. I was out at Grey Ladies this afternoon. Pink and I were the only ones who went today and of course we had fun at it but she always insists that she by me a candy bar and that is just more than I should eat at one time of such sweet stuff, neither good for stomach or figure.

Tonight the radio says the finish of the war in Europe is just a matter of days away which is good news for our waiting ears to hear.

Had written Mrs. McKellar after I got your letters of the 12 and 14th,Tom and today I had one from her saying she was glad I had written for it was longer ago that she had last heard from Klegg and I had told her that the letters were quite full of Klegg. We may not go up Sunday for the weather has been so unsettled and sort of nasty but if we do not go Sunday then we will put it off for another week or two for the next Sunday there is a High Mass here at nine and I could not go before that.

Jack Walker has gone up to Fairbanks, Alaska to that base where they start the planes off to Russia. He will be there a while and then comes back to Edmonton, Can. so Ann is not going till he gets back there I believe. They say that this is a very good opportunity for him.

Tom you have never said a word about the air model but is that not routine after five missions and an oak leaf after 10?

Your letter to Dad at the office came this morning Bill telling us about the nurse named Sisson whom you and Bob made it a point to see in order to know that she is worthy of the name. You did not tell us much about her. Where is her home? etc maybe she is a relative. That would be too bad since she is a good looking girl and a possibility. The nurses off the hospital ship really showed you a good time. Swell of them to have to dinner on the ship. Saw Horace Todd in the PO last night when I went in with your letters and he was asking all about you. He is especially interested in your doings, Tom for you know he is learning to fly. Says he has in about 46 hours.

Will run along now for I want to get home early and to bed. We had a little party last night after all. About six thirty the Richardsons called and said they were coming down for a game and in a few minutes the Moberlys also called so then I called the Kendalls and we had an eight some. They went home about 10:30 but I am tired tonight anyway.

*   *   *

Letter No. 69

Tuesday May 1, 1945

Dear Tom and Bill:

Your letter of the 26th, Bill came this morning giving us your change of address which means the Pacific for you, I guess. Glad that you got a date with the little Sisson person before you left there and also glad that you had a grand time. You really must have had some sort of mix-up when you found yourselves with two girls apiece. Usually you do not even have one and to have financial trouble beside, well you really did have a time. Anyway you will have all that to think about if and when you are farther away. Do wish we could know where you are heading but will just have to be a patient and in some way we will guess. Do you remember our little plan?

Bill and Julia arrived last night on schedule and now Julia has already gone back. I wish she could have stayed longer but Bill thought best that she get back to her classes. Think she would have stayed till tomorrow if he had okayed it. She is a very charming girl but has not changed much since the last times we have seen her. A little more sedate and quiet, perhaps but just the same Julia. Bill goes on tomorrow morning by plane at 9:30 to Wichita. He looks fine and they seem to like N.Y. very well.

We read your three letters, Tom and your one bill to them and they seemed to be very much interested in what you both are doing etc.

This, Tom is Bill's new address in case you should get this before you do one from him.

G-10 Comp 62
% Commandant N U B Navy#3256
%FPO San Francisco

I cut out some clippings of air raids made on the 16 and 17 of April and guess from some little clue that you were among those present, Tom to give Germany her last good beating from the air on those days.

Am glad that you have straightened us out on how you and Clegg are still together and not with the rest of the Caspar gang. Surely glad that there is occasionally some nice sunshiny weather over there when you can be out in the sun. Does not sound so bad when you tell about the boys lying on the lawn in the sunshine.

Dad seems to fare very well on the cigarettes but perhaps being in the drug business has something to do with it, it should have some advantages.

That trip like the one Jan. 1 in Caspar must have been quite an experience. Wont you have a lot to tell us when we see you again?

Guess I had better get my two men some thing ready for the supper as it has to be early for I go to the Library board meeting at seven and then I want to go to church so will let the two fellow have a good visit till I get home.

*   *   *

Letter No. 70

Thursday May 3,1945

Dear Bill and Tom:

The letter yesterday did not count in my numbering for it was not a community letter but hope you get it just the same.

I have just been down to the store to get them to weigh a box which I had ready to send to you, Tom and darn it was four oz. too heavy so took out a package of raisins and put in a package of cheese there being a difference of 7oz in the two so now it should be within limits. I wish I could get the dried fruit for I imagine that is what you would like best but it is just not to be had right now.

I am going to get some of those cans in which you can send candy and stuff to the Pacific with safety and send you something this week Bill so that in a couple of months after you have arrived where you are going you will have a package coming to you.

I read in the Colorado Alumnus that Dick Counley is in the Phillipines and had been out in that direction for 31 months so I wrote him a letter to Sterling and asked that it be forwarded to him in which I gave him your Address, Bill. Ofcourse you probably will not go in that direction but thought that it would do no harm anyway.

Everybody asks us what you have to say about what they are to do with you, Tom. So many think that you will be sent back to the states for some other kind of training etc. They ought to know that you will be about the last to know what the plan for you is but there are so many rumors going around here that everybody is asking everybody else everything.

The Rotary party last night was a big success and "they say" the decorations were simply beautiful. Justine take a bow. We did not stay for the dancing so did not get in on the really big party it seems for the report today is that it did not break up till about three this morning and as you can guess was a bit hilarious.

I went to Margs this morning to return the candle sticks which I had borrowed so could not get away without making a date with Bob for Saturday. He wanted to come home with me then but I had to get the dinner so the next best thing was a promise that he could come Saturday. Bud has been moved again so suppose that he is still further into Germany. He says they now have the best billets that he has had since he went into the army so he must be pretty well established. Marg says that the reason that she did not want to go to the Rotary party was that she went Christmas and it made her miss bud more than ever so she just wont go again.

The rotarians are making a strong pull for an international building (permanent headquarters) in Denver. It seems that the only other place that is making a strong bid is Chicago but that the committee of investigations unanimously approved Denver to the board of managers. It would be a something over a million dollar establishment so would mean quite a thing for Denver if they should be successful in getting it.

Will fix Dad a sandwitch now for I will be having to go to church ere long.

*   *   *

Letter No. 70

Friday May 4, 1945

Dear Tom and Bill:

Have just written you, Tom a little V-mail letter for if possible I want you to see Bud and Hem so thought that you would get that more quickly than you will this one.

The news tonight sounds as if the war in Europe is over and perhaps tomorrow they will actually declare it so. How I wish so much could be said of the Jap conflagration but maybe too we can hope that this cessation in Europe will affect the struggle over there. I should truly think that Hiro Hito would be at least a bit jittery.

I went out to Grey Ladies today and it was pretty warm, very different from yesterday and last night. All day yesterday I had to have a little fire going to keep the house warm enough to be comfortable.

So glad Tom that you finally got the flashlight for no doubt you have been needing it. I suppose now the evening are so light that you probably no longer have to use it to ride after supper.

We did not know what Flack leave is that the other boys in your barracks are on but Dad asked Mutt and she thinks that it means that they have gone on a rest leave. Dad will ask some of the overseas-returnees when he has a chance. We find out lots of things that way.

What you said about going to a party with Charlie Belt when you get to the states made us think that you might be trying to tell us that you may come if the big news you might have for us about the first is that.

I surely cant imagine your eating two and maybe four eggs for you breakfast but hope you can keep it up when you get home.

Bill I am going to write you some V-mail letters for maybe you will get them a little sooner than the others and I surely want you to get mail as quickly as possible when you arrive at you destination.

Will stop now and eat before I have to go to church.

*   *   *

5/5/45

Dear Dad & Mother,

I'm again enjoying an ocean voyage, that is I'm making an ocean voyage and making the best of it.

As usual the navy is giving us good chow. We have no waiting lines—The only prerequisite is that we have to be there on time.

The time does not go too slowly. Most of the day is spent in developing the melanoplores (Sp) in our skin. I have played some chess and bridge. I've read several books and am now reading David Copperfield which I've never read before. It is much like Dickens other books and is entertaining.

This shall have to convey my greetings for mothers day and your birthday. You know I will be thinking of you as I do everyday. I haven't much other relatable news.

All my love, Bill

William R. Sisson, Lt.jg, USNR

*   *   *

Letter No. 72

Monday May 7, 1945

Dear Tom and Bill:

The radio just said a little while ago that Churchill has announced that V-E day will be tomorrow so suppose that it will take place over here at the same time. It is so good to think there will be mo more fighting in at least one theater from now on. Hope the Japs get thoroughly scared by the thought of all the power which will soon be sent on them and pull out of the fight but I dont think they have sense enough for that.

We heard the report first this morning as I was getting breakfast over the Alex Dryer program so I just took out and went to Mass as my V-E day celebration of thanksgiving.

When I got home I thought that I would start the laundry but because it was cloudy and a bit wettish did not hang the clothes out to dry and now I wish I had for about noon it cleared up and is nice but a bit cold yet.

Have decided to have the club this Thursday so want to get that out of the way so as to have lots of time to chase the dirt out of the corners. Really there isnot too much yet after the house cleaning. I was up set today when I took out Bill's tux to air before I stored it in the basement. For some reason it had been in one of the closets upstairs. I found that about one dirty little moth had set himself on the inside of the legs and made two little tiny holes so I must get the rest of your things out and look them over lest there might be some more. I dont think that these little holes will amount to anything they are just pin pricks like, and I can draw them together but if I had not gotten them out I spect there would have been more damage.

I wrote Dr. Carter a letter this afternoon thanking him for his thoughtful note to us.

Dad asked a fellow down town this morning what a flack leave was and found out that our guess is correct, a rest leave which he said you get after 15 missions so you should be in line for it. I should think that Jim Ballard would be coming home for he was near his 30 missions but say Mrs. Leroy at church this morning and asked her if she did not think so and she said no that he said he might get to come this way and see the baby and all again but that he would go to the Pacific. Maybe he does not know.

Aunt Fans hearing has improved so much that she does not have to use the aid and hears quite well when we talk in a normal tone of voice. If her back did not hurt and she was not so stiff she would be really pretty fine now.

Aunt Hazel said that they had had such a good letter from you, Tom and they are hoping that you will get over to Belgium again and can see Ed. Lea has asked to be transferred to Denver or the Springs so they had written Shirley not to come on out so they must think the change will take place pretty soon. Ofcourse Hay is hoping it will, the sooner the quicker for her.

From reports over here the 9th army is to be kept there for the occupation. I think that would suit Bud lots better than going on to China except that it might be for a longer period.

Will write more tomorrow.

*   *   *

Letter No. 73

Tuesday May 8, 1945

Dear Tom and Bill:

Two of my letters have the same number, two 70's so yesterday I numbered the letter 72 so that I would be straight again, so if you dont get a letter No. 71 just remember there was no such animal.

This morning Mrs. Cranson called and as it had been a long time since we had had a conversation we had a lot to catch up on and talked an hour, maybe. Anyway she could tell us quite a few things that we had not gotten from your letter, Tom and visa-versa I think I was able to tell her some things Walt had not told them. I know how busy she is all the time so I dont call her very often and when I have there was no answer or else she was not at home.

Aunt Fan went out to the ranch this afternoon and I am glad she is there, she called about four, for it is getting to look as if it might rain. She said there had been quite a little shower at the head of Iron Canyon and a little even as far down as the house. At the head of the canyon it had made the water run and there were still some places where the water was standing so it must have been quite a little shower. Hope that there was enough to make a little water in the reservoir.

Mary was in at noon today too and had a letter from Dud which she read to us. He had not been very busy but had had three ambulance calls. His brother Claude had been thru Denver and he and family had gone down to see him and ofcourse Judy had made a hit with her uncle. Claude was on his way out to Oregon where he is to be married.

Dad saw Primo today down town and he asked about you boys and asked Dad to be sure and say Hello to you for him when he wrote so there it is.

The Hornings will be moving in to their new apartment soon as it is about finished. They made three rooms out of the place where the back porch used to be like this

(Sketch not available)

There was no mail this morning but think that tomorrow will probably have a letter from T. We will be surely glad when we can hear from brother again and it is now only about two weeks since he left Hawaii and it seems ages as if he had had time to go clear around the world.

Our spring is just now looking like real spring. The trees are finally quite full of little soft green leaves. Guess you in England have had later snows than we have. Mrs. McKellar sent me a clipping about a snow over there on May 1st.

Dad and I will now go and eat some of the good food that Aunt Betty gave us this noon when Fanny was leaving. She brought a cake for Fan and it was too big so we got half of that. Then she deliberately gave us a loaf of fresh bread.

*   *   *

Letter No. 74

Wednesday May 9, 1945

Dear Bill and Tom:

If you could see your mother now I think you might turn away your heads for I have been cleaning all day everything except myself and I am a horrible sight. As soon as I finish your letters I will go clean up a bit for this is the night that we have the Novena Devotions.

Dad came home this eve with the refreshments for the club tomorrow night, nuts and candies and also a package of Whitmans which we will take to Mrs. McKellar when we go up Sunday. Mrs. Lagerquist is going with us to visit with Fred Jones. Helen Cash is not going for Bill is coming home that week end. Per haps we will find some one else who would like to have the ride.

Yesterday afternoon Kathryn Kroeber, sister-in-law of the

Lt. who has been with you so much since you have been in service, Tom came up and spent the afternoon with me. Have I ever told you that they are expecting the stork? In September. So she is going home in June and stay back there till after the baby arrives.

I was talking to Mrs. Mann this afternoon, asking her to accompany some of the folks on the Mothers Day program at the USO Sunday. She could not do it for they are expecting Bob at any minute. He was due to arrive the first of May but has been delayed so his time till now extend till sometime in June for he is to have a 30 day furlough. When he goes back he goes to New York for some reason or other and they hope that Bill Mays will still be there so they can have a little visit.

Did I tell you, Tom that Kroeber has only nine missions? So he says that he will not be due for 1st Lt. for a while. So guess the boy who told Dad that they had to have about 15 knew what he was talking about.

The Hively deal finally is to be settled tomorrow. Uncle Earl is handling it and you know how that is to get him to get at things, anything except his farming. Poor Eleanore has really had a big job going through all the letters and things that Aunt Hi saved. There was one letter which she herself had written to some woman in Kansas City and which was returned to her. Now who but Aunty Hi would think of keeping a thing like that. I guess she had every letter she had received in years and years.

You will be hearing from this same station tomorrow so till then "Good-NIght".

*   *   *

4/10/45

Dear Mother & Dad,

I've not had any sea sickness; so I don't think I'm subject to the disease although I've not really had much of a test.

The day is pretty much of a routine now. In the mornings we have a little fresh water so I shave. After breakfast. I go up on the deck in the short I manufactured out of a pair of trousers with the aid of the little sewing kit. The trousers above mentioned and the slippers Tom gave me are my entire wearing apparel except for the meals when I have to slip on a shirt.

The rest of the morning I usually read. After lunch I find a space to lie out flat and take my siesta for about an hour. Then I become a sun worshiper for the rest of the afternoon until shortly before supper when I shower and wash my under-shorts in salt water. After supper, I read or play a game of bridge or chess. In the evening they usually have a singing bee interspersed with abundant talent we seem to be bestowed. We have a different picture show every three days and so far I've seen no duplications. The big event of the evening is watching them dump the garbage. The trip is not bad except that it is a little crowded.

After Blackout I go below and read or as I'm doing this evening write a letter. Though I've plenty of time I've not written many letters as there is very little to say.

I'm surely glad the war in Europe is at last at an end. I hope that Tom does not have to come over here very soon. Perhaps he will be in the States within a short time. I may even run into him over here somewhere.

I have made quite a little more letter out of this than I expected, though I doubt that it conveys much information. Till later.

Love,

Bill

William R. Sisson, Ltjg USNR

*   *   *

Letter No. 75

Thursday May 10,1945

Dear Bill and Tom:

While Dad finishes the act of dressing I will write a quickie to you. I am all ready and we will go in a little bit to the hotel. We are not eating in the gold Room tonight for there is another party there so I do not have to put on decorations or place cards so we do not have to get there quite so soon.

Was talking to Marguerite in the store this morning and find that Harold is on Hilo but ofcourse flies all around there. He too thinks it is very pretty over there.

There was no mail this day but the Cransons had a letter from Walt so know that you were probably having a little leave in London as he was and he wrote from London so if you did not write till you got back to base we will not get it for a day or two.

Naomi Davis is being married tomorrow in Pueblo for there is no minister of their church here. Dad says Clyde has been very busy today getting things all straightened for them, such as calling and making the arrangements in Pueblo etc.

Yesterday afternoon, after wanting to do it for a year or more, Mrs. Mays took Bobby down to see and get on the Desil. Marg has not wanted to let him go for she kept telling Mrs. M that it would frighten him but you know Mrs. M. She was sure he would like it for all their children did. Mr. M. took him into the engine and when he looked into the fire box and saw the flames that was the first thing that scared him and then, I think that the whistle blew loud, and worst of all the engine started up and he was just frightened to death. Poor Mar felt like I did when the people in Missouri persuaded me to take you, Bill into the cave. She could just have kicked herself for not holding out for what she knew she should. Well to make up to him she took him last night to ride on the Merry-Go-Round which has just set up this week down on Bradish. Legion I guess has sponsored its coming here.

Well I had better quit now for I dont want to be late in receiving our guests at the hotel.

*   *   *

Letter No. 76

Friday May 11,1945

Dear Tom and Bill:

There is no party tonight or anything else that causes me to hurry or curtail my letter but the lack of news may be the reason that it will be short.

I went out to Grey Ladies this afternoon with Pink and Mabel Fertig so without our boss, Mrs. Needham, that is what we call her for you know she has a way of telling one what to do and when and all about it, we had a good time and guess we must have done a lot of loitering for it was almost five when we got home. Saw Ann and Mrs. Bell a minute at Pinks and Annie asked about you fellows.

I saw Mrs. Oberling today and stopped to ask about Mr. Oberling, he has been sick for some time, is better now, and she was telling me that Roy who is the Chiropracter but is in the Navy now for about three years and over in the Pacific for some time, 18 months I think it is, seems to be with the Marines and now is on Okinawa. All the folks whose sons have been in a long time like that are figuring up their points to see what their chances are to get to be discharged. We all think that John Todd will be one of the first ones from here to get it since he has two children with all his overseas service and all. Too bad Bud does not have about three children instead of just one, and if Justine and John just had a few he might get out.

Dad just said that Helen told him today that Blanch Todd was figuring up John's points and the way she has it he has only 78 but I bet she does not know of all his combat credits.

Last night Miss Backer called me and asked if I would give a little reminiscence at the dinner they are having for Mr. Herron

Monday and asked that I make it as humorous as possible so I have been raking my poor brain for something to say. I cant remember anything funny that ever happened if there were such events while I taught. Guess I will have to get Dad to get some good stories from Mac to tell. Do you think Mac's stories would be suitable for such a company of notable people as the Junior High teachers?

Aunt Mayme was in a little while ago, just about ready to go back to her ranch but she did not have any news, had not had a letter from her kids this week but could tell me all about all the little calves that are arriving out there and what a time Jack has at the "confinements".

Harold Hancock of Rocky Ford has brought home an Irish bride from Belfast, Ireland. They were married over there and since she could not travel with him she came along to this country. Lucile and Margaret Driscoll had a shower for her a few nights ago. They say she is pretty and charming. I guess she finds this country as queer as you do England, Tom. Bet you Bill are about to find your new location a little queerer still. Gee I can hardly wait to hear from you but guess I will just have to hold my horses a while yet.

*   *   *

4/13/45

Dear Mother & Dad,

Today is Sunday the 13th—Mother's Day. As usual on Sundays we said the Rosary in the Troop Mess Hall. I've thought about you today Mother—even more than usual being a special day to remember mothers. And as always I thought of Dad—for how can I think of Mother without thinking of Dad.

We are now nearing our destination and even when you get this note I may be there. The trip has been without event and are anticipating no causes for worry.

My watch has been running perfectly ever since I received it except for several times when I forgot to wind it. Since leaving my last station however the band has become very tarnished. I procured some polish this morning and I did a fairly respectable job of shining it. Looking at it this evening However I find that I have not been such of an artisan or it tarnishes in less than 10 hr.

Today some of the fellows have been fishing with only minimal success. One such enterpriser let me sit and hold his line for a good part of the afternoon, but my efforts were unsuccessful. I thought how grand it would be to be in the mountains of Colorado near a mountain stream equally unsuccessful. I believe the type of fishing I really enjoyed the most was spear fishing on the Island of Oahu which was of course equally unsuccessful.

I surely miss ole Robert Inman and am wondering how he is doing without me. I don't think there were very many days when we weren't together. I didn't get to see Woody before I left, as I had wanted. I'd seen him a week previously.

I'm looking forward to my new job. Oahu was grand and I didn't have much work. Perhaps I'll have more work than I wanted.

Till Later, All my love, Bill

William R. Sisson

*   *   *

Letter No. 77

Monday Mar 14,1945

Dear Bill and Tom:

Here it is five oclock and I still am not sure what I will say at the dinner when I am called on to make my speech. I do hope that I get inspired or I will be a disgrace to all my family. We are going with Carolyn and Art McCune so Dad will have some congenial companion to talk with at least and I dont think that it will be very long so maybe he can stand it.

We made our trip to Canon City yesterday and really had a good day. Aunt Betty and Mrs. Lagerquist went along. We started at ten and had a flat at Rocky Ford which delayed us a little while. Glad it was only a hundred yards or so beyond that filling station at the west end of the city so all Dad had to do was turn round and drive in there and get it changed. When we were ready to come home Vincent lent us a tire from the prison garage so we would have a spare on the return trip. Fortunately we did not have to use it and Dad sent it back this morning. We got home at about ten thirty having had a little bite to eat in Pueblo at the drug store on the way. We saw the Jones who used to live here in La Junta and at Aunt Maymes when you two were little fellows. They have a little pomaranian dog and we got to talking about pets and I asked it they remembered Trix and Mrs. Jones said "Yes and I remember an imaginary cat too" They used to get a big kick out of the "Mit Game" it seems. But she could not remember what you called it

The Donahues piloted us out to the McKellar ranch so we had no trouble finding it. Mrs. Mc was expecting us and just from her letters and telephone conversations I would have recognized her in a minute. She was just as I had pictured her. We had a grand time comparing notes on our sons and I had taken along all the pictures we had (in fact the scrap book which I guess I told you I have started for each of you) and also we went out to the Cransons Sat. eve and Mrs. C. let me take some of Walters letters which I thought would be particularly interesting to her. She had some film and so got Dad to take a picture of her and myself so when we get one will send it on to each of you. She showed us pictures of the old family estate in Scotland where Cleggs grandfather lived and do hope that Clegg can get up there to see it before he comes home. It looks as if it is really lovely. Clegg has a grand, aristocratic back ground and I am sure must be very proud of it.

This morning the mail brought us a letter from you, Bill and it was grand that you had a chance to write us while still at sea for otherwise it would be so very long before we would hear. Of course you could not give us much news but just so have the letter was a lot. We have been guessing where it might have been mailed and perhaps our guess of Guam could have been right. Now I suppose it will be another two or three weeks before we get more news but we will be patient and oh so happy when we do get a letter.

This morning Margaret Strain called up. She had been trying to see us yesterday but we were ofcourse gone all day. It seems that some one had told her that Deans plane had glided to earth and in some way it got all twisted up that you, Tom had reported to me that you had found that out in going to Deans group. Isnt it strange how distorted things get in being retold a few times. Any way for some reason she seemed to have gotten a new feeling of hope and had out to see the Cransons to see if they knew if you had found out anything from his group over there.

We cant just understand why we have not had a letter in quite a while from you, Tom but ofcourse there are so many things that could cause the delay and knowing you are not in combat now we do not have the feeling of anxiety we might if you were.

Aunt Mayme was in this afternoon but she did not have much news. Aunt Fan called Trinidad yesterday to see if Aunt Nell would not come out to the ranch to help with the gathering of the cows and calves but found out that she had left for San Francisco the night before so guess the wedding is approaching.

Must go now to the party so till tomorrow ta-ta.

*   *   *

Letter No. 78

May 15, 1945, Tuesday

Dear Tom and Bill:

Since yesterday afternoon we have had a little moisture. This morning it was coming down as snow but melted as it hit the ground. It is quite chilly and the weatherman says that it will be near freezing tonight. I have some flowers in the porch boxes and think that I will cover them tonight just in case. We need the moisture so are really glad to see it.

Poor Dad has had to be the janitor at the apartments today. At about 7:30 this morning Dr. Farnsworth called him that they were all cold down there. The stoker is out of order and the janitor is away so Dad made the fire and got the steam up so that they had heat. It is supposed to warm up tomorrow so he will not have it to do very long. Am glad he does not have to earn our living that way for shoveling coal makes his back hurt.

Had announcements this afternoon from Rosie Herron for commencement the 23rd. It does not seem that she can be graduating. That means that little MacDonald is also one of the class so next time you are home, Tom maybe she will be a college girl and not too wee to date. Ann McCune went with us last night to the dinner for she was to play while we ate. I really have not talked a lot to her in a long time and was surprised what a young lady and how very attractive she has become. Lots on the ball too.

Helen Cash is quitting the abstract company the first to go work at the F& A or rather I guess manage the F&A for Boots has gone to California, I think the place is. Dad has a woman who is going to try it. Dad is a little dubious for this woman has been a teacher and he is suspicious of all teachers since he had such a bad deal in his personal life with a teacher. (I can say that ofcourse he would not dare.)

Still no mail from T. Perhaps when we do get some it will all come in a bunch. The Cransons have not had anything either since the letter written the third. I have wondered if the shot you were having was a hay-fever or if it was malaria and you were being processed for the Pacific. Maybe you are in India by this time. Perhaps you two will be meeting out there some where.

My speech last night was all right, so Dad said so guess I must have been inspired. The party was very nice. Mac sang some Scotch songs so it was worth going to according to Dads way of thinking. Mr. Harren didnot want them to give him any gifts so the Teachers club just gave him life memberships in the different school organizations and the Junior High teachers gave him pictures of the force which he had indicated he did want. They are still going to live here and he is to go over and give a lift whenever he has the desire.

It is about time now for Dad to come and to hear the news so will stop for this time.

* * *

Letter No. 79

Wednesday May 16, 1945

Dear Bill and Tom:

Better not mention it for it just means that I am 56 years old and so I just as soon forget my advancing years. Dad did not spank me yet so guess he has forgotten about it.

I sold bonds today and sold one to my youngest son. Dad made out the check and I the request slip for it so you have another $100 worth, Tom. I also sold $1000. to Mr. and Mrs. Sisson, they are nice folks you know to buy from me. I am supposed to sell in the mornings on Wednesday but Ella Jane called me yesterday and asked me to change with her so she and Jewel could go to a party this afternoon and I was very glad to do that for I got the ironing done this morning, or most of it so that I finished in a little bit this afternoon when I got home.

The sewer pipe is being laid so part of the time we cant use the toilets or the sink but hope they will be thru tomorrow or the next day.

Just talked to Aunt Fan at the ranch. She says her stiffness and soreness is some better. Dr. Cooper had had her taking vitimin B-4 so maybe it is helping her. The hawk had killed one of the young chickens today and saucily came back and ate it. If there had been anyone there to use the gun she thinks that they could have killed it.

The boys are branding and she had been up to the corral to see the calves. She thinks that they are fine little fellows and the cows are in good shape and giving lots of milk. Now "if we just have one more good rain" they should get along fine. Manuel told Dad yesterday that there is to be a big calf crop this year. When we have a spare tire we went to go out to see them. The ration board condemned the tire which went flat on us Sunday so now we ought to get a new one some time.

I may not get a letter written to you tomorrow for I have a full day. In the morning I have my hair set, in the afternoon tend the snack bar at the USO and in the evening we go to the club.

Mary Lou Mc Donald was all upset today after the Senior-Rotary Lunch. When she went in Laurence Thulemeyer grabbed her and took her in to sit with him. She did not say anything but she had wanted to sit with her dad. She went home and cried about it. Said she had planned for a long time how she would sit with him on this occasion and then did not get to. Dad had Rosie Herren and the Pike girl for his guests.

I am hungry tonight, guess I sort of short changed myself at noon, so will go now and fix some supper for Dad and me.

*   *   *

Letter No. 80

Friday May 18, 1945

Dear Bill and Tom:

Have just finished our bite to eat, ice cream and some of my birthday cake so will write you a little and then go mail the letters and also take our two graduation gifts to the girls, Mary Lou and Rosie.

I had been the hottest day of the season so far, about 89 and that is about as hot as it gets in summer at Trinidad. I was out to the hospital this afternoon and even as hot as it was, there was heat in the radiators, can you beat that, I nearly melted just going into the wards and dont see how the poor patients could stand it.

Another letter from, you, Tom came this morning. It was written the 6th, Sunday and you said that you flew that day. Guess you must be doing a little transport work.

Dad tried to get your bars today Tom but they had none at Roaths but they thought he could get them at Goodmans so he went there but he had to get them from the base. That is Bob Hurt did have to get them from the base so Dad does not have them yet. You may not get the full five pairs this time but if not we will send more when we can get them. Aunt Fan will be going to Pueblo next week and probably White and Davis have them up there.

There was a report got started around here today that Russia had told Japan that if they dont surrender to the U.S. Russia will start war on them. That would really be good news for think that there would not be much Japan could do in that event but surrender.

Had a letter from Frank Leonard today in answer to one that I had written him telling him that, you, Bill could not look Bob up in Hawaii. He says that Bill Grant is on Guam and he was all excited that you might be going to the same place. Ed Leonard on the air plane carrier gets into that port occasionally and he sent me instructions how you could know if you are on Guam. I dont think that you are for if you were think that we would be hearing from you. We have it figured that the letter at sea which we had last week was mailed there on your way further out.

Had a letter from aunt Gertrude today telling us that Marsdon got home last Monday and they are a happy family. He has till the 27th of June. It took him a month to make the trip from New Zeland and part of the way was by plane.

Aunt Mayme was just in and had had a letter from Olive. The family up there seem to be fine and happy. Mary plans to go up to help celebrate the birthday the 12th of June.

Charlie Belt and Hazel are to be married at Raton where her sister lives, tomorrow and Pink and Ann are going with them.

Tom, you asked who was elected mayor. Evidently you have not received the letter in which I told you about the election. I wrote you on the 4th that Al Miller had been elected but that I did not think that it would make any difference in buds being the city attorney. It did not for when the council met they appointed him again.

Mr. Hollis was up today and told Eleanor that he had sold his other house and that he would like to get into this one the first of June. She does not know what she is going to do or where she is going to go and Dick is coming in June some time for furlough. I guess we will have to take them in. If it is the first of June he comes I think that she will just stay in the house in spite of Mr. Hollis.

The plumbers got through with laying the new sewer pipe into the house today and I am glad that is over and hope that we will have no further trouble with it.

Had a letter from Hay today. They had had their first letter from Ed and it was from Germany where he and 25 of his Fighter Control boys were in charge. Ed was mayor. He had had a letter from you, Tom.

Well tom your papers were only a month old when you got them. Maybe you will get more now that they have started.

Will stop now for tonight.

*   *   *

21 May 1945

Dear Mother & Dad,

There is not much more news to relate that I have already told you. I feel now that it will be really grand when I get to our destination and can walk all around on land. I think I'm very fortunate to be land based as this ship living is not what its cracked-up to be.

I did have an enjoyable afternoon the other day when I went swimming and enjoyed an ice-cold Coca-Cola and some beers.* We also had a fresh water shower. It would be good to have such things happen every once in a while.

I'd surely like to hear whats the news at home and hope there is mail for us when we arrive.

There is not much more news for the present.

Love, Bill

William R. Sisson

* We stopped at the island of Ulithi but could not say that.

*   *   *

Letter No. 81

Monday May 21,1945

Dear Bill and Tom:

A chilly spell is upon us again and the weather man is warning that there will be frost tonight. It rained a little last night and more at the ranch than here. Aunt Fan had planned to come in today but was a little skeptical about starting so waited till noon when it seemed to have dried some. She had no difficulty for the road after leaving the head of Iron was practically dry. She says that the grass all the way in looks fine and the cattle are doing very well.

Aunt Fan is feeling much better. In fact she says her stiffness is improved so much she no longer dreads to move about. I guess it is the vitimin D which Dr. Cooper has been giving her that has done the work. How about that doctor? Anyway it is surely fine to see her so much better.

Got your letter of the 11th today, Tom and glad to know that you are conducting "Cook tours" now. Walter had written his folks about your trips to show the devastated country to the ground crew men so from the two of you we got quite a picture. I bet you fly right over Bud and Ed's heads but still we do not know just where they are. If we did you could drop a little note to them like Walter did the toilet paper over London.

Joan has the mumps for the second time in her life. It is rare for anyone to have them the second time but Dr. Cooper had seen cases of it. She had a perfect attendance record for the year she could have gone this afternoon and this is the last day of school. Claude said that she had cried most all the afternoon for she was disappointed about it.

When Dad was getting your bars from Bob Hurt the other day Tom he gave Dad a patch for you so will send it in this letter. It is a very fussy one but I doubt that you any longer wear this kind as you have your own 8th air force patch.

We heard tonight that the First Army is already on its way to the Pacific but will come by the way of the USA. John Todd is in the first so suppose he will get a furlough on the way if he does not get out.

Yesterday the Hollis family came and put in a big garden in the back yard over at the Hively house. They had taken out the old dead tree back there so it makes a nice big garden. Our back yard looks a little the worse for wear since the plumbers got thru out there but has improved in the last two days so think that it will come out again in a little time.

Well will mail these now and then read a while before we hear the news and go to bed.

*   *   *

Letter No. 82

Tuesday May 22,1945

Dear Tom and Bill:

As yet no news from our little "Willie" from the big Pacific. Guess we are just a little too sort of in a hurry but no doubt it will come pretty soon.

The Sabins have not had a letter from Justine for about 10 days which is rather unusual for her but since she has become a little more acquainted there she has more to do and not so much time on her hands so guess that is the reason. If she had some good news like Johnnies being discharged I am sure they would be hearing promptly from her.

Aunt Betty had a letter from aunt Nell yesterday giving the details of the wedding plans. It seems that George didnot get into San Francisco as they had expected he would but made Portland instead so Friday the 25th Nell and Ginny wound their way up there and on the following Sunday the marriage will take place. believe it or not Uncle Charles has planned all along on going out to San

Francisco for the occasion and they are in hopes he still can make it to Portland. It seems that Ginny has an apartment rented in San Francisco but now ofcourse the newly weds cant use it for they will stay in Portland till George has to leave again but Aunt Nell will come back to San F. and wait till Ginny comes and then stay and visit with her for a few weeks so then they can make use of the apartment. I guess after that Ginny will go back to the Residence Club.

Aunt Fan is going to Pueblo tomorrow and I would accompany her but I have to sell bonds at the bank in the morning. I think she may have to go alone for so far no one has indicated they would like to go along. I need some new curtains for our bedroom very much but cant get any here. Perhaps I would not be able to get them there either but there would be no harm in trying anyway.

I went over to see Joan this afternoon and she showed me her collection of movie stars pictures that she has. I think now she has about 75 and is very proud of the ones (two or three) who have autographed theirs this way "To Joan, Sincerely So-and So." That is a very personal touch and she likes it. Then Bing Crosby does not send them out so her wrote her a note to explain, quite personal too.

Guess I am going to the commencement excersises tomorrow night but think that Dad will probably be going to the poker club for Mac ofcourse since his daughter graduates has to go to the exercises so they will have a vacancy at the club.

Yes, Tom it looks as if we will all have the pleasure of seeing our Dad at the presidents seat at the rotary meetings next year. He did not tell you boys this but if the war is over by that time and conventions are in order again he and I will get to go the InterNational wherever it is held. He said not to bother telling you that for it is so remote and perhaps just a dream. But I said you would get fun out of dreaming that might happen to your mom and pop as we do.

Fibber and Molly now have the floor so guess I will concede to them.

*   *   *

Letter No. 83

Wednesday May23, 1945

Dear Tom and Bill:

Your letter of the 14th, Tom came this morning but still we have heard nothing from Bill. Do hope we can soon hear that you have arrived at your destination and perhaps if you cant tell us where it is we can guess. It really has not been so long but it seems ages since you left the islands. I wrote you a V-mail letter today for I began to think that it might be a little speedier getting to you than air mail tho every one say that the contrary is the ease. I thought it would not hurt to try anyway.

Your letter was good to get for since the censorship is less rigid you could tell us more of those trips while you were flying combat. Wish Bill could have the letter we got today but no doubt you have written him too much as you did us. On May 1st I sent Bills new address to you, Tom but since I now know that you do not get all my letters I am going to put it in again and again till I hear that you have it.

G 10 Comp 62
%Commandant NCB Navy 3256
%FPO
San Francisco, Calif.

I figure Bill left on about the 25th but guess you had not had my letter telling you of his change, not at least up to the time that you wrote on the 14th. I am glad that you got the stationery, finally and the few eats which I put in with it. I will get the combs today and will get another box off to you probably tomorrow. I think that there is not much use to send you, Bill a box till we get a permanent address for you for Mrs. Cranson sent one to Walter to that first address he had and it did not get to him till after some of the others which were sent much later. Tho I dont have to have a request to send things to you, Bill I hope you will tell me the things that would be good for there is no use to send the things that you may have some of there. Like fruit or canned ham or raisens or candy or just what.

Aunt Fan had for passenger today, Mrs. R. Sabin. She hears from bud right along again now but there is not much change for him as yet at least but like you, Tom we all think it would be a better set up to stay there than go to the Pacific.

Two boys, returnees, who have been with Roscoe called Mutt a few nights ago and assure her that He will be home in June but that they are definitely going to the Pacific. She says when she hears that he is coming form Roscoe himself then she will believe it but just the same she is pertty excited about it all.

Neither the Greens or the Strains have heard from the boys. Custis is supposed to be a German prisoner and it seems as tho they should be hearing of his release soon. They have been waiting expectantly for him to call them from New York for very often that is the first the family knows of the boys release. They are becoming jittery about it.

Frances Horning was just telling me a little while ago that Hal's wife is here and she had a good visit with her. The Harrisons have bought a house in Albuquerque and so are moving and Jean is very busy so will leave Roger here while that is going on and then too she is not very strong just now for they are expecting the stork again.

*   *   *

Letter No. 84

Thursday May 24, 1945

Dear Bill and Tom:

Goodie, we got another letter from you, Bill today even tho we did not know much more after getting it than we did before it still was mighty good to get it and made the old folks feel good.

For your benefit, Tom I will repeat a little of the contents. The days schedule was the most thing it contained. Shave in the morning for there is a little fresh water then, dress in the shorts self constructed out of a pair of trousers and the little sewing kit, read all forenoon then don a shirt for meal time, a siesta in some quiet spot, if one can be found, the ship is crowded, for an hour or so. The rest of the afternoon spent in worshiping the sun till time to shower and wash shorts in salt water, supper, bridge or chess or picture show which changes every three days, song fest and then watch the dumping of the garbage, the big event of the day. I can just imagine that for I recall how we watched the gulls up the coast from Santa Monica last Christmas time. But perhaps you had other than just gulls struggling for a bit of it. Sharks perhaps?

Aunt Betty called a little while ago to tell us that they had a letter from Justine today and she said that there was much excitement there for the points necessary for discharge for the air corps had been lowered. A pilot got out on 58 and Johnny has 68 so she thinks there is a good chance for him. Jim Sterling is out except to go to Ft. Logan for the final say. They are starting from San Marcos tomorrow, I think she said. Well it will surely be good to have some of the kids around and maybe it wont be so awfully long till more of you will be getting out too. Perhaps we can scare the Japs will all this bombing they are getting now, and more in store for them.

Walter's letter of the 10 is published in the Democrat tonight and I will send it on to you, Bill for he tells the story differently than Tom and so you will get two angles on their doings over there from it, and Tom.

Last night after the graduation poor Mac had a terrible for some boy by the name of Jones with whom Marylou has been going asked him if he could marry Marylou. Mac did not tell Dad what he said but that the kid is a nice kid but expects to go to college to study medicine and cant you just hear Mac say" H—I might have to put him through Medical school" Marylou is just about 17. Dad went to the poker club and came home the winner of 1.85. I did not hear him come in nor light the light or anything till he came to the bed and kissed me and that woke me up and about scared me to pieces, just for a second.

I put out some petunias in the little spot where I usually have them, last night and hope they do good. Marg and Bobbie just came in so I will close this now and they will go with us to mail the letters.

*   *   *

Letter No. 85

Friday May 25,1945

Dear Tom and Bill:

Have just heard Van Der Cook say that most of the B-17 and B29s are already on their way home. Could it be that our Tom is on his way? Well if not then the set up he has over there is not bad I think so we will be satisfied either way.

Aunt Fan just phoned, would have called earlier if I had been home, that she arrived safely and sound at the ranch about 2:30. She did not start till after dinner so made good time. She goes over the bombing range now all the time and the road is very good, kept up by Uncle Sam.

I did my Grey Lady duties this afternoon. Just Mrs. Needham and I went out this afternoon so it took us a little longer than when we all go. Pink had to stay home and help her children. Charlie was moving(he and Hazel have one of the Kendalls apartments) and Ann is going back to Pueblo in the morning to stay a while longer with Her aunt, so Pink had to do some sewing for her before she left.

We are having Forty Hours Devotion at the church for the next two days beginning this morning so I have to go this evening. I told my husband that he could go to the Elks but he seems to think that he will not take me up on it.

I have a package ready to send to you Tom with some Bunte candy in it which Aunt Betty got for you, also some candied nuts some cheese and raisens. I dont seem to be able to get much of a variety into these boxes. raisens are the only dried fruit that is on the market now. Guess you can make away with what I put in anyway even if it is about the same each time.

Am so glad that you have gotten some of the papers. Have you had any boxes in which I have put the funnies from the Denver Post. I put them in for filling up the corners but thought you might be able to straighten them out enough to read.

The grass which was so covered up while the men were working on the sewer and which seemed about dead when they got thru is beginning to look much better and in most places I think will eventually come out.

Last night Aunt Fan and I thought that it would be sort of fun to call the bride to be so put in a call to Miss Sisk but after waiting for a long while canceled the call so we could go to bed and be undisturbed. She and her mother were going up to Portland today.

Will go now and fix Mr. Sisson a sandwitch.

*   *   *

Letter No. 86

Monday May 28,1945

Dear Bill and Tom:

The mail man brought only a magazine this morning so I thought that there should be more this afternoon and have been out there to see a dozen times but as yet, five oclock, he has not been to our house for I put a letter out there to be mailed and it is still there.

Suppose that Dad told you(I dont get to censor his letters like he does mine) that Ginny's wedding is all off. It seems that about five days before the date George called her that because of something that had come up at home he could not be married till he had gone down there(Los Angeles) and could not get leave for nearly two weeks so ofcourse Ginny thought that it was only an excuse guess she has called it all off. He said that the next time he would be in would have about a month and they could be married then but she evidently did not think much of that idea.

I had a letter from Dick Counley in answer to the one that I sent him so now have his address and will give it to you Bill. He said that he would write you and perhaps there might be a chance you would meet but he seemed to think that probably the Phillipines is not your destination.

Capt. R.T. Counley

Hdq.251st AAA Gp

APO 75, San Francisco

The Greens have heard that Custis has been released and will be home some time soon. How I wish the Strains could hear something good like that about Dean.

Bettey Ballard called me today to tell me that in a clipping which her mother-in-law had sent her from Louisiana it gave the group numbers of the 8th air force which would be sent home immediately(30 to 60 days) and both the 392 and Jims group were given in it. It also said that some of the groups could come by boat so we wonder since you, Tom went over that way if you will be coming home in the same manner. Any way it looks as if you will be home before too long. whoopee!

This is ASO night for Marg and me and Dad had thought of going to the show while we are there but since I would like to see it too and it will still be here tomorrow night he has consented to go to the club instead and wait till I can go with him tomorrow night to see the picture.

It has been showering just a little bit and a little thunder. There was quite a bad hail storm yesterday near Denver which caused some damage to gardens and the like, so the paper reported.

Bud Lane was here over the week end but as yet is not out of army. However I guess he thinks it is coming soon and so put on his civvies and paraded around yesterday. Said he just wanted to see how they would feel.

Will stop now and try hard to think up something interesting
for tomorrow night.

*   *   *

Letter No. 87

Tuesday May 29,1945

Dear Tom and Bill:

All day it has been threatening to rain and a few times has
actually misted a little but that is all. It is quite cool and maybe too
cool to rain. Fanny would surely like to see just one more good rain
as everything out at the ranch is so far going along fine this spring,
but ofcourse she is fearful that it will turn off dry for the summer.

No mail today and am getting very anxious to know where you,
Bill have landed. Had a permanent this morning so had a talk with
Mr. West. He said that Harold wrote them that one morning there
was quite a commotion outside of their tent and one of the boys
went out to see what was causing it and found two native women
stark naked taking a bath in their water supply. Guess it must be
furnished them in limited quantities for they were pretty sore at
the "ladies".

I was already to go with the "girls, Jane, Bertha, Pink, etc" so
plan for a picnic in the Richardson back yard tomorrow eve, this
morning about nine-thirty when Mr. West called me that this was
the day that I had made an appointment to have a permanent, I had
forgotten or rather got mixed up and thought that it was to be
Thursday morning. Well they met and gave me the salad to make so
did not load me too heavily as punishment for not being at the
meeting.

There is still lots of guessing what this field is now to be. It is
definitely in the 2nd Command and was supposed to be a transition
school but now there is talk that it is to be a fighter school. Anyway
Bob Green is to be stationed here. Yesterday was a red letter day for

the Greens for Bob got home here to be stationed here and they had the word the Custis is released and to be home.

Buck and the promoters of the Koshare Ceremonials are having quite a time for their dancers keep joining the army and leaving on a moments notice and the program has to be rearranged. And too they are having quite a time to get the teepee poles. They cant get the four-by-fours that they have formerly used and so thought they had it all arranged and some fellow from Salida was to bring them down at .50cents a piece but that fell thru and now it will cost them 75cents a piece to get them if at all. So Poor Buck has his worries too.

Last night at the USO Bill Swentzel and the Stangl boy came and showed me their cards that they are enlisted reserves so could use the facilities of the USO. It hardly seems yesterday that Bill Swentzel was over across the street and had not yet started to school. Do you remember when they lived where the Lacy's do now?

I want to take some shoes down to the fixer when I go down for Dad so will close now and go get them ready. It has gotten very dark and I hear some thunder so maybe we will have rain after all.

*   *   *

Letter No. 88

Memorial Day, Wednesday May 30, 1945

Dear Bill and Tom:

Although it has been cloudy today there has been no rain to spoil the days parade etc. so it has really been nice for it has not been hot enough to weary the poor participants. Dad said it was really quite a parade for there were cadets and Wacs from the base in goodly numbers. I did not go down to see it but was up early and on to the cemetery to put flowers on the graves for the Garlingtons and the Winchells. I also took some to the Noble graves and wanted to put son on Aunty Hi's grave but as yet it has no marker so I could not find it. I left two boquets on the Noble lot and told Eleanor that one of them was for their lot so hope that she got it on.

I have the stuff ready to put my salad on the platter but dont want to fix it till just before we go so an already and when Dad comes home and while he gets himself beautified I can assemble it. I saw a picture in a magazine that I want to copy for it looks so pretty. Just vegatables but it is the way they are put on that makes it look nice so it will take me a little while to do that.

Tom your pipe is finally here but now Dad thinks we had better keep it here for from what we hear you will probably be coming home before it would reach you there. I have to pinch myself when I say you may be coming home for it is just too good to seem true and then I dont want to let myself get excited about it for fear they might decide on some other plans for you. As you say in this army one does not know anything is going to happen till it has actually taken place. I dont see what they want you in the Pacific for as Dean says there are so many more pilots there than they have planes for that they dont get their missions in but very slowly and as there is just nothing to do the time go so slowly, and the papers say that the Willow Run plant will not make any more B-24s after June 15.

There was a bad hale at Rocky Ford yesterday afternoon which did a lot damage according to report. They say that the greenhouse up there had almost every pane of glass broken and that many plate glass store windows were broken. Mrs. Mayer told me this morning that she saw some of the hail stones which some woman who was up there at the time had brought home with her and that they were like a little hen egg. Sure glad that they did not get that at the ranch.

Mrs. Halsey had a reception for her daughter-in-law yesterday afternoon at the Presbyterian church parlors but I did not go. After I had the mix up about my permanent I got sort of out of schedule as to time. I guess now I will have to go call on her to make up for it. I had asked Marg if she wanted to go with my but she said that if she did not care more for the daughter than the mother she did not think there was much sense in her going.

Last Sunday Marg took bobby to Mass with her but had to leave for then our beautiful choir began to sing he began to cry. I did not think it was quite that bad. She says that he always does that when he hears singing. Nice of her wasnt it to make that explaination?

Bob Mann is home now. I have not seen him as yet. I also saw by the paper that Wert Roberts was the first local boy to be discharged under the new point system. He went into the army in 1940, so the paper stated.

Hope we get a lot of mail, two very important letters tomorrow.

* * *

Letter No. 89

Thursday May 31, 1945

Dear Tom and Bill:

At noon today Mrs. Mc Kellar called me and seemed a little upset for Mrs. James(I think that is the name of Kleggs co-pilot from Estes) had called her. They both had had V-letters from the boys in which the fellows said not to send any more packages over there and they seemed to think that probably meant that the boys were headed right over to China from there. I told her about what we have been hearing and reading about 392 coming to the good old USA in the next 30 to 60 days and she was thrilled and hardly waited for me to hang up she was so anxious to call Mrs. James and tell her. So that once at least I guess it was a good thing that we had been corresponding with each other.

We had a good time at the picnic last night, and ate much too much as one usually does at a thing of that kind. We later went in the house and while the ladies indulged in a little bridge the men had a game of poker and your dad came out the winner and paid for the food which I had taken up there.

Aunt Fan came in today and as usual brought some eggs to sell. This eve when I took them down to Zellers I was about mobbed for it seems that right now the hens are on some kind of a strike and there were no eggs for the ladies to buy so they circled around me and took the hen fruit off my hands before I had time to sell them to the grocery. When I got home and told what had happened Dad scolded me for he said that it was not right for me to sell them to the women there in the store so now guess I will have to go back and make it up with Bill. Oh! my.

Still we have not had those two letters that we are waiting for so anxiously but they will get here one of these days. Marg had three from Bud today but he still did not know what is in store for him. His letters are not censored either now. The last one was written on the 19th.

Aunt Mayme was in today too, but did not have any new news. She is still planning on going to Idaho Springs for Judys birthday the 12th.

Father Bertrand was to call this afternoon. He was telling me that he is giving instructions to a Grenard girl from Swink or out that way somewhere who is going to marry Phil Abbott.

I have to go to the USO tonight for a committee meeting and another one down there tomorrow night and as I am not dressed up this eve I would rather just stay here and not have to go change my clothes and go down there but—so since it is near 7 now I had better stop and hop along.

*   *   *

Letter No. 90

Friday June 1, 1945

Dear Tom and Bill:

Well I still cant answer any questions for either of you for as yet that awaited mail has not arrived, so will just have to confine the information herein to facts and events of the city and family. The weather is always a good subject so will start by telling you that it clouded up this afternoon and has sort of teased us but as yet has not favored us with a single drop of rain. At least the temperature is quite perfect so we can be thankful for that. Some of the people who have been here at this base almost from the beginning are being transfered to Luke at Phoenix and at this time of year they dont relish the idea very much. Do you remember the Moberlys (Major) who lived in the other half of the duplex on Colorado Ave where the Nortons lived? They are one of the couples thus favored? They have been very popular here and so that too does not help them to like the change. We too regret to have them leave. They have belonged to the Thursday night club in place of the Todds who have not been able to come because of Mr. T's illness.

The boys at the ranch butchered a calf today and (no they did not butcher it but brought it to the packing Co to be butchered to-day) so if you, Tom get home about with in a month of six weeks you will be lucky in getting in on some good meat. So many over here that that the Japs industrialists are not going to like all this de-struction to their industries and will be giving up or asking for peace before too long. Let us all keep that thought in our minds and prayers for it would surely be good if they could see the handwriting on the wall and call it quits.

Your English instructors would not think this a very well con-structed letter. Look at all the subject matter which I covered in the last paragraph.

Pop came home with a new sprinkler for the hose, today and it does a swell job of hurling the water a long way. That is fine for it can be left longer in one place without running off into the street and gutter. The city dads threatened us last night telling us that if the waste of water continues we will have to have watering hours.

Mrs. Horning was brought home from the hospital yesterday and is getting along fine. She had about the same sort of operation that I had some years ago.

There has not been a single scratch from Ginny or Nellie since the one letter we had telling of the flop of the wedding. Perhaps Nellie is on her way home for she thought that Ginny would get out and go places more if she came on home.

Julia Belle and her two kiddies are coming for a weeks visit soon and Pinkie is all excited about their arrival.

Will go now to meet with the Activities committee of the USO and help them line up the proper things for the boys and girls to do down there.

*   *   *

6/5/45

Dear Tom,

I am sitting on my sack in a camp on an Island half-way round the world from you. The best thing I can think of is that no matter which direction each of us goes we will be getting closer together.

The sea voyage was quite uneventful except for the length of time—over five weeks. However as I look back on it—we had all the luxuries. Right now we don't have so many. In addition we haven't gotten all our gear to where we are. We've had to hunt around a little but now have a fairly decent bed on a wooden floor in a tent. The biggest difficulty has been the infernal mud. We got to our ambulance today and procured some of the gear and now have golosses—so perhaps I'll be able to leave a little of the mud on the outside of the tent.

You son of a gun now you as much rank as I only I think a 1st Lt is quite a bit higher than a Lt(jg) for I've found that I'm just a button somebody pushes. That is swell Tom and I'm proud of you. I was also glad to hear you may stay on for some local flying. I hope that you can stay out of this place.

When I got here there was quite a little mail and two letters from you. You asked about a rash under your arms—I imagine that it is gone by now—I doubt it is being scabies.

Perhaps after the war sometime you will get that package. I'm looking forward to the end of the war when we can have that big vacation together. How about this little English girl? Still hear occasionally from Betty.

Must end this while we have a chance.

Love, Bill

*   *   *

6/6/45

Dear Mother & Dad,

I've been reluctant to try to tell you much about this place because I didn't know the censorship regulations. Now that I know them I find that I can tell you even less. Later perhaps these regulations will relax. I can say I'm on an Island in the Western Pacific North of the Equator. You both are very intuitiative and doubt that you need any further information.

In Oahu I procured a good little radio and brought it along. It was in my sea bag which was dropped from the ship about 30 ft to the boat that brought us ashore. Today I opened the sea bag and found it undamaged as far as I could see, but I don't have the facilities to test it now. I surely brought a lot of junk with me and I know that the next time I'll travel light. It wouldn't have been so bad except for the mud. Today it hasn't rained and there are a few fairly walkable paths.

I went on a sanitation inspection and saw some of the Island which is really quite green and pretty. The soil is good here and there is plenty of rain; so there is an abundance of vegetation. I've seen a few natives from a distance who are Orientals.

When we were on the ship they exchanged what money we had for Invasion Money. There is nothing to spend it on, but I don't think it'll be too long before such things are available.

I don't really believe there is anything very much that I need. We have all the necessities so all we could use would be a few luxuries that are unperishable. Don't waste your ration points on me however you can use them better at home.

I had a letter from Tom yesterday telling of his promotion. That's really swell. I hope he gets stuck in England. I am getting ready for bed and you have just gotten up this morning. Tom is having lunch this noon.

Something happened to the lights so until later,

Love, Bill

Airmail stamps are hard to get.

*   *   *

6/8/45

Dear Mother & Dad,

Only a few minutes till dark and am sitting on a little porch in front of the tent smoking a pipe and writting this note. I am now prepared to sleep well as today I procured a cot.

Keep sending things please as I really like receiving them. The box with the golf balls arrived after I left my last station. I received an awfully swell letter from Aunt Fan when I arrived here.

I had a swell time today looking at the latrines and out-houses. They go to a lot of concern that didn't impress me much at the ranch. We saw two white women today—an army nurse and a red cross girl. The first I'd seen in about six weeks.

No more rain today and everything is drying up pretty well. I only went up to my ankles. Hope it continues.

After all my boy scout outings this really seems quite civilized. However I miss ole Tom. I'm surely glad that Dr. Carter wrote to you. He is a peach of a fellow. He is married to a doctor and they have a baby girl he has never seen. I would surely like to go spear fishing again with him.

We surely don't have anything to spend our money on so should save a little. I shall enclose a sample of our Invasion money.

Almost dark now so I shall close and write again Later.

Love, Bill

*   *   *

6/9/45

Dear Dad & Mother,

Everything here is coming along just fine. We have managed to fix up a radio and are now listing to some good ole U.S. programs. We don't have any plugs to use for the electric equipment; they are scarce around here. You might put a female plug in the next package. I have neglected to mention that I have really appreciated the Denver Post Sunday funnies in the boxes.

Today went over to see about some of our gear which seems to be in better shape than I had hoped. Ran into Dr. Hartson who had been with me before. Also, saw Dr. Walsh. He is another G-10 unit. Still haven't got a job. Been in the navy eight months and yet have to get a job. I wonder if I will be worth a hoot when I get out.

I enjoyed the clipping of Cransons letter. Ite gave an interesting account of their flight. His however letter was not as entertaining and interesting as Toms. Tom is really a good letter writter.

You are surely having your difficulties with help Dad. I hope that you have good luck in the procurment and maintenance of personnel.

Some of the boys are quite souvenir hunters, but I don't find myself so inclined. I shall keep my eyes open for some sort of good handicraft. There isn't really much here worth having. I have seen a few goats that look fairly healthy, but they are rapidly disappearing. I saw a horse the other day and it was really decrepid. I've seen no natives at close range, but they say they are poor physical specimens.

The soil appears quite fertile. Our camp is right in the midst of an old farm—I think we slept in a rice field the first night and you've seen pictures of them. They grow other vegetables, but because they use night soil (human manure) sanitary measures prohibit its use. Our food isn't too bad dispite no fresh fruit. The only milk I have had since I left the states was at Hilo. I am not complaining only meditating.

Will write more later. Love, Bill

*   *   *

6/11/45

Dear Mother & Dad,

The last two days I've been sort of checking up on some of the sanitary facilities around the camp. Hope to have showers in the not too distant future.

I didn't get near enough to Bill Grant to call on him. You can't tell who you might meet out here so I am keeping my eyes open. There are probably a lot of old friends around that I just don't know about.

The priest didn't get around yesterday; so I haven't been to Mass since I left in April. That was so long ago it seems that it was the next to last station, I was instead of the last.

I had a letter from Inman—surely miss him. Also one from McBurney. The scoundrel had been on Oahu for some time and by the time he looked me up I'd gone. Also had a letter from Bill Davidson. He'd been in San Francisco and out to the Marine Hospital. He'd seen some of the Doctors—Haines and Graham.

I surely hope this war ends soon.

We don't do much in the evenings. There is a movie about a mile away; so may go over there one of these evenings. There also are some nurses and Red Cross girls, but the odds here are a lot more than in Hawaii.

Til Later, Love, Bill

Am wondering how long it takes any mail to reach you. The latest letter of yours I have is May 25th.

How about that Virginia. I guess she is married by now.

*   *   *

Letter No. 1 (single)

Tuesday June 12th, 1945

Dear Bill:

What greeted my eyes when I went out this morning to look for mail made my rather wild with joy, for I could see an airmail letter in your handwriting. Wonder if you can guess just how I felt. It sort of seems to me from the tone of it that perhaps it is not the first letter you have written us since you got to the place you are now at. We have guessed from your saying it is in the western Pacific and north of the equator, very rainy and muddy, loss of vegitation no harbor, or at least you did not land on one, and the natives are Oriental that you are in Okinawa. Am I psychic again?

I wonder since you speak of getting a letter from Tom if you have had any mail from us. We have written as usual, I on the week-days except Saturday, and Dad on Sunday. I surely hope you have for I am sure that mail must be very welcome. I am going to put a few stamps in each letter rather than many in one letter for I sent Tom stamps once or twice and those were the letter that he did not get so we have learned by experience the better thing to do.

Also I think that even tho I am not having to send a carbon copy I will write on the type writer for then I can keep a copy of your letters and have them for reference, and while Tom is here I will mark them single and number them that way and then when he goes I will start in where I left off a week ago when I wrote the last letter in unison to you both.

Well this was really a red letter day for us for first your letter came and then as we were eating dinner the phone rang and Tom called from Denver. He will be here tomorrow. Aunt Mayme and Nell went to Denver today and as Mary did not much want to drive back alone (Nellie is coming back tomorrow, Mary Saturday) she was wishing Tom could drive the car down. She took it up for she had bought it there and there was something that she thought that they could do in the way of repairs on it otherwise she would have gone on the train for Judy's birthday, also today. Tom called a second time and as she had made this wish in the meantime and had already started off, I told him to call them tonight at Idaho Springs and maybe he could get a drive down tomorrow. He was going to call Shirley Garlington and thought that she might go dancing with him tonight.

Guess I did not tell you yesterday that Jim Ballard called Betty yesterday morning from the same place that Tom landed, Bangor Maine and will be home in a week or so.

I am so very glad that you were able to get a radio for I have felt guilty ever since we failed you in not taking yours out to California with us when we went at Christmas time.

Think this will take care of todays happenings so will write again tomorrow so ta-ta and

*   *   *

6/13/45

Dear Mother and Dad,

We have moved from the rice Paddie to an adjacent hill—formerly a graveyard. Though we've a tomb in the back yard. It is much nice, as we have trees, bushes, and grass and a swell view over the water. It's quite a walk up here from the chow hall, but to have such a swell camp site it is really worth it.

I've been spending my time trying to learn a little about the water situation. It is a lot of fun and something interesting to do. It won't be long before we have showers. In our new tent we don't have electricity, and Aunt Fan's careful instructions about these kerosene lamps has surely come in handy. I imagine we'll soon have electricity. We have a head (Chic Sales) right in back without a house around it. It is about the best view around—It's really the prettiest toilet I've seen.

I know something you could do. I've left my check book in the cruise box and the rest of my money is Invasion currency or a $20.00 Bill. The Times Magazine has a Pony Edition for Overseas subscriptions. It costs $3.50 for one year. The address is

> Time
> Circulation Manager
> 330 East 22nd Street
> Chicago 16,
> Illinois

I have seen issues out here less than a week old.
Well I've about cleaned up all my stationery.
Till Later

Love, Bill

*   *   *

Letter No. 2(single)

Wednesday June 13,1945

Dear Bill:

Today your letters of the 3rd and 4th came and now we are sure that our guess of yesterday, the first one, is correct other wise you could not look for Harold.

Am so glad that mail was waiting for you and such a goodly number. You really had an experience right at first at least but I hope that by this time you have things fixed up so that you have a little comfort. There is such a very interesting article on that island in the May Geographic so we can know something of what you are seeing in the way of vegatation and natives etc.

Will try to think up something that is not perishable and get a little box off to you this week.

Tom will be in on the early train tonight but it is a little late so will arrive about 8:30, that will give Fanny and me time to go to church before he gets here. Can hardly wait for the time to arrive. Dad says to tell you that he is going to mix Tommy a Scotch and Soda when he gets in. We went down and got some steaks out of the locker and intended to wait and all eat our supper together but when the train was reported late we thought he would no doubt have eaten by the time he gets here for they have a diner on that train.

Dad was telling Mr. Wheeler about your having arrived at your destination and he wants to publish your letter telling about all the mud and the state of things as you first had them.

Really I think you could be in much worse places in the Pacific than where you are and feel sure that soon the Sea-Bees will have things fixed up so that you can get along nicely.

Harold is with the Personnel Section of the 106th Infantry. His best friend is with the Medical Corps and his name is Jack De Wald. Bud Hartmann is in the Medical Corps, Headquarters of the 10th Army. You might happen to run in to some of these fellows. Glad you found one fellow that you had seen once before on the ship. Gee! I bet you were sick of riding the waves after more than five weeks of it. We have a sneaking idea what took you so long probably waiting for a spot to open where you could land with safety.

Dad talked me into using some sugar to make drop cakes for Tom this evening but think he had just a wee little selfish motive in it.

I must run along now so more of this old stuff tomorrow.

*   *   *

6/14/45

Dear Mother & Dad,

Today I managed to get the light plug; so you can cancel my order. I tested my radio and found that the 30 ft fall had not hurt it at all—so as soon as We get electricity I can hear the radio.

I got the package today with the golf balls, tees and glove. Also the latest Denver Post Sunday funnies which I really enjoyed. Perhaps I can soon get to the local country club for 18 holes.

Also received two letters of the 30 & 31 in which I learned that Tom expected a change. I surely hope he goes home.

This pen is about to run out of Ink so shall close.

Love, Bill

*   *   *

6/14/45

Dear Buck,

I have recently seen a lot of the La Junta boys including Bob Inman, Tom woodruff, James Louthan, Von Harold Dixon, and John Mayhew. Were ever a fellow goes he finds someone from home. More than fellows from the towns it seems to me.

I've wondered why—of course that is where our homes are. there seems to be more however for we have many friends in the town. I believe this marked feeling of-home town spirit is responsible by your swell work with us boys and the other swell people in the town.

I'm now using some of my scout experience and I've found that this is the life of ease compared to a scout camp.

Thanks a million, Bushy, I hope I can always be as good a scout as you would want.

Sincerely,
Bill

P.S. I meant to write this letter to thank you for my registration card and the news letter. Thanks a million.

*   *   *

Letter No. 3(single)

Friday June 14,1945

Dear Bill:

I am sure glad tonight to know that you have a cot to sleep on for even tho I know that you are not cold I cant think sleeping on the floor with one blanket under you could be the utmost in comfort. I have wondered what you did that first night when you did not have even a floor nor any dry ground for a bed.

At noon we heard that Japanese on Okinawa had mutinied against their Commanders orders and surrendered but no other commentator has mentioned the fact. It sounded so good that we hope it was true. Of course we know that there is only a small area where there is fighting going on so your safety does not worry us but the fact that some Japs would surrender might mean much in the whole duration of the war over there for it could become epidemic and the whole thing blow up.

Tommy is waiting for Bob Mann, Bob McNeil, and Elton Thomas. He says that he will write you a letter tomorrow. He got around quite a little today and saw a good many people. The Norton family was out in front as he came by there so ofcourse he had to go in to say hello. He shook hands with Annie and then when Julia Belle and her mother came out Pink kissed him and Julia B. followed suit and then he said he thought that he should make it unanimous so he kissed Mrs. Walker. Do you think Jack would like that? No fear he knows his little Annie.

You had a letter from Paul Dukes today and as Tom wanted to read it I let him so we will put it in another envelope and send it on to you. I know you will enjoy reading it. There is so much Phi Psi news in it.

We did not get to bed last night till midnight and then went reluctantly for we had so many questions to ask Tom and he so much to tell us. He has kept a good diary and one that he says we are free to read so that will save him some breath. I have not yet had time to read it all and I am so anxious to do so. His log too is interesting and all these things will be here for you too when you come sailing home.

I could kick myself not that I know your address is just the same as it has been all along for not sending you a package every week as you would have several coming along and as it is you will have to wait quite a bit for one as it has been so many weeks since I sent one thinking you would not get it anyway. I realize that I cannot send you many of the things that I sent to Tom but will try a package tomorrow and after that I will get one off every week.

I expect that over there is the latrine question is one of great importance because of all the various germs which that warm climate cultivates but hope that it wont be your continuous duty to have charge of them. Are there any other doctors around that place for you do not mention any people as if you might be a lone man "sort of Robinson Cruso(I sure cant spell that name tonight). We do know that there are two women there for you mentioned a nurse and Red Cross girl. Do you still have the same corpsmen that you had in Hawaii for John said you were very fortunate to have such good fellows.

Will close now so Dad can get this mailed before he wants to listen to the nine oclock news.

*   *   *

6/15/45

Dear Mother, Tom, & Dad,

I surely hope this note finds you all together at home. This has been a swell day, for I got Dad's letter telling of Tom's arrival in the good ole USA. That's really grand and I surely wish I could be there with you. After the 30 day leave I hope Tom gets stationed close by in Pueblo for a long time. That was really grand news.

This morning I put in a phone call for Woody Brown, but was unable to contact him, so I left a message. So about noon or shortly after who should appear, but ole Woodrow himself with a two month old mustache. We spent the afternoon together and evening chow. He isn't far away so hope to see him often.

You all are just getting up this morning and we're getting ready for bed. Some system!

Was going to write a note to ole Tom this evening, but can make this a community note.

Till Later,

Love, Bill

*   *   *

6/17/45

Dear Mother & Dad

Well it looks like I may get my dispensary set-up soon for which I'll be glad although it means moving out of this comfortable place where I now am. We are surely fortunate for we have nearly all our gear which amounts to about 60 tons. Still have the jeep and ambulance. Although the stearing wheel of the jeep was really badly bent unloading.

I have been looking at the water-works most of the time and find it interesting, and will perhaps be very useful in the near future.

The new censorship regulations permit mention of air raids in general—which is big of them, and we don't have any. That get through. Our only complaint now is the heat and no rain. I surely wouldn't have said that two weeks ago.

Last night I went to a picture show at a near by army camp and saw a fairly entertaining picture. We are having a picture here tonight and if I can get the pass-word shall take it in.

My pen broke the other day and one of the mates fixed it up for me.

Hope you've been getting my letters.

Till Later

Love, Bill

PS Saw in an old "Times" a newspaper item in the Rocky Mt. News from a lady in L.J.Colo.

*   *   *

Letter No. 4(single)

Monday June 18,1945

Dear Bill:

You have had quite a little rest from letters from me for three days now I have not written. Friday Tom said that he was going to write so I did not then the rascal did not get the job done but on Saturday he wrote and Dad on Sunday so you have been fairing well anyway. Sunday we got the letter you wrote on the ninth, thanks to the office box, and am glad that you are seeing some of the fellows whom you have known before for they seem like old friends, I imagine when you run on to them again.

Hope you find the spot where they need you after a while as I think you will like things better when you have something definite to do.

Evidently the mail from here is getting to you in pretty good time for you mentioned the clipping of Walter Cransons letter and it was not so very long ago that I sent it to you as it had to be written after VE day(the eighth) and could not have reached here for at least a week later.

We have just figured up that you were landing in your present station the same day that Tom landed in Maine, the third of June.

I am sort of glad that our sons are not souvenir hunters for just as you say often the things are not worth being bothered with lugging about with you and if you are like your mother you could spend all your time trying to find something then not do it. I think it is to do like Tom did and spend that time trying to see something of interest instead of wasting it trying to find something to bring home with you. There is just one thing that we want from that country over there very much and you can guess what it is, one big boy.

I can imagine your first night there must have been a honey wallowing around in the rice field and think of the poor infantry who have had to live in spots like that for ever so long. Dont think that we will think you are complaining for we like to hear the facts as they are, it is interesting and we dont think you are so fragile that you cant take a little hardship.

I sent you a package Saturday and in it I put a can of candied nuts, some cheese, some raisens and a can of tuna. In the bottom of the box I put some clippings, cut at random so dont know how much of interest you will find in them. From now on I am going to cut some continued stories out of the Sat. Eve Post and Colliers and send them so let me know if any of these things are to you liking for when it goes such a long way one wants it to be the best possible. I am so glad you mentioned the Funnies for I have wondered if it was just was to put them in.

Today we got a letter you wrote on the 21st of May while still on the ship and Tom got about ten of our letters returned to the states, one from you, written just after you had left Hawaii.

The Toms are playing cribbage but think the younger is about ready to go hunt up Bob Mann and step out for the evening and as I want him to mail this as he goes will close for this time.

*   *   *

6/19/45

Dear Mother & Dad,

I have received your letters of 6/8/ which I got several days ago, but today I received the letter of the 6th so that's the way it goes.

Yesterday I did my laundry. It will be a great day when I no longer have to scrub my fingers to the bone and have nice clean laundry. Such a minor point when I was home seems now to be quite an item. Of course I wear green which require my especial effort and do not bother to iron.

I went over to where our supplies are today, and drove around a little in the jeep which has been repair and now runs as well as ever. It almost seems like ole religion to me now. Am surely glad that it got through the trip at all. The ambulance—however is our work horse. It is a fine automobile though somewhat over shown by the daintiness of the jeep.

I imagine you are all home now. Boy that would be grand to be there. That ole Tom a 1st Lieut.—He'd better not pull his rank on me.

So Dad you are the Rotary President for next year—I hope you will take me down to the Luncheon. Thats swell and hope you and mother go to the convention and hope it is in Rio de Janeiro or Buenas Aires.

If you have sent me any V-mail it has not yet arrived. I've been looking back and through your letters and noticed that ole Tom called from Maine the same Day I arrived here. I'll bet you don't have much to worry about Tom's finding something to do—I'd just sit at home and the office loafing.

I shall drop Eugene a line for he may have a better chance of finding me than I would have finding him.

Not much more news—

Love, Bill

*   *   *

Letter No. 5(single)

Tuesday June 19,1945

Dear Bill:

I have been playing nurse maid this afternoon to Eddie Garlington while Shirley went out to the base with Nancy Gardner. I dont know that any of the family have told you that Shirley came down last Friday. Her folks are on the move again this time to Oklahoma or Calif so they started to Okla and came this way so Shirley and that baby came this far with them and will stay here for about a week while Bonnie Groth's husband is home on furlough. After he goes the two girls are going to live together till Hay and Lea come either to Denver or the Springs. He is getting a transfer to one or the other of these places, he thinks in the near future.

Aunt Mayme shoved up this afternoon and had been to a horse sale where she bought a riding horse for Aunt Nell. Olive and Judy had come down with her from Idaho Springs but had stayed out at the Lusks (Olives sister) till this eve when she was going to take them out to the ranch but just for overnight. They go to Pueblo tomorrow.

Mrs. Stone helped me with the laundry today and dont know just how I would have gotten along if she had not been here for I am tired as it is. Perhaps one of the main reasons was that my labor of the afternoon was out of the ordinary.

Tom has gone down to swim with the Scouts for a little while. I think it will be a very little while for as yet this Colo. weather especially at night is quite chilly. Even as old an old timer as I am has never seen the like. Had a fire in the furnace a few days ago and in some parts of the state quite a little snow and freezing in some parts of Wyoming. Anyway it had not been too cold for the millers which have been plentiful. The last few nights there have been only a dozen or so in the house in place of the usual four or five dozen.

Just talked to Aunt Fan at the ranch. She had had Manual's wife's sister who is staying out there with them come down this morning and help her clean out the bunk house and tomorrow she is going to help clean the north porch. I hope that the girl proves such a help that "Fannie J." will let her help her a lot.

Tom has been playing a little golf with Mr. Mann and Bob the last few days but he says that his form is terrible. I am glad now that I did not send all the balls to you for dont suppose you can use them over there for a rice field might not make such a good course.

The Hollis's were moving in some chairs this eve so it looks as if we would be having some new neighbors over there in the near future. Mrs. H. was planting some flowers on the south side of the front porch too.

Little Bobby(Frances Hornings baby) has taken quite a liking to me since I bring him over to see the chickens. He says my name now by screwing up his mouth in a great fashion, putting his tongue against his front teeth and sort of hissing. Frances has heard from her husbands gunner that he rode with "Chuck" to the hospital and tho he was still alive he was unconscious. At least Frances was glad to know that he did not lie out in the field somewhere uncared for.

Must go now and dampen the clothes for ironing tomorrow.

*   *   *

Letter No. 6(single)

Wednesday June 20,1945

Dear Bill:

This will have to be a quickie for I have just come from church and brother wants the car to go dating and imagine with whom? Ida Ordner, at 8:30.

When dad went to the office this morning there was your letter of the 14th and of course we thought that would be all for today but when the postman came there were two more, one of the 11 and the other of the 13th.

Just too bad that you missed seeing McBurney in Hawaii. We knew Bill Grant was on Guam from the Leonards. It must have been good to get Davidsons letter with news of the doctors in Marine Hospital.

We have figured that you are now getting our letters in about two weeks but yours come thru in only about five or six which is wonderful. I think by this time you have had letters which I wrote you after we knew that you had landed. I hope you have had the one telling you about the failure of Ginnies wedding to take, this time I guess it was because George got stage fright.

In one of your letters you told about your new camp sight in an old grave yard and so I know just what it looks like for the Denver Sunday Post had some picture of Okinawa. I will put it in the box so you can see what we think your living quarters look like.

I wonder if you need stationery for I noticed that one letter was made up of several different kinds. I am glad that you will have showers and electricity soon, probably you have them by this time. Hope you did good for the Navy in your inspections of the sanitary condition of the water etc. but not so good that they would want to give you that job permanantly.

It was a rather odd coinsidence that a letter came from Time this morning telling us that the subscription which we had ordered for you had started with the April 16th issue, in the very same mail with the letter from you requesting us to send it to you. I sat right down and sent Time an air-mail with your change of address so you will be getting that some time too we hope.

Aunt Mayme and the Farthing family came along but only stayed a little while. that Judy is one cute child and as pretty as a picture. I took her out to see the Horning dog and little Bobby was out there so they took up with one another pretty good. He seemed to think she was fine and wanted to love her but she was a little standoffish. Olive went on to Pueblo and will stay there a day or so to have her eyes tested.

Tom is here for the letter so ta-ta.

*   *   *

6/21/45

Dear Mother & Dad,

Yesterday I received mother's letter of the 10th and learned you had received a letter I'd written after I'd arrived here. It was not the first I'd written, but imagine you've received several by now. It takes about two weeks to receive answers to any questions you may ask.

I surely enjoy your letters mother. I can just see you writing them. Especially the account of your carbon copies to me, Tom and your record etc. Also enjoy the accounts and descriptions of the parties etc. Also Dad's weekly letter for there are just like Dad. Letters surely mean a lot out here. Bill Davidson is now in the Phillipines land base and know he likes letters; for he has written me three without a letter from me. Also had a note from Dr. Carter enclosing some pictures we took there.

I received the box with the cake and popcorn and raisins. Though not quite like being home, it was surely good. Also getting the funnies was like sitting home on Sunday morning. Sundays were the best days. I haven't been to Mass since I left, but they are having Mass here now so shall soon be in the groove. Also, I got two issues of Colliers which I really enjoy. You are very intuitive, mother, in more ways than one for you surely know what I like.

It is now getting dark and without lights tonight, I'd better close so can drop another note to the office.

Love, Bill

PS: Also, thanks for the stamps.

*   *   *

6/21/44 no 5

Dear Dad & Mother,

I received your weekly letter today and as always I enjoyed it very much.

I'm now sitting in front of the tent in the cool of the evening. Tom is now home. It is like the evenings at dusk on the ranch. I would surely like to be with you at the Rotary Club to here Tom & Walter tell of their experiences.

Enjoyed your account of Aunt Nell's visit and the difficulty between Ginnie and George.

Am surely glad your Business is good. That's the way it goes. When Tom and I can really help you don't need it and when we were burdens and money scarce you really had a tough time. You've surely done everything for us.

Some of the Boys have procured a horse which is about 1/2 the size of those at the ranch. They once in awhile use it to carry a sea Bag up the hill, but that is about the most it can do.

Well had best close

Till Later Lots & lots of Love, Bill

*   *   *

Letter No. 7(single)

Thursday June 21,1945

Dear Bill:

This is the longest day of the year and for La Junta the hottest so far but at that I would say it is probably about 90. The boys have been out playing golf all afternoon and Tom just came in with a little too much sun but I dont think it is enough to blister and spoil his already growing tan. They had a five some for Bob, Jack Roath, Mr. Woodruff, Jim Ballard and Tom went. Jim just got here yesterday.

We all are ready now to receive Miss Winchell, except that Mrs. Sisson does not have the supper quite ready but still I have about three hours to get that on so should be prepared for the gal when she arrives. Marg Larson and Bob are going to eat with us after Julia gets here. Hope the train is on time or otherwise they will be starved. The kids will probably not want to go anywhere for Margery is so big for Bob and he is very conscious of his height.

At noon today the Toms heard over the radio that Colorado Springs is to be the Headquarters for Doolittles Eighth Air Force and since we are now in the same command Tom could be stationed here for a little while if he had lots of luck. Too the same broadcast said that there is a possibility that Okinawa will be their overseas Headquarters. That really made Tom dance even if it is just more or less of a rumor and probably not a thing to it, but just the thought was good for him to hear.

Now that Okinawa is really in Allied hands maybe it wont be too long for any of the boys and we surely hope and pray that that is true.

Just read a letter Buck had from you thanking him for your registration card and news letter. He showed us the Rocky Mt. Council bullitin in which the Koshare history is featured and all the credit for starting the thing is laid right in the lap of you and Bob Inman. Am glad that at last your efforts are recognized, and we had nothing whatever to do about it, in fact knew nothing about it till buck showed us the bulletin.

I have a cake at Mrs. Raneys so must run over there and get it so will close now and go along and will be telling you tomorrow how the first evening that Julia is here came off.

*   *   *

Letter No. 8(single)

Saturday June 23,1945

Dear Bill:

There was just too much doing for me to get a letter off to you yesterday. Shirley and little Eddie came down about 2:30 and were here till about five. I tried to take most of his attention so was not wanting for something to do. While they were here we had other callers. Perhaps you can remember of hearing us talk about Dr. Brunk. They left here when you were about four years old and have not been back in the meantime so Mrs. Brunk and Naomi Davis called. It was interesting to hear her tell about the changes that have taken place in the town in that time. They come so gradually that we do not realize how much has really been done in the way of new buildings etc till some one who has not seen the development, like that comes along and reminds one of it.

Then we went to dinner at the Old Country Club with the Lloyd Larsens and Margorie and to their house for the evening afterward. We stayed rather late, nearly twelve when we got home for some reason I could not go to sleep when we did retire so have felt a bit groggy today. Julie stayed with Margery last night but was over a little after lunch and we(Dad, home because of Saturday afternoon, Tom, Julia and I have played bridge all the afternoon. Now Tom and Julia have gone out to the base and I am supposed to be making waffles and ham and eggs to be ready when they get back. Things are pretty well on the road as far as I can go till time to set it on so am now having a little talk to you.

We got two letters from you yesterday and it always amazed and thrills me to see how quickly they come. One was the 15th and the other the 17th, just five days. There was a special del. stamp in one of the letters and we wonder why it is there, perhaps just an accident.

I was nice to know that you know that Tom is here and it was grand news to know that you and Woody had gotten together and are close enough that you can see one an other often, to hear that the dispensary is about a reality and the jeep and ambulance stood that trip well and you still have them.

The kids just came home and so will stop now and fix the supper so we will have plenty of time for the train.

*   *   *

6/24/45

Dear Mother & Dad,

As I write this I realize it is Sunday though it seems like only another day. Yesterday we were very busy as we moved to another camp which is very new. We had quite a day loading the trucks and then the boat and journey here. Fortunately all the unloading was done for us.

It was surely a good feeling to arrive here, and meet a friend by the name of Robbins who was expecting us. I've known him for some time and he was on the ship with us. He had a place for us to sleep and eat as well as a tent in which to set up our dispensary. It was surely a grand feeling as we were really tired.

Today they have been putting a deck in our dispensary and hope its not long before we get set-up in working order. This is what I've been waiting for 7 months in the navy. It is a lot of work, but find myself enjoying it.

Our address remains the same.

More later, Love, Bill

Have already had a patient-minor gasoline burns. William R. Sisson

*   *   *

Letter No. 9

Monday June 25th, 1945

Dear Bill:

The Toms are all in a flutter for they are going out to a party that Art McCune is throwing for the soldier boys, a sort of a rush party for the Legion, we think. But anyway papa is invited too so Maw does not have to get any supper. I go to the USO since I dont have any company for the evening otherwise I would have skipped it this time but Marg does not want to go tonight either for Gerry and Ag(Bills wife) are here and are leaving tomorrow so thought that I had better go and do the duty for the two of us.

Right now the rain is pouring down, about like it does in Okinawa, perhaps? It started to rain a little last night and all day has sort of threatened but did not get the job done so hope that now we are really going to have it.

Tom had a letter from Ginny today in which she told him that she is coming home for a little vacation and will arrive the ninth which will be fine as he does not leave till the 14th and so can see her. Fred and family will also be here after the first so it will be quite a gathering of set.

Today about five of the letters which I had written to Tom in England were returned and for the first time he found out that Marsden is home on leave. Dont know whether he has read all of them yet and he may find out some other things which are important.

Guess Aunt Betty is going to go down to see Justine if she can get a reservation. She would like to fly but Uncle Earl is not air minded so does not approve too much. Getting down there on the train is a hard job, we know for we went to Bonham and in the time it took us could have gone clear to California.

Was over to see Gerry Guthrie this afternoon. She is leaving tomorrow for her station. She perhaps will have a new assignment when she gets there but for now goes back to where she was.

Tom has just fixed up a big date for himself and Bob Mann with two Rocky Ford girls (Erlene Blotz and Eleanor Jackson) for tomorrow night. I think the big date is to include a trip to Pueblo for dinner etc. I believe Wilson Cooper is going along with his date a Van Cleave girl from here.

I am sort of cross at myself tonight for procrastinating. Aunt Fan has been wanting to buy another jersey cow for hers will go dry in a few weeks so I saw an add in the paper for some but when I called this afternoon (several days after seeing the add) the cows were all sold. The boys want to go now so I have to take them down so I can have the car so will sign off now.

*   *   *

6/26/45

Dear Mother & Dad & Tom,

I hope ole Tom is really having a great time and I know he is. I'm surely looking forward to that time when we can all be together again.

After a good nights sleep things look a little better around here. When we arrived we did not expect much and got more than was expected. The camp has only been here a week. The area is on the shore. It is not as pretty as the other camp for everything has been destroyed.

I am the only navy M.D. There is an army doctor not far whom I've already called up for help. His name is Ranson and got his MD at Johns Hopkins. The company and men I'm to take care of are all color except the officers—This is as I expected however. Dispite the difficulties we are getting things lined up and are not in too bad a sanitary shape now. I live with three other officers (all white).

Our dispensary will soon be in order to start setting up shop. It is really quite an experience, though perhaps I'm not getting a good deal of medical experience. I think I'm learning a little something.

It is now very hot and I am in my shorts. I will really like a good bath. We are situated next to two main highways and it is really dusty now.

Just met another navy doctor—Wehr, who had duty with Grant and Lucas. He also met Woody Brown. I think he'll be doing my lab. work for me.

There is a nice breeze now which surely carries the dust, but makes it a lot cooler.

I now have five corpsmen. Two colored and three that have been with me since Oahu. Two came with me from the States. They are pretty good boys.

I enjoyed Paul Duke's letter and am glad Tom got a chance to read it.

Til Later, Love, Bill

*   *   *

6/27/45

Dear Mother & Dad,

I am writing this letter from my desk in our nearly completed sick bay. It is really quite good I think. The boys from the company built it for us. It has a wooden deck, and for the top it is a tent. The boys know quite abit about carpentry. It has 3-partitions with one for office, examining room and sick call—one for minor surgery and a ward (10 beds if needed or more) and one for storing gear.

The navy really equipped us. We've got practically every drug we need and many we don't. We have lots of electric fans, but we don't need them as we have a fine breeze and screen all around. We have had several cases, but weren't ready for them. I think we can handle anything now, but probably won't be very busy. We have an autoclave, surgical lamp and instruments enough to do an appendectomy, but I doubt that we do any.

The ambulance and jeep still run, but the jeep wouldn't run without the ambulance for it needs a push every morning.

More doctors are here now and I've met several young fellows. I thought I had lots of news but guess I dont.

All of my love,

Bill

I got Toms letter and really enjoyed it.

*   *   *

Letter No. 10

Wednesday June 27,1945

Dear Bill:

Yesterday we received your letter of the 19th in which you said that you had had my letters of the 6th and 8th. Seems strange that you had not received the one dated the 7th as well as the 1st,4th,5th. But they will be along, old slow pokes when the spirit moves them. Hope that by this time you are really at work for you have been off the beam so long I know it will seem good to be busy again.

Dick just came in a little while ago. Had just arrived a little while before from his station for a 15day furlough and of course was looking for poor Tom. I dont know how T. will manage to be busy all the time but I know he is going to have to do some fast talking as well as thinking if he is not to be bored a lot in the next two weeks. Dick thinks his mother should go out and live with Marie or Ellen. That might be fine if they were all a little more congenial.

Aunt Betty went to Pueblo this afternoon to catch the plane for San Angelo at 2:40. Tom would have driven the car up for her but he was going to Rotary with his Dad and she had to leave about 12:00 to get there in plenty of time so Uncle Earl took her up. Bill that trip to the Rotary international is just a pipe dream for your dad might not even be the pres next year but being vice this year makes day dreaming a pleasant pastime.

I went to a party for Ann Clare given by her sisters yesterday. It too was a sort of farewell from Mildred to her friends here for she leaves for Belen, N.M. where she is going to teach next year. It will be nice for the two sisters to be down there together but we do not like to see Mildred leave. Sat next to Opal Harrison who ofcourse was telling me all about the Hals. The new baby is expected about the 12th of Sept. and like the other one will have to be a Caesarian. They had to buy a house to find a place to live and now are having all sorts of difficulties getting the necessary equipment to keep house with.

Mrs. Inman called me the other day to tell be that Bob had called the night before. He cant be a Captain till September for Floyd cant move up till then. Bob said that the school is going along fine. Ginny is keeping house for her folks. Her mother works at the state house in Helena.

Last night Tom, Jay Cahlfant, Bob Mann and Wilson Cooper all had dates and they went out to the old country club where there is a new out door dancing spot. We went out to look at it when we were out there with the Larsons. They have cemented all the back for tables and in a little place about as big as this little dining room have made a smooth floor for dancing. It looks very nice back there with some landscaping around the edges and little tables and booths all around but I should think that the bugs would be terrific. I forgot to ask Tom about that part but since he didnot mention it guess they were not too bad.

I got Tom a date with the girl the Leonard wrote me about who is an exray technician at the hospital for a while. He was a little dubious but said that they got along well and she could dance. Their little party with the Rocky Ford girls did not materialize for the Blotz girl has poison ivy poisoning so does not feel well enough just now to do it, and as Bob leaves Saturday guess it will blow up all together.

I got a luncheon set to send to the young Humphries for the Sisson family so must get it off tomorrow. Also hope to get a package off to you but must first get some cans so I can seal the stuff all up so the bugs cant get in and spoil them.

*   *   *

Letter No. 11

Thursday June 28th, 1945

Dear Bill:

We are so glad to know that you know that we know that you have arrived where you started for from Hawaii. We had your two letters today one addressed to the house and the other to the office, both written on the 21st the longest day of the summer. You speak of only an occasional letter as if you do not get many of the letters I write for you know I write every day except Saturday and Sunday for I leave the news of those two days for Dads Sunday letter, so it seems as if there are many you dont receive. Perhaps they will get to you pretty soon.

I know it is good to get letters and am glad that you have had letters from Davidson and Dr. Carter. Aunt Fan has one ready to send to you which she wrote at the ranch. She came in today and will stay at least till sunday for she is going to the dinner Saturday night that the Woodbridges are having for Lt. Sisson and his family. they have asked Marg to be his girl that eve. Hope we dont stay too late as I imagine the Lt. would like to go out to the dance at the Lake that night with the girl I found for him. they evidently got on fairly well for he had another date with her last night. Think that they went to the show.

Just as I was about to put the dinner on the table today at noon Dick appeared. when we were ready to sit down and asked him to have a bite with us he said that he had had his dinner but you may know that we did not have to twist his arm to make him sit down for a glass of ice tea. Well if he had eaten before he got here I dont know how much he would have eaten if he had been hungry for he did as much justice to the food as any of us. Poor T. guess he was stuck for the whole afternoon and am afraid that it will be that way all the time. Surely am glad that he is not next door for perhaps T. can make a sneak once in a while, since he is so far away.

Your saying that that cake packed in the pop-corn was good if not like it would have been at home surprises me very much for when it did not catch you in Hawaii I thought of all the mess it would be when it did reach you. It must have been over two months on the way. Just a minute and I will look it up in my carbons and see—Yes it was April 12 that I sent it so that makes a good two months but if I try it again it wont take it so long I think and might be in better shape. would you advise my trying it again?

Glad that you got some of the stamps that I have been sending. I put a few in nearly every letter so you ought to get some of them. You said that you were sitting in the front of the tent "in the cool of the evening". Do the evenings and nights get cool enough for you to get some sleep. Pomp has told me that the climate as far as he can judge from what Junior says is about like it is here except for the humidity. AND RAIN.

So you know that the Ginny-George wedding did not take place. Poor Ginny. I guess this really did hurt but she is very sensible about it and all the family think that it was fortunate for her that there was a slip.

Little Bobby Horning Johnston has taken quite a fancy to me since I have some chickens to show him out in the back yard so now if I am in a hurry doing my work I dont dare go out the back door when he is out side for he comes right out the minute he hears me and then I must take time out to go with him to see whatever the queer word is that he has for chickens. He is really getting very cute and you know me and little kids. If I could I would spend all my day with him. The Bishop is here today to give Confirmation tonight and the poor choir(six of us) the rest wont come, have had to learn some new hymns for the special service of Confirmation. there will be a reception directly after the service when the Bishop will talk and the mortgage on the church will be burned.

Dr. Cooper would like very much if the Bishop would give consent to the Sisters building a hospital here and says that he would make the first donation toward it of quite a substantial sum(I would not dare say for I did not pay very much attention when Freda told me). She says that many of Dr.s patients are not happy in the Mennonite Hospital and that is one of the reasons that he is so anxious but Father Bertrand told me that he did not think with two other hospitals here the Sisters would want to undertake a hospital. that is all just gossip but Dr. was going to try to see the Bishop today while he is here.

Just called for Uncle Earl to see if he would come eat with us this eve but he was not in the office just then will call later. Too I wanted to know how Aunt Betty got along with her first air-plane ride if he has heard and I bet he has for I imagine he made her wire him as soon as she arrived. will go iron a bit now and then get the supper. aunt fan and Dad are at a bank meeting this afternoon and dont know just what your brother is doing, entertaining Dick, I imagine.

*   *   *

Letter No. 12

Friday June 29,1945

Dear Bill:

While the Toms and Mutt and Marg battle it out at cards I will have a little conversation with you. They thought that Murial and Eleanor were coming with Mutt but when she arrived she was alone so I phone Marg as I had not written to you yet and wanted to do so before the day closed and so Tommy could mail it after the little party is over. I intended to write when I got home from Grey Ladies but Mrs. Garvin came just as I got home so then because I had to go practice a little singing for the First Communion, next Sunday I did not have a chance before Mutt came so Having Marg come in saved the day for you and me.

Aunt Fan and Mrs. Guthries (she is always ready to go) went to Pueblo today and saw Frank while there. He said that he and Polly want to come down while Tom is here so I must write to them and set a date. They also told her that Ed got as far as Hawaii on his way home and there he was stopped and is there yet. Do hope that they are not going to send him back for more combat duty. Mrs. Guthrie had a good time and got a lot of little things that she went after. Mariam has the mumps and now Marg is wondering if it would not be sensible to let Bobby go up and play with her and maybe he would get them before he gets any older. The only reason that she hesitates is that she has not had them either and she would not like to be sick with them, if she should get them at the same time he might be sick. Bet if they went ahead and did not think about it neither of them would have them.

I went out to the base hospital for Grey Ladies today for the first time in about three weeks and my what a durth of soldiers there is out there. Hardly any in the PX even when we went over to do the patients shopping. Of course there is much, much talk about what is to happen out there. One of the wildest that we have heard came this morning when some one told Dad that he heard that they are to make a Navy training school out here and make a canal to the gulf or dredge out the channel of the Arkansas so it could be used for a waterway. Did you ever hear anything so silly?

Pink told me today that she and Annie are going to have us to dinner some night next week as they want to have a long visit with Tom. Ann goes to Canada about the 20th. She wants to drive and even tho a young girl about her age is to go with her Pink says no unless they get some one else to go along. Lots of people would like to go if there was a good chance that they could get back home again but the railroads keep telling us that civilian travel is to be cut shorter and shorter as time goes on and military travel gets heavier with the redeployment of troups to the Pacific.

Dick did not show up here today but maybe the big chocolate cake I had Mrs. Raney make for him had something to do with it. Perhaps he was not hungry. I bet he ate about half of it without stopping. His mother does not have much of a stove for baking so that is the reason I wanted to give him the cake as I did not think she would be baking one for him and any of the fellows like a good cake.

Aunt Fan said that Dr. Lassen asked today where you boys are now. He seems never to have lost interest in you.

The Confirmation Services went off fine last night except that the Bishop was terribly long winded. He started in asking the children questions on their Catechism and he was so slow waiting for each answer that he was at that alone 50 minutes and every body got so restless and tired we thought we'd go wild. They say that the music was good. Ofcourse we could not tell except that we knew that we got off in a few places. Wilson Cooper and Dr. Hudspeth, the Vetinery here, a convert, were among the 45 adults and children confirmed.

Bob Mann leaves tomorrow so Toms closest playmate will be gone but there are still quite a few of the boys around so he will have bowling partners for a while yet.

Guess I had better see how the game is coming along and then slip off and say my night prayers so I can beat them to beat them to bed when the guests leave.

*   *   *

6/30/45

Dear Mother & Dad,

Today we started our sick call which fortunately was very light. However we managed to get one emergency. I would liked to have taken care of it myself with Dr. Ranson's Help, but better judgment told us to send him to the hospital. We can take care of a lot of things now. Since we moved to this place we surely haven't been getting much mail. It'll be coming in one of these days however. Because of the rough roads we don't go up there very often.

I went for a swim this afternoon and it really was good to get wet all over at once. It was salt water—I didn't think I would enjoy a salt water bath ever again after being on the ship.

The wind didn't blow much today and it was rather hot. We have electric fans however; so it is not so bad. We don't get so much dust when the wind isn't blowing as we have a highway in front and on the side.

There used to be a town about the size of La Junta here, but there isn't one now. We had our laundry done the other day by some of the native women and it looks a lot better than the way I've been doing it. The shoes for these people—at least what looks like snikers which they wear have two compartments for toes— one for the big toe and the next toe and one for the rest. They look something like this—> =3.

The skipper of this company has been swell. They have a typewriter which they don't use much; so they let us keep it, for it isn't pecked at and we have a lot of use for it

I have five corpsmen. Two belong to this company and are temporarily under me. I don't as yet know their capabilities, the other three are fine boys. One has had quite abit of experience in an operating room. He keeps our little autoclave busy. One boy keeps the medicines straight along with many other duties. The other does my paper work for me along with other duties. I'd surely like to see Brown, but I'm pretty well confined which no doubt he is too.

It would surely be grand to be home with all of you. Perhaps it wont be too long.

Till Later,

Love, Bill

*   *   *

6 no 7/1/45

Dear Mother & Dad,

Tonight we have one patient in our sick bay. He isn't very ill, I hope.

We haven't been too busy. Tomorrow we have scheduled a big operation—a circumcision. We have a good autoclave and a good boy working it; so I'm not much worried about it. Have another patient in his tent. Did a little suturing today so am having quite a time. My boys have a lot on the ball and are well trained. Am really having the time of my life.

We have five electric fans in our shop. It is good to have them for there isn't as much breeze as there was. The fans are big and oscillating.

This being on my own is really good for me. No telephone to call for help and the only transportation about is our own vehicles—that is for our transportation. When I get back perhaps I'll be more sure of myself.

Hope Dad is having good luck with his hip.

Till Later,

All my Love, Bill

I got to Mass today at an army place.

*   *   *

Letter No. 13

Monday July 2,1945

Dear Bill:

All the afternoon tom has been sitting around waiting for the boys to come and to start for Denver but as yet,4:15 they have not arrived.

We got your letter written the 24th, a week ago yesterday, today and surely were glad to hear that at last you have some sort of duty even tho you did not yet have the dispensary perfected. By now you should be pretty well established and hard at work. Hope the first patient, the boy with minor burns got along fine.

You did not say that you left that island so suppose you are on the same one only in a different place. I'll bet it was a very different feeling to have some one expecting you than when you first landed there and had nothing at all for you not even a place to rest your weary head and mud mud everywhere. Now time will not hang so heavy on your hands and before we know it the Japs will be licked and we will all be readjusting to civie life. Oh what a pleasant dream!

Tom just came out here to me sat down and said he had made a decision. It seemed to be a weighty one so I stopped everything to listen and he had said that he had decided that he would not go to Denver with the boys for he thought that he would rather just stay at home and play around with the small town folks so he has gone down to inform his Dad of that idea. It suits me swell.

Earl called me this morning to say that Aunt Betty and Justine would be coming home as soon as they could get some sort of reservation. This is a secret but since you wont be talking to any of the home town folks to give it away I will let you in on it. The Lloyds evidently have a "little secret" and because there was a possibility of loosing it was the reason Justine was in bed. The doctor says it is now safe for her to travel so she will come home till the weather cools off a bit down there. Poor Johnny I know will be lost without her but on the other hand guess it worried him to have her there in the heat and getting all faged out. this is the day that the 2nd air force took over this field and there have been planes flying over all day and so it does not look as if they are to close it as the rumor, or rather one of the rumors had it.

Aunt Fan went out this morning and went the long way for when she came the other day the army boys were working the road the short way and she knew that it would be hard to drive on today for they were piling the dirt all in the middle like they do so many times. That is another thing that makes it look as if they will not give up the bombing range either. Ofcourse it is for the Pueblo base and not this one, so is really no indicator of what if happening to this one.

This weather here can change in a big hurry. this morning we had to have a little heat in the house and this afternoon it would be good and to have the cooler on. While we were enjoying our fire in the fire place last night we heard over the radio that it had been 103 in Amarillo and Albuquerque yesterday.

The Hollis family are hard at work over at the house today and from the sound of things I think that they are making the door from the room that used to be Aunty His bed room, into the dining room for they are going to make a kitchen out of that and use the old kitchen for a bed room. The arrangement will be much better that way for then the bath room will be off the bed rooms instead of the kitchen.

The other morning when I woke I saw a little yellow bird out the north window so I lay there watching it and noticed that it would fly away and them come back and soon found out that it would fly away and then come back and soon found out that there were two old birds feeding a young on that was sitting on a branch right outside of the window. I must have lain their 15 minutes watching them and thought that little fellow must be so full he would burst but he never refused to open his mouth and gulp down the bug they brought him. I hope the cats did not get him for the next time I look to see what was going on he was no longer there. I think they must have had the nest close by and am sorry I did not find it just so I could see what sort of nest they had. that would help me to tell just what sort of bird they are.

Tomorrow is wash day and still I do not have the last weeks ironing done so think that I better stop and run down and finish it up it wont take me but a little while.

*　　　*　　　*

7/3/45

Dear Mother & Dad,

Today we had our first operation—a circumcision. The patient seems to be doing very well. It was surely good experience even thought it was surely a minor procedure as there was no one to call upon. The Captain paid me a visit today. He is my senior medical Officer. I hope he was satisfied with our set up. I think it is pretty good if it weren't for the dust. He didn't say much even about my elective surgery. There is surely too much Red Tape to this job—That is its only drawback. I don't know very much about the forms and no book to tell me. So I have to rely on the corpsmen's experience. They have surely been good boys and seem to fit in to the set up just fine.

I got the June 18, Time yesterday and see that you had already anticipated by slightest wish. In the boxes you send me you might put in a medical Textbook. They will probably be out of date by the time I return anyway. The ones I would like most are Medicine by Cecil, Surgery by Christopher, and Fractures by Key and Conwell. There is one other book I don't have and that is Surgery on the Ambulatory Patient by Ferguson. If you happen to be in Denver Sometime you might pick it up for me at the Book Store in the Medical School.

We have the radio working and are listening right now to Bob Hope. My Electric Razor also works on our generator.

I got the third band for my watch today since I've had it and hope this one lasts a little while. It is cloth. The climate out here is surely hard on bands. The watch runs well and fits all my needs.

I had a letter from Bob yesterday and will enclose a few pictures we took at Hilo. Isn't it a funny car.

All my love, Bill

*   *   *

Letter No. 14

Tuesday July 3,1945

Dear Bill:

We were very glad to get your letter today and learn about you and your colored company and know that being like your Dad and mother you will get along fine with them. Your Dad always got a big kick out of the colored boys and liked to be around them and hear them talk etc.

There is one thing we are sure that you are learning and that is to take responsibility for being the only one there you just have it to do and will have to go ahead and act. Am glad the other doctor appeared to do your labratory work for you or you might have had to work night and day and while it is good to be busy one does have to have rest once in a while.

You said that you live with three other officers(all white) by that I would judge that there are some in the company that are not white. Hope you get some bath facilities set up before long for when it is hot there is just nothing like a good bath. Is water plentiful around there? I should think it would be if there is some way of holding some of that which falls in such quantities at times. If I can find a map of the island I will be looking for two main highways and near the shore to try guessing where you are.

Am glad that your good corpsmen who went from the states with you are still there. John said they were really good boys, especially one of them he thought was a big help to you for he really knew the Navy.

About one oclock last night the boys arrived from Oklahoma and Tom gave in and went to Denver with them but said that he would be back tomorrow on the bus. He had a date tonight with Pat (she is the technician from Pueblo) and asked me to call her this morning and tell her he would like to change the days for tomorrow night so I got that little job done in good shape this morning.

We suppose that Fred and Jean are either in Trinidad or coming but have not heard a word from Nellie to that effect or to any other effect, in fact. We just have not heard from Nellie, period. Mary was in today but neither had she been informed about the arrival of the junior Sisks.

Aunt Betty and Justine will get home tomorrow eve, by plane to Pueblo and then on the train down here. Marg and I are going out to get their house ready for them in the morning.

Mr. Todd died today after being so bad so long. They were trying to get the boys home through the Red Cross and it is just a shame that they could not have arrived. John will be discharged when he gets here for he has 104 points.

Am going to a board meeting and then Dad and I are going to see Mrs. Todd for a little while.

This morning Jackie Lacy and Charla Rea Bickett came to see me selling chances. Of course I took one from each, that kind where you punch out a number and that is the price you pay and I got hooked for .29 and .33 cents. Rather costly dont you think just for being a kind neighbor. Must run now.

*   *   *

7/4/45

Dear Mother & Dad,

The sick call has enlarged from a first aid station to same old sick line. Backaches, etc. I don't spend much time with them. But being on our own away from the gold braid is a big compensation.

In Bob's letter he said his father had resigned. I'm surely sorry to hear they are leaving L.J.

I am surely glad you are getting my letters so quickly. I get yours usually in about 10 d—2 wks. I think we are now getting them a little faster.

I haven't drawn any pay since I left in April so now have quite have quite a bit on the books. I don't need any money here As a matter of fact you can't buy anything except stamps and you send me them. Have the checks been coming from the allotment I made.

Ole T. has a date with Ida. She is a good gal and a lot of fun. It was surely nice to have Julia come down, I'll bet.

I haven't seen Brown since that one time, but hope to get away soon. Woody and Wally Gist are in the neighborhood somewhere. There are several other people out here I've met along the way and hope to get to see them soon.

4th of July. I wonder if Tom went to the Sunrise Dance at Holbrook.

Till Later,

All my Love, Bill

*   *   *

Letter No. 15

Wednesday July 4, 1945

Dear Bill:

I surly have taken myself a holiday today. Just done not one thing for me or for my country or anything else. I had the good excuse this afternoon that Tommy was sleeping in the basement and so I just Had to be quiet so lay on the davenporte and the Denver Post for once. Most of the time I disgrace my husband by not knowing what is going on in the world for ordinarily I just read the headlines if I get at it at all.

Then for a little while I had callers. This Pat girl at the Mennonite Hospital had her folks with her this afternoon and stopped for a few minutes. Think they wanted to meet Tom but I did not wake him up for having had practically no sleep for two nights I knew he was a bit tired and would like to feel a little perker for this eve. They are the people who live next door to the Leonards so I was glad to meet them. They seemed live very nice people.

Tom had quite a good time in Denver for he saw quite a few he knew at Lakeside last night. He will have to tell you about it for I dont remember all of those he spoke of the only one I remember is Bob Mertz. But getting to bed about two last night and getting up at six to catch the bus did not give him a very full night of rest.

Dad has been working at the office most of the day on some certificates that Uncle Earl wanted him to get out "Immediately". You know how Uncle Earl loves those people who want him to do something in a big hurry. Well Dad told him he could not get them done till tomorrow so he has worked today in order to try to fill his promise.

It is thundering a little just now but dont think there can be much of a cloud for it is not dark so guess it is just local like most of them are. Talked to aunt Fan at noon today and she was some what discouraged for after all the vaccinating they did out there this spring there have been two of the cows that were vaccinated have died. Dont know what the vetinary will have to say about it. They brought in the ear of one of the animals that died for him to test as he had told them he wanted it in case there were any died.

We have had very little fourth of July celebration in the way of fire crackers, however I think that it was Jackie Lacy who woke me this morning with some rather loud ones. I heard the commentator over the radio say today that some cities in the south who have never celebrated fourth of July since the Civil War did so today. Guess they have finally decided they area part of the USA. There have been no parties that I know of among our friends. I think largely because of Mr. Todds death yesterday and the Kendalls are still waiting for news from Dean. Jim Sterling told them rather reassuring things about the number of islands where he went down and the slow way of getting information about the fellows who have bailed out which made them feel more hopeful.

I will celebrate the evening by going to Holy Hour and I believe that is a rather fitting way under the circumstances. Dad just came in so guess it is time for me to get busy with a little food for the supper and to wake Tom up. He has had a good sleep so should be wide awake for the evening.

*   *   *

Letter No. 16

Thursday July 5,1945

Dear Bill:

My conversation with you will have to be a little short and snappy this eve if I get it ready for the Lt. to take with him when he goes dating at 8:15. We were a bit late with the supper for Tom was bowling and did not get home till a little late and I did not get to the letter writing while I waited for him as I should have so that is the explaination for the briefness of the letter.

We went to the funeral, Mr. Todd today, Dad was a pallbearer, so I did not do much else this afternoon but when I got home I washed the sox etc.

Tom said that he was hitting a pretty good game this afternoon and twice had in the 80s. Dick was there too and Tom says he bowls a fairly good game, averaging about 150. We havenot seen a sign of him up this way since that first day and we are really surprised. Perhaps the rank of the Lt. sort of scares him tho it does not affect any of the other boys.

Wonder if you have started to getting any of the publications which we send you, the paper, Colliers or Pony time. Two boxes which I had sent to Tom came back today. The raisins in them were just fine and of course all the little cans of minced ham etc and a box of candied nuts was in fair shape but a few crackers I had put in were just a mess of crumbs. There was also a box of candy which aunt Betty had sent. It looks all right but dont think that he has opened it yet to see.

Aunt Betty and Justine came over a little while last eve after they got home. Aunt B. thinks air travel is just the thing and said that she was really rather proud of herself for she did not get at all sick and lots of the passengers did. Justine is fine but a little thin, it seems to me. She will go back after a while as they kept their apartment. Johnny will stay there so she feels better about that for the barracks are much hotter even that in the little city of San Angelo.

Tom has put in a call for the Sisks hoping to have a talk with Fred. They have not seen each other for about four years no it is three years. I guess for we have not been in the war four years yet.

Archie Sierks and Bob see each other now in Hawaii. Archie is in and out of there now for a while. Mrs. Inman gave us a picture of you that was taken when you had the hired car over on Hilo. You are sort of draped over the front fender and it is a marvelous picture of you. Because she thought it so good was the reason she gave it to us. Did you not get any of those pictures? They all seemed to be fairly good.

The Toms have gotten into a cribbage game. Dont think Dad will want to take me on tonight for last night I was all luck and skunked him three times but ofcourse luck like that cant hold up all the time. Will close now and get this ready to send along on the date.

*   *   *

7/6/45

Dear Mother & Dad,

Tom has a little over a week before his leave is up. Then it would surely be swell if he were sent to the Springs.

Things are pretty quiet here and we are settling down to a nice peaceful existence. Even our sick call is not very large.

The other day I went over to see a Doctor in a CB Battalion and to my great satisfaction he gave us a cold beer. It surely did hit the spot. What would be better however is an ice cold Coca Cola. It won't be long till watermelon time at home. An ice cold watermelon would really be good.

There are four of us in a tent and we all had lots of gear so I moved into a tent with just one other boy. It is better for there is lots of room now. I didn't realize how valuable the mosquito nets were—They are just the ticket because you can be absolutely bug free. I am now using the bedroll I brought from Oahu which is better for it has sheets. Really living royally now.

Till Later,

All my Love, Bill

*   *   *

7/8/45

Dear Mother and Dad,

I 'm having a little rest spell. I might as well tell you the whole story else you might worry. I had quite a pain in my right side so consulted one of the doctors close by and he decided I should come to the hospital where I am. I passed a little stone last night. X-rays this morning are perfectly normal so am perfectly well and hope to be back to the dispensary in a few days, but you know this hospitals.

It really has been a vacation for as I arrived the pain stopped. The only disagreeable part was cleaning out my bowels for the X-ray. One swell thing is that the Dr. in charge of the ward is Walsh whom I've been with in Hueneme, crossing to Hawaii, and Oahu. He fixed me up with stationery and reading material. He has a little dog he picked up in his journeys which really made this place seem like the States. I had a good shower last night and saw a good picture show—so this has been really a vacation. I missed Mass this morning as was having my picture taken.

Another nice thing about coming here is that I've sent several patients here and have been able to follow them up.

It is quiet pretty here—reminds me a lot of the rolling country of the Ozarks. Tom has only 6 more days on leave.

Not much other news,

All my love, Bill

*   *   *

Letter 17,(single)

Monday July 9, 1945.

Dear Bill:

Dont see how you have gotten along for I see that your mother has not written you since last Thursday. Tom wrote Friday, Dad on Saturday and no one yesterday. I will have to make a good, good letter today as a result of all this silence on the part of your mater.

First I will tell your about getting three letters from you this morning. One of 6/30 telling of your first emergency which you sent to the hospital so by that we know that there is a hospital somewhere in the reach of you. Sorry that the mail has been sort of held up on you but it must be some where so you will get a lot when you get any perhaps. How far is it to the place where you have to get it from? You spoke of the rough roads going "up there". Glad you got a swim and bet it really did feel good even if it was salt water.

Guess we should be able to guess where you are since there used to be a town there about the size of La Junta but I am not so sharp that way.

I spect you will be wearing the sort of shoes that the natives wear when you come home. I should think that strip between their toes would be very uncomfortable. I suppose that is what keeps them from coming off. Glad that you can use the skippers typewriter for it must facilitate your report work if you can make carbons of things for I imagine they have to be made in triplicate if not more.

Seems from what you tell of the duties you have for each of your corpsmen that you have things very well organized. Glad that they are good boys and know their stuff for that must be a very great help to you. We are guessing that an autoclave is and mine is that it is a sterlizer. Well what?

In the letter of July 1 you told about having one patient in your sick bay another in his tent and an operation scheduled. Am glad that you wrote the next one on the third for then we knew how you had come along with the first operation. This first visit from your Captain evidently went off all right and from the fact that he made no complaints I think indicates he was pleased with the set up. The dust is not your fault and just cant be controlled if those two high ways are there. Evidently there must be quite a little traffic over them. The forms must be a nuissance and the darned red tape but I guess there is a reason for it or otherwise they would do differently.

I will see about sending your test books for I think that I am allowed to send scientific books to some one in the Navy who needs them. We might possibly take Tom to Denver Saturday if he wants us to but so far we have not discussed it. We could get that other book for you then if not will have a chance some other time.

The snap shot you inclosed is the one that Mrs. Inman had given us but she had told us that if you sent some we were to give this one back to her so shall do that very thing now that we have our own. I will put them in your scrap book, which I am keeping for you.

My! how glad I am that you got a radio for I was so upset that we had not taken the other one to you. It is grand that it and your razor work on that current.

Our trip to Trinidad yesterday was a success and the baby is one big fine baby. We had a picnic dinner out in the place west of the house that they have sort of parked with trees and flowers etc. and it was so nice out there. No flies and nice and cool. Tom stayed to be godfather for Chuck today after Ginny would get there for she was to be the Godmother then they will bring Tom home tomorrow morning and I think stay over till Wednesday. Aunt Fan is coming in tomorrow morning so she can get a glimpse of the off spring and if Mary gets my letter she too wants to get here.

Tom and Walter Cranson are to be the program at the Lions club tomorrow so he has to get here in the forenoon. Tom and Fred had gone out to play a little golf when we started home yesterday afternoon. There was a little shower but guess it did not stop them and made it nice and cool.

When Tom wrote you he let me censor the letter and I noticed

that he did not tell you that Bob Mertz was using old Religion. He said it stood out there and finally he tried it out and with a little fixing it went all right so he had been using it.

Got the card today telling us that your clothes are at the Express office, no freight office, today so we will get the package maybe when Dad comes home.

This is my USO night and probably the last one for the base is closing up all but for just a few to look after things. It is being put on a stand by basis so guess my war work is about over. I called to see if it was necessary for us to go down tonight but the director said yes and if there was just not anything doing she would let us come on home.

Time out—Al Diming was just here to tell us good bye for he is like most of the others, leaving, heading for the Pacific in due course of time. I told him if he got to Okinawa to write me and I would send him your address. He thinks that he will not be doing Link Training from now on for as he says the need for them is about over.

Guess Mr. Horning will have three apartments to rent after the 15th. One is already vacant.

It is time for Mr. Sisson now so will close and listen to the news with him.

*   *   *

7/10/45

Dear Mother & Dad,

Shall try pencil today as my ink supply is about gone. I haven't received a letter for several days but hope to soon.

I am still a patient, but believe the red tape will be settled soon and will get back to work. I guess I haven't been very sick. Dr. Walsh has belittled my little stone. He thinks it can only be called sand. Today Meserole—one of my corpsmen, was up to see me and says everything has gone along very well without me.

This evening Walsh and I may get up a bridge game. First I'll have played since the ship. One of the patients has a radio that works fine. We've been getting all the latest news. There are lots of good transmitted programs out here. They lack only the advertising.

Last night saw a picture show—John L Sullivan. It was a good diversion.

Wonder where Ole T will go now. That would be grand if he went to Colo. Spr. I've spent most of my time asleep. I really don't need the rest, but am surely getting it.

Not much other news,

All my love, Bill

*   *   *

Letter No. 18

Wednesday July 11,1945.

Dear Bill:

Tom has gone(5:30 PM) down to the opening of the Kit Carson bar with two ladies, Bette Morse and Ann Walker. Mrs. Frey has put it in where Dr. Morse used to have his office. Perhaps you can recall that there was a door in the east end of the lobby(I had never noticed it) so it made it very handy. Mother Frey did not like the idea at first but guess she has been sort of talked into it by now.

Yesterday was a big day for the family for the Sisks came down, Aunts Fan and Mary came in so the family had a picnic last eve in the Sabin house, it had to be inside for the rain fell in torrents. Every one enjoyed it very much and all ahed and ohed over the baby but Jean certainly does not let him appear much. Kept him in seclusion most of the time and dont think that any of the fond aunties got to hold him at all, or talk with him altho he was in a very talkative mood. Not once during the whole day did he let out even one little cry.

Got you letter of the 5th yesterday and glad all is going fine thus far. Dad checked with Mac about Mr. Inmans resignation and he says that there is nothing to it. Mr. Herron resigned. Could Bob have meant that? Maybe that board does not know his plans yet.

We have decided to take Tom and Walt to Denver Saturday for then we will have a whole day longer with him and its a little easier than the train too.

Hope you get to see Woody and Wally Gist ere long.

No, Tom did not go to the Sunrise dance for he was in Denver that night.

I went down to see about sending your books and I can send 70 pounds so that will take care of all you want us to send. I am writing to so Jess Humphries tonight to get that one from the Med School book store for us so we can pick it up when we go to Denver and then I will send them all together next week. I have to show them your request for them however.

Tom has a date tonight with the girl at the Mennonite Hosp., the red head he calls her. Think he really has had quite a good time with her since he met her. He says at least he feels that he is not imposing on her when he asks her to go with him.

Will run now and try to have the supper ready when he gets home. Bought two silver salt and pepper shakers for a wedding gift for Nancy Gardner today. We will not be at the wedding for it is to be Sunday afternoon.

*   *   *

Letter No. 19

Thursday July 11,1945

Dear Bill:

While the Toms get ready for the dinner party at the Nortons, I got all fixed before they came home, I will write to you.

We got your letter of the sixth this afternoon and I judge from what you say that it is really hot there now. Your strong for a good cold drink would indicate that or the thought of good cold watermelon. As yet there are no home grown melons for sale but today I weakened and bought two cantaloupes, 24cents a piece. One was good and the other I threw out for it just had no taste at all. We bought one watermelon when Tom first came home, in fact it was the night that Julia was here and I threw out most of that so you see as yet you are not missing those things by not being here.

You spoke of things being dull in the dispensary. Well it is like that you know the old saying it never rains but it pours. When you do have some business it will all come at once.

The fellows had a big time last night at least Tom Jr. did for he had four women to take about. As I told you he had a date at 5:30 to take Ann Walker and Bette Morse to the new cocktail bar but they stayed so long there he had to get his other date too then the Mac Donalds were down there and May sort of attached herself so they all went up to MacDonalds where the men had gathered for the poker party. Guess John Mullins was feeling a little too good, had been to the bar too, to want to settle down to poker so they danced and played around up there till about ten when Tom and the ladies went down to get something to eat. It seems that they had had no dinner till that late hour. Dad got home early for the poker players, about 12:45 and T. came not so long after.

Aunt Fan went to the ranch today and found that the grand rain we had here the other night as usual missed the ranch much to her disappointment. However the rain they had had there a few days before had filled up some of the reservoirs around the head of

Iron and Minnie canyons which helps a lot for they were having to take some of the cows out of that pasture as the iron spring at the head of Iron did not afford enough water for them all.

Mrs. Stone came this morning and so we got the laundry all done and now I will iron Toms shirts, little Toms, so he can pack them tomorrow. Your box is here but I have not opened it for Tom left it in the garage and I have to have some one bring it in for me and I just cant remember to put in the request.

We still have not had any warm weather. The nights get down in the fiftys but we keep thinking that as all good things come to an end we are just about to get it. However it will have to hurry or the summer will be over for already the days have started to get shorter.

Got all excited this morning for I could not find my ration books anywhere. Looked all around here so thought they would be at the store so went down there but no they did not have them. Looked all over here again and about gave up when I remembered that I had gotten those cantaloupes in a big sack and had just put them in the cooler in it so looked there and sure enough the books were in the sack, safe as could be.

Better go now as the boys are about all set for the party.

*   *   *

12 July '45

Dear Mother & Dad,

I am back on the job in this dusty corner of the world. On the way back I stopped in at my previous camp. There they had a sign with the distances on it to the various cities of the world. That really made me think how far I am from anywhere except perhaps a land that I am not very fond. It is about 3000 miles closer to London than it is to Washington D.C.

The stay in the hospital was really a lot of fun and I'm surprised that I was able to get out in 4 days, and glad. It was ole Walsh— I guess he was glad to get rid of me.

Everything has gone along very well without me. Thats no feeling of being a necessity around. A couple of Dr. from a CB outfit took care of my emergencies.

Haven't had any letters for awhile, but imagine I'll get a bunch of them one of these days.

Not much other news,

All my love, Bill

*   *   *

Letter No. 20

Friday July 12, 1945

Dear Bill:

You might think that Tom had been busy today packing but tho it is now about 7:30 PM he has not even started. However since we are driving and do not start till noon he will really have time enough in the morning for he does not have a great deal to get done. I did little washing and ironing for him today and mended some socks but that is about all I did.

Dick was up this afternoon to say good-bye and tell us that he is going to Pueblo tomorrow and "he wished he knew some one that was driving up tomorrow". I dont know whether he had an inkling that we were or not anyway I did not even peep tho I thought at that time we probably would have room but I was not going to inflict him on the boys if that were not too eager about it. Since then we learn that Walters girl from Nebraska is still here so think she will probably be going up with us so then we would not have room for another especially this hot weather three in the front seat is just too much, so guess it is a good thing for once I kept silent.

Mutt had a telegram this afternoon from Roscoe from Brazil on his way home. He will be here in about three weeks so Dad is out looking for another girl. Mutt is all excited. At first she was afraid to open the message not knowing what it might contain.

_____ The Mac Donalds asked us for dinner tomorrow night, a little late but we appreciated the thought just the same. They did not realize Tom's leave is up.

I took our gift up to the Gardners this eve and ofcourse had to go in and see Nancys gifts. They were getting ready to have the mother and father-in-law to dinner so I only stayed a minute.

Shirley Garlington and Bonny Groth and her two children are coming down tonight for the wedding. That little house of the Gardners must be made of elastic for it always seems to accomodate all that come.

We heard that Mr. McCartney had a stroke down at Dodge last night. Have not yet learned how severe it was but I intend to call Hazel soon to find out. He should have retired some time ago but felt it was his duty to keep on when they need men so much.

Guess Aunt Gertrude wrote you that Marsden is to stay in this country and that Marion had a miscarriage at one month.

Bud had a nice break recently when the Major came to him and asked him if he could drive a car that he had a business trip down south into Germany. He asked Bud if there was some place along down that way he would particularly like to go for they could do that too so Bud said he would like to see Bill Guthrie and the Major said sure they could go to the place Bill is and see him. Will be anxious now to hear how the trip turned out. Too he thinks perhaps, there is a rumor to the effect, that they will be allowed to make a trip to England when they are stationed at Deauxville if they did not take one to the Rivera which was allowed to them but which Bud passed up.

We had a nice evening at the Nortons last night and can you believe it when all the good-bye kissing was on that young woman stuck her face up and gave your brother a big smacker. She is still quite a kid even tho married.

We will start about noon tomorrow and stay all night. Mrs. Frey got us a room at the Albany.

*   *   *

7/14/45

Dear Mother & Dad,

Today Tom's leave is up if I remember correctly. Hope he gets good duty. The mail has been slow, and I haven't had a letter in over a week, but when it does come I'll probably get a bunch all at once.

Our dispensary has not been busy; so we did another circumcision yesterday. They seem to do ok.

It is surely hot and dusty here now. They are building a big Highway right by us and when it gets finished we may have it a lot better. You have to keep everything closed or under something to keep from getting a big layer of dust on it.

Last night we went to an Army Camp show made up of army talent. They had some clever boys in it and it Was very entertaining. After the show the jeep wouldn't start, but fortunately an army or CB mechanic knew the intricacies and with our pleas the little jitney perked to life and brought us back.

We have a nifty water system in the dispensary. It consists of a 50 gallon water barrel on the outside of the dispensary with a spigot sticking inside. It is luke warm all of the time. We have a little burner to make hot water. A truck comes by every morning and fills it. We have oiled the floors which surely seems to decrease the dust. We have screening all the way around the dispensary which with the fans keeps it fairly comfortable. This is really the best structure in camp.

When we do our surgery(circumcisions) it is a far cry from the Mennonite Hospital. I think we manage to keep our sterile technique but it is pretty tricky. The most patients we have had at one time has been two. We usually don't have any as they get well or we send them to the hospital. We have evacuated several patients from ships and other nearby camps. We have had a case of meningitis, pleural effusion, several accident cases and numerous other minor things. No native diseases as yet however, except for possibly dengue; for I've had several cases I don't know exactly what they were, but they get well in a shorter time then Dengue should.

I went over to another G-10 outfit who are running a hospital for the natives. The doctor has been very busy. He had several interesting cases including tetanus—the first I've ever seen. We of course are all immunized against it.

Have not much other news

Till later

Love & Kisses, Bill

*   *   *

7/15/45

Dear Mother & Dad,

Today we got lots of mail—18 letters myself. It was surely a wonderful Sunday afternoon, sitting down and reading all the latest from Home. Had letters from Aunt Fan, Ginny, D. Duffy, McBurney, and Davidson in addition to those from you. The last letter was the 7th of July. It was surely good to hear that Tom may get C-54. I was about to write and tell him what to bring and what not to bring to this place. It wouldn't be much help as all I could suggest would be not to bring anything you don't want to lose or ruin, don't try to bring too much gear, but bring anything else you think you might like to have. Good clothes are of no value. The fewer clothes the better—Being in the air Corps however is quite a bit different I imagine. We have our laundry done by native women. I guess they surely can't understand English or read it for I never get anything that I send down back. Every week I have a different ensemble.

There is not cross road where we are, but we are on a coast highway. We are right near a pier—there are two roads running To it and we are right between them; so we have roads on three sides. We are on the site of what was formerly one of the main cities.

Hoped to get to Mass this evening, but in the middle of this letter we got a patient—a boy who almost drowned. He is all right I think, but don't feel like going too far away.

Surely did enjoy all the letters. Till Later,

All my Love, Bill

*   *   *

Letter No. 21

Monday July 16, 1945

Dear Bill:

Dad and I got home about 45 minutes ago. He let me out here and then went on to let Walter and his girl out and when I tried to get in I could not work the key. I saw Mr. Land on the porch so went over thinking I would telephone to Dad but first Mr. L said he would come over and see if he could work it and sure enough he got it to work. It is just hard and I did not have the elbow grease, I guess. It is now 4:30 so I did not want to wait all that time outside. There was no letter from you when we got here as I thought there might be but Dad says that I am just spoiled for you have written us so often that I think there should be a letter every change of day time.

We left Tom with Klegg and some of the other boys who go to Sioux Falls, to leave about two-thirty this afternoon. There were many whose orders had been changed so were not going there, but since the pal Klegg is everything was fine.

Walter got an emergency extension of 15 days and so he and the girl came back for another visit. Dont know whether this might mean he would not fly with Tom or not but am sure it wont make a great deal of difference to T. if he does not.

We went up to Idaho Springs just about 1:30 and about seven miles out of Denver passed an ambulance and felt sure it was Dud but went on thinking we would see Olive and Judy and the home etc but when we got there all was locked up tight as could be. We waited around about two hours and then decided to leave a note and come on back to Denver but about five miles out of there again passed him so turned back and arrived a little while after they had. They had been down to Denver to see Fred and family who were on their way back to Michigan. We did not know that they were to go thru Denver as they had come out via Santa Fe. Ofcourse they wanted to feed us so Olive whipped up a meal in no time. We were so glad that we did catch them for Dud seemed as happy as a kid with a little red wagon to show all his set up. He was recently installed in the first chair of the Elks Lodge there and that had really pleased him more than most anything that has ever happened to him, he said. Judy, being in her own surroundings was more friendly than usual and hawled out all her dolls and filled the arms of each one of us with them. when Olive started to set the table and got things ready to feed us she was right in there helping like a little old lady.

There was a picture in the Democrat Saturday of an LST landing on Okinawa and from it I can just imagine it looks like that place you are. I will put it in this letter and you can tell me if it does.

We got the book for you. Jess had it and I will inclose the note he had put with it explaining how he got it. Will get them all off to you tomorrow or next day. Tom went to Lakeside Sat eve with Roy Black and saw Jess and his wife there also saw Ed Meuller.

Last night I think he and Roy just had a big gab fest and he came in early for we were to get up at seven this morning.

Guess this is all the news for this time so will sign off.

*　　*　　*

Letter No. 22

Tuesday July 17, 1945

Dear Bill:

Three letters from you today but sorry to hear about the stone however it sort of sounds like it was from you view point sort of a break in the monotony of life on the island. I remember that once before you had an attack like that but at that time dont believe they were sure it was a stone but rather thought so. I imagine if it was a little gravel as Dr. Walsh says that you dont want any stones for I bet the pain was a plenty. That letter the first from the hospital must have dropped into the fuel tank of the plane for it was oily and smelled of oil, not gasoline. so guess it must be a new way of sterilizing things over there but really it made us wonder how it got that way, but guess it does not make any difference just as long as we got it and can read it still.

I must have seemed good to have that shower and see a picture show and all. Think they did very well to keep you for four days for evidently you were not very ill when you were going to shows etc.

We think that perhaps your CBs are making a new harbor and that is the reason you are right on the beach where it is so dusty. I also guess from your FPO number that you are not too permanently located there. Well the way things look from here the Japs are getting it hot and heavy and it sounds like their home island will be occupied before long. If it were not profane I would say "The Fools" Cant they see that surrender would be better than annihilation. Surely there are some smart japs left whose eyes will open soon and give up the war so we can get all our fellows home. From what you said about the distances from the large cities to the place you are now at it would seem that you are about the same distance from London as you are from San Francisco for it is about that distance from Frisco to Washington.

Doesnt your radio work or cant you get the good programes out there that you heard at the hospital? I think it was swell of your corpsman to come out to see while you were at the hospital with the news that all was going well in your domain.

Hope you got in the bridge game. We only played once while Tom was here and that was the evening that Mutt came to call.

Wonder where the letters got stacked up but you probably have had a lot of them by this time. The last of the three letters we got today was written the 12th and here this is the 17th so you see it was just five days ago that you wrote that letter. Surely wish you could get ours that quickly.

I got all the books ready this afternoon, all in one big box. So in the morning Dad will take them down and get them mailed and your ought to get them by the first of September, in the meantime you will have to consult the other doctors, I guess.

I had an appointment with Dr. Brown Monday morning at ten so when we decided to stay in Denver and sent the wire to Aunt Betty I told her to cancel it. Well it was not necessary for he had gone to Colorado Springs with out letting me know he was going and I was not the only one for a woman from Fowler called Aunt Betty this afternoon to ask if she could tell them anything about him for they had come down to keep an appointment and could not find him so he must have gone away without doing anything about his appointments. Isnt that an odd thing to do. It would not be surprising if I did that for I am that absentminded but one would hardly expect a doctor to do it. I will surely have some "ribbing" to do on him.

I just talked to Aunt Fan but could hardly hear her. I did understand that they had had a little rain at the head of Stage canyon and there is some water in a couple of the ponds up there which helps.

From that little clipping at the top of the other page you will now know that we know what an autoclave is. As we thought it is your sterilizer.

Aunt Fan said that about seven or eight of the cows out there have died so it looks as if it is not anthrax since they were all vaccinated by the vet this spring.

The Driscolls do not like living in Rocky Ford so now are combing the town for a house here. They were looking at the house north of Aunt Betty Sunday and as the people who live there are away they went to the Colonges and got the key and went in and all over the house. The neighbors out there think that was a bit nervy. Mrs. D. asked Ruth Draper at the party yesterday when she was going to be ready to let them have her house and since Mr. Larsen is not very well the folks who heard her did not think that was a very tactful remark so the lady is sort of getting herself in the dog house it would seem.

I spect that Tom is in Sioux Falls tonight but doubt that he knows what he is to do next yet.

Roscoe phoned Mutt yesterday from Charleston So. Carolina and will come to Ft. Logan and then be home. He is relieved from his group which means that he will be discharged and Mutt is walking on air. She had figured that he will get to Denver about Friday so is going up there to be on hand when he arrives. Ofcourse it makes Dad trouble for he has to get another girl. The new girl in the office is working on some of the girls she knows so perhaps they will find one. The greatest difficulty is that it has to be some one who knows the business and who is really accurate and good.

Dad and I both had the big eye last night so think that we will turn in pretty early and so will close now and get this nailed before time for the news. We got the great big heavy boards from around your things this evening so now tomorrow I can get into them and see what needs attention.

*   *   *

7/18/45

Dear Dad & Mother,

Not much news from this place. We have settled down to pretty much routine.

The other day I picked up a few surgical instruments from some Marines. They are Jap instruments and will constitute my souvenir of this place. There isn't much here of any value. It took a long time for these natives to fix up this Island and only a few weeks to tear it down. But now there is a reconstruction period and I doubt that the natives will recognize the place.

The other day I went up to see Brown and on the way picked up Walsh and his dog. Unfortunately Woody was out. Walsh, the Dog, and I then went for a swimm. The water was grand—the only difficulty was that it was a long way out to deep water so we never got much over our knees. I had lunch at the NUB and supper with Walsh. It only took 45 min to get back here. Some difference from the first time when we came by boat.

Your letters are coming through good although it is usually sporadic. I've had letters in as short a time as 8 days. The Colliers and Time are coming good—the paper however not so well as I haven't received a copy since I left the States.

Our camp has changed quite a bit since we arrived and are now well situated.

Have not much other information—till later,

Love, Bill

Note: After finding a Japanese language officer, I learned that they were veterinary instruments.

*   *   *

Letter No. 23

Wednesday July 18, 1945

Twins—Nell
and Mayme

Dear Bill:

The twins just left here for the ranch and are not accepting the kind invitation of Mrs. Sabin and Sisson for luncheon on Friday. We are just going to have a few for Mrs. Richardsons house guests but thought it would be nice if Mary and Nellie came too. But they thought that it would be more fun at the ranch.

Father Bertrand was over to see me this afternoon just for a friendly call and to tell me that he had asked his uncle to get me a box of those big sweet cherries. Hope they get here but it is getting rather late for them.

Dad is going to the poker club tonight so I will have things to myself for a while. Dr. Brown is still away so Dad is taking his place at the club.

The Parhms sold their house over on Rice for 7500 dollars. So I told Dad we had better sell ours for if that one was worth that this one should be about 10,000. but he is satisfied to stay here and be poor, so think I shall stay with him. Judge Miller bought one of the courts where Pink lives (they are selling them in separate units, Pink had to buy hers) so guess their big house on Colorado will be for sale so maybe the Driscolls will be after that.

Aunt Betty and Justine were at a party at the hotel today which Betty Inge was having just for sort of the family. think that Bess and Marg and Justine comprised it.

The Hollis's next door are still working on it so ofcourse have not moved in. It seems to take so long to get things done. The yard as yet does not look much better than it did before but guess it will if they ever get to living there.

Think Shirley Garlington has about decided to get an apartment down here now that apartments are easier to find. I hope that some of the tenants will move next door and she can get one of those. Then I could have Eddie once in a while.

This is church night so had better run along. It got rather hot today and the paper tonight says that it was 95 which is about the warmest we have had.

*   *   *

Letter No. 24

Thursday July 19, 1945.

Dear Bill:

Your mother is worse than the absent minded professor. Last eve when Dad and I came home I put my car keys down and when I started to church I could not find them anywhere so had to use Dads. this morning I looked and looked again but no. So guess Dad ordered Mr. Glatz to make me another set after he had gone to the Post Office, the only place that I had been and they were not there. This afternoon I moved a piece of carbon paper which was sitting on the desk and there were the keys right in almost plain sight.

Then I told Aunt Betty we could use some towels which I got along with the luncheon set which I sent to the Humphries for a wedding gift, and when I went to look for them I could not find them anywhere and sad to relate I still cant find them so we had to buy something else. I fear now that I did not take them out of the box and sent them along with the luncheon set to the Humphries which would have been more of a gift than I had planned to give them. As yet they have not said thank you so perhaps when they do I will find out if I made that mistake.

This has been real summer and the paper says that the thermometer went to 98 this afternoon and it has felt like about 198. There seems to be quite a little humidity in the air and that always makes it seem hotter. the paper tonight says that the Air Base is going to open again the first of August. The report is that there will be P-38s here. So I guess those who did no want to see it close are happy again. Ofcourse it has never closed entirely but the town has been pretty quiet.

Manual was in today to get the truck on which the pistons were being ground and brought me some eggs but no cream as Aunt Fans cow is about dry. She is trying to get another one and is on the trail of one two year old, fresh last May, but has never been milked so they do not know just how much milk she will give but it does not have to be so very much for just Fan.

The twins have been riding since Nellie has her own horse at Marys now but I wondered if they could stand the heat today or staid at home. Think that Nellie plans to go up and see Fan before she goes back to Trinidad. Maybe they will ride up there from Marys.

Had a letter from Aunt Kitty today in which she enclosed a clipping of the wedding of Renard Fitzgerald. He has just gotten his wings as a Navy flyer and is an Ensign, to be stationed somewhere is

Florida. Up to the time that she wrote the letter they had not had any hot weather down there but I bet is hot today. Dont think there can be too much hot weather for in August the days start to getting quite a little shorter and the nights are usually cooler.

Sort of sounds to us like there is something brewing in the war game. The newspapers today are full of the possibility of peace feelers etc. Some reports have it that Stalin has taken to the big three conference a peace offer from japan. For some uncanny reason I have the feeling that it is not to be too long. Guess the fact that the Japs have put up no fight at the shelling of the home island accounts for it.

Dad was not lucky last night and came home minus about 1.50 so I told him he could not go again if he could not be better than that. Think that he is a little sleepy tonight despite the fact that I let him sleep this morning till eight oclock.

More tomorrow after the party.

*   *   *

7/20/45

Dear Mother & Dad,

Last night we had quite a little wind & Rain. It was surely good to have the dust settled, but we again have this awful mud. We are better prepared for it now.

Yesterday I painted my first picture with the oil paints. The painting wasn't too hot, but it was a lot of fun.

We get enough food out here, mother, even candy and gum. And it takes such a long time for a box so think it would be better not to send edibles. I am getting the stamps just fine. I haven't drawn any pay since I left. The only thing we can buy is stamps. The cigarettes though very inexpensive are free. The only thing I have bought so far is a box of Jap surgical Instruments from a marine. The marines and soldiers surely have been making a good business out of the souvenirs. They were doing good business on Jap flags, until the CB. started making them and selling them.

We now have a shower; so who could ask for anything more.

This company has three white officers—No colored officers and one white Chief Petty Officer, and no Colored Chief Petty officers. There are also two red cross men and my 3 corpsmen that are white. The Chief and I now live in one tent, the 3 officers in another, and the red cross men in another. The corpsmen live in a tent beside the dispensary. We are a long way from the gold braid so it is pretty good duty. I do get a big kick out of the boys in the company—except those who come to sick call—They have a good sense of humor. They all have been good to us and given us all kinds of help.

Till Later,

All my love, Bill

*   *   *

Letter No. 24

Friday July 20,1945.

It is pretty hot again today altho it was cloudy when we got up this morning and staid more or less so till about noon. There seems to be so much humidity so guess that is the reason that we feel it for the paper says it was 92 today which should not really feel too hot.

Aunt Betty and I had the party today, ate at the hotel and then went out to her house for the bridge. Her house seemed nice and when it did get a little stuffy we put on the fan so guess the ladies did not melt at least we checked out as many as we did in.

One of the Richardson house guests is a pharmacist so when Rena Woodbridge talked to her at Mondays party she told her that "We need a lady pharmacist at our drug store? and that the lady should get in touch with Mr. Woodbridge at once. When the lady told Bertha about the lady whose husband owned a drug store here who wanted her to take a place in it Bertha got a kick out of it, knowing Renas ability to give impressions of the Woodbridge importance in the community. The next morning Rena called Bertha to tell her to be sure to have her friend go see Ned about taking the position. Well Dad had heard nothing about it so guess Ned probably knows nothing about it either.

We feel a little excited tonight about the possibility of Buds being on his way home for a read in the Denver paper that the Hdq of the Ninth Army would embark at LeHarve today. Hope it is so but the Sabins do not know either if it means Bud is among them but that is his station, or section of the army or whatever you call it.

I am going to put a clipping from tonights paper in this letter just to show you how good your mother is getting. Now I expect that there will be a great rush to get my services.

I am going to have a little girl to help tomorrow with the work. She is the sister of Manual's wife and helped Fan a little while she was out there with them. Hope it proves to be a good arrangement. She is to work for me three mornings and for Aunt Betty the other three.

Have not had a scratch form Tom yet but think that tomorrow will bring some word and may bring another letter from you.

Shirley called me a little while ago. She has come down to look for an apartment and intends to stay. Dont know why she gave up living with Bonny. So far we have not had any luck but when the word gets around that she wants one maybe her friends can run one down for her. There are no vacancies over next door unless it would be the third story one and she could not take the baby up that far.

Jackie Lacy brought over some beets out of their garden last night but we were out at the Sabins and Madeline told me today that he was so disappointed not to be able to give them directly but had to leave them at the door. He and Charla Rae have been selling chances on things so today she brought over one of those "Witch and children" barometers which she said I had won on my chance so maybe the 33 cents that my punch cost me was not so high after all.

*   *   *

7/22/45

Dear Mother & Dad,

I got to Mass this morning ok although was a little late, We went to a CB camp for it and they have built quite a nice little chapel. Afterwards we had a fried chicken dinner which really did make it seem like Sunday. Our chow is getting better all the time. We are having fresh potatoes occasionally and also butter. Have had some fresh meat. Had fresh eggs once. We are having a little fresh butter now.

Today Walsh, Dog, and a Dr. Ayers came down. We took a drive over to the city, which isn't far. I wish it were like some other towns taken in Europe. There is nothing there now at all. It would be nice to go to dinner somewhere or visit native shops.

Our business has surely slacked off. Perhaps I've scared all the patients away.

I have grown a little mustache which isn't very becoming, but is something to do. Am also smoking a pipe once in awhile.

The mail has surely been slow again—only one letter in the last week, but it will come all at once again as it did last time with 17 letters. I wonder where Tom has gone. There is some cold beer tonight. I guess we have about everything we really need to be comfortable.

Til Later,

All my love, Bill

*   *   *

Letter No. 91

Monday July 23, 1945

Dear Tom and Bill:

Again we are back on the double letters for we have at least a temporary address now for you Tom since the letter we got this morning. Today was good to us for we had letters from each of you. Had not had any from you Bill for several days and from Tom ofcourse not since you had left and ofcourse we were so anxious to know what your position was to be. Yes it was very good news to us that you will be in this country and also in the 2nd Air force for there might be a chance that way that you would be stationed not too far from home. You did not say what you would be doing in the permanent party but suppose it will be an instructor job.

I called Walter but talked to Ada Beth instead for Walt was not there just then for I knew they too would be anxious to know what you had found out. Just in case you Bill want it the address is

> Group 392 Squad 578
> Sioux Falls AAB
> Sioux Falls, So.Dak.

Dont suppose Tom will be there when you get this even but thought I would send it anyway for they can always be forwarded.

Your letter, Bill was very interesting. You seem to be getting quite a bit of experience in the circumcision operation and glad to hear that they are OK. Hope it does not take too long to finish the highway which is responsible for so much of the dust that you get. It surely must be hard for you just cant keep the windows closed when the weather is so hot. It was a good thing that you found a mechanic who knew what was the matter with the Jeep when it would not start after the show. Glad that you got to the Army talent show and enjoyed it.

The water system in the dispensary of which you spoke consisting of the 50 gallon barrel on the outside with a spigot inside must be quite an innovation but you did not say whether that was the source of your drinking water or not but if it is always luke warm I hope not.

From the list of cases you have had it seems to me that you have been fairly busy and perhaps it was because of the excellent care that the cases you thought might be dengue got well in such a hurry.

I had the party for Shirley and little Eddie this afternoon and had about 16 ladies. We just sat and admired the baby and he showed off in good form for he was very good while they were here and so they thought that he was a marvelous child and "How much he looks like Ed" was what every one of them said.

Shirley is looking for an apartment here for it looks as if it may be quite a while till "Pomp and Mom" get a transfer. We thought that there would be some available now that the base is on a stand-by basis for a while but so far have not found a thing at all desirable.

This is my night at the USO but since Marg wont want to go if Bud should come and since one of us can take care of all that there is to do she went tonight and I will go the next time, two weeks.

Aunt Betty had a letter the other day from a boy who graduated out here in one of the first classes and whose mother staid at the Sabin household while she was here for the graduation. He is in India and said that "there is such a fine chap here from La Junta, perhaps you know him. His name is David Hill". Aunt Betty wrote back that her two nephews know him well. Mrs. Kendall says that it is because Marie Louise keeps putting the wedding days off that the case there has sort of cooled off rather than that David is not still strong for her.

John Todd called today from Denver so Blanch and the two boys left this afternoon to meet him there. Ann Norton went along just for a little visit up there with Julia Belle. It is about decided now that Clyda Todd is to drive to Edmonton with Ann when she goes which will be shortly after the first.

The little maid did not appear at Aunt Bettys this morning as she had said she would and now I am wondering if she will come here tomorrow. I need her for I plan to do the laundry and have to be at Dr. Klobs at 10, so will have to rush if I get there on time. Dr. Brown is back I hear but so far he has not called me up to apologize for breaking his appointment with me. It will be just as well for then I will be saved making any explanation about going to Dr. Klob. The latter exrayed my teeth Saturday when I went down so tomorrow I am to know if he will fill that tooth or pull it out.

We feel rather excited tonight about the conference in Berlin being over and that things went very satisfactorily. No one knows where everybody has gone and if our guess is correct we think that the American delegation have gone to Moscow to meet the Japanese. If that could only be true and there could something good develop. Oh! could we celebrate in true fashion.

This afternoon every lady here hugged me and told me how glad they are that you Tom do not go over seas again. We really have much to be thankful for through it all even if we have had to be far apart and not very happy about it.

Will stop now and we will mail this and then gone home and call Aunt Fan. It is still hot and no rain though my little witch comes out every day. Dad says he thinks she just does not like the heat inside of her house.

*　　　*　　　*

7/24/45

Dear Mother & Dad,

Yesterday was a good day as we had quite a little business— Mostly evacuating patients from the ships to the hospital. We have quite a bit of fun as there are quite a few Diagnostic problems. Sometimes I'm right.

I got four of your good letters yesterday, one from Gene Rourke, Koshares, and 7/9 Times. We go several days without mail and then get several letters period. We have to go up to NOB to get our mail, but that is easier than changing our address as we may even have to change our location again someday—not very soon however.

The typewriter unfortunately has been taken away from us; so we have to do our paper work by hand. We are looking for one, but doubt if we ever get one. Are busy again today as we have three patients to evacuate. Cancelled another big operation.

Was glad to hear that Religion is still moving. It really sounds like Tom did the town up proper. Would surely liked to have been with him.

We had a nice rain—I believe I told you that the dust is not nearly as bad now. Looks like you are having a pretty wet year. It looks like we may have a little rain this afternoon. The days are pretty warm, but the nights aren't so bad—Sleep with a sheet over me—Yes even have sheets.

Glad to hear Roscoe is coming home, but sorry that Dad will have to find another girl as Mutt is surely a good one.

Yes Aunt Gertrude gave me the latest news. Glad Marsden will be in the states; so they can have another try.

Not much other news.

All my love, Bill

*   *   *

Tuesday July 25,1945

Dear Bill and Tom:

Another letter from you, Bill today and also one to Aunt Fan. It was grand that you got all those 18 letters and what a time you must have had reading them. Bet you had to stay up half the night after reading all Sunday afternoon on them. Your letters have not come quite as quickly lately as they were for a while this one was 8 days on the way and 10 from the time that you wrote it, but even that is good I think.

Had a letter from Hay this afternoon and Lea is finally out of the Army, or will be as soon as they can get to Ft. Logan after the first, the day that they leave Spokane. She is all excited about it and how they would like to go right into their own home but ofcourse Mr. Harms wont be gone till the USO is over here and that may be some time yet. Ofcourse they will drive and bring George with them.

She also enclosed a letter from that woman who was a Jap prisoner after the fall of the Phillipines. It was very interesting. They are now with relatives in California, and getting back to normal. The husband had beri-beri very badly but is coming out of that at last.

This morning as I was a little suspicious of my maids coming to help me with the washing and I wanted her for I had to be thru so as to get to the dentist at 11. I drove over there for thought then I would be sure of her coming but no she said she had to do the washing there today so I had to come home and really get to work. I got thru all right so it just shows what a fellow can do when she is pressed.

Frances and little bobby leave early in the morning for California so Dad said he would go over to the drug store this afternoon and get a little present for him for the trip. He had to come over when he spied me out hanging the clothes this morning and hand me the pins to hang them with. We will miss seeing him around when he leaves.

Aunt Fan got in this morning and will go out to the King ranch in Smith Canyon tomorrow with her ranch hands to look at some broncoes that are for sale. Friday she is going to Pueblo and I think that I will go along for my glasses need straightening. The Herrons are going to go too. Rosie is to be home from Springfield on Saturday and I think is to go to work in the telegraph office at Rocky Ford.

The Driscolls were to go look at the Klug house at 801 Carson today. Mr. D. was in here last night to talk to Dad after they had driven by and looked at it from the outside. They are surely trying hard to find a house here. Guess all the family is off with Rocky Ford and determined to get back to La Junta before school starts.

Will go now and take in the clothes and when Dad comes he may have a bit of something to tell you.

After supper—Dad did not have any news but the twins came along just as we were eating. They wanted to know all the news too about you fellows etc. and were as thrilled as the rest of us that T. is to be in the states. They are going to accompany Fan and the boys up to see the horses tomorrow.

*   *   *

Letter No. 93

Wednesday July 25,1945

Dear Tom and Bill:

No mail today but after such a good supply of the last few days we really did not expect any unless T. had some news for us and then we would be expecting a letter. Guess it is as hot at Sioux Falls as it is here and suppose that in Okinawa it is even hotter. I have not found a record of the temperature there in any thing that I read. After your last letter, Bill in which you spoke of being where on of the principal town used to be and knowing from other things that you have said about the general lay of the land there we have figured out that you are where Naka used to be. Are we good guessers?

Yesterday Aunt Fan went to Dr. Cooper to have a check up to see if she could or should continue the medicine and found that her blood is up in good shape and I think that she has put on a little weight this summer. While she was there Dr. C. got to talking about the possibility of a Sisters Hospital here. It seems that when the Bishop was here for Confirmation a while ago he talked to the Bishop about it and got his approval. He thought since he had heard that Aunt Fan is worth a half a million(she thanked him for the compliment but denied the truth of the assertion) she could build it for them. Anyway while talking about it he asked her if you, Bill would possibly be coming to locate here after the war. She said she did not know what your plans are but supposed that if there was a good opportunity here you might be interested. He said "I would like Bill to work with me. I think that he and I could get along fine and with the new hospital that would be fine." So you see he is doing some day dreaming too.

Was talking to Mrs. Lane this morning, in fact I did not get any work done for I went to Mr. O'Conners funeral and then was out in front gathering up some leaves off the lawn when she came along so the morning was about gone when I came in. She told me that Bub had met a girl down at Pampa that he is very much taken with. Did He tell you, Tom any thing about her? Mrs. L. seems to think that she must be some girl. Her folks live on a farm in Oklahoma and she was working in Pampa.

Irene Klein wants to get some of the young girls started singing in the choir so they are to go practice with me this evening. It would be grand if we could get them started for then the old ladies could be relieved and I think that it is about time.

Aunt Fan bought four horses today and guess she would have bought more if there had been any more for sale. The twins and Jack went along from Higbee.

Dad just got a girl for the office he thinks. Rita Lopez's sister who is married to an American Lieut who was out at the base here but now over seas. She is coming down in the morning.

The Driscolls did not buy the house up here on Carson. Suppose that it is not quite classy enough for them.

Dad is going to the poker club tonight and Friday he is going fishing, yes I said fishing but you know how much fishing he will do, with Mac, John Mullins and Dale Earnest, Montgomery Ward manager. He says that he will get some good "belly-laughs" even if he does not get any fish. They are going to Eagles Nest Lake above Taos, N.M. Do you remember it and how pretty we thought it was when we first saw it the time we drove to Grand Canyon?

*   *   *

26 July 1945

Dear Mother & Dad,

We are having a little respite from the dust—surely wish we could share some of our moisture.

The other evening Dr. Lockward from a CB. Battalion had me over to dinner. We had fresh meat, butter, and Ice cream for desert. After dinner we had a couple of cold beers. He has a pup that was evidently born during the fight. It is really a cute little thing. They have a real good medical set up with X-ray and laboratory facilities. The CB can really get things done. They are taking care of our laboratory work as well as the Jeep and ambulance. Our main duties now are sick call and evacuating patients for ourselves and everybody else.—So it keeps our ambulance pretty busy.

Yesterday I took a boat trip with the Chief in a search for fresh food. We found it but didn't have a boat of our own to get it back here. Our contact was a Dr. for whom we evacuated a pt. He has similar duty to Cowgill and knew Joe in New York. Maybe Cowgill & I shall meet out here. Am also keeping an eye open for Gene Rourke.

Till Later,

All my love, Bill

*   *   *

Letter No. 94

Thursday July 26,1945

Dear Bill and Tom:

Last night we really had a hard rain and lots thunder and lightening. The paper says that there was an inch and a little more of moisture. So do not know whether it rained out at the ranch or not but there was heavy rain at Timpas and Delhi so perhaps Stage Canyon got some at least. The twins were supposed to come in today for Nellie was going to go home but as yet they have not appeared so maybe there was rain out there and the roads are bad. It got nice and cool afterward and coat. Then it has been so hot today.

Well Roscoe and Mutt got home from Denver today and John Todd and his family too. The paper also says that Custis Green is back in the State so suppose that he will be coming before long. There seemed to be something strange about his being held over there so long after he was liberated for her seemed to be in good health and even he did not understand it. Well that water is over the bridge now.

The radio has had lots to broadcast today with the defeat of Churchill and the ultimatum the other three, Truman, Churchill and Chiang Kai-caek(I will be very proud if I have come anywhere near spelling that right) sent to the japanese. Oh how wonderful if it brings them to their knees. You really had the political situation sized up right Tom when you got back from Europe. I remember that you said that Churchill did not have a chance. Today the big boys are all saying over he radio that it is such a surprise etc.

Dads new girl was on the job today and guess she is very good. Hope he can keep her a while.

Dad had a letter this morning from Albert Burbank telling him that you, Tom had been in-to see him and that you were to go to their house the next night for dinner. After that he said he can drop in at any time. Hope they can find you a good date once in a while. Am anxious to hear your version of it.

When Shirley Hardy Shunders got a bad burn yesterday from ammonia when she was opening a bottle of it for use at the Band Box cleaners some one picked her up and carried her in to Dr. Coopers office as she was about to succumb. The office was full of patients but Dr. C. dropped everything and rushed her to the hospital. He worked over her and finally had her in pretty good shape when Jeff came in. The first thing he said was to the nurse "Go call Dr. Davis". Can you imagine even Jeff Saundres doing such a thing?

The weather man says that tomorrow will be cooler and I do hope so for we are going to Pueblo and I dont like the trip much any way but especially when it is so hot that one bakes.

Dad is going down to a drug store meeting about 8:30 to check over the accounts so I will send these letters down with him to mail.

*   *   *

7/27/45

Dear Dad & Mother,

Looks as though we are going to have a nice warm humid day. Last night was grand sleeping as it rained all day yesterday and it was nice and cool.

Am getting the Time and Colliers pretty good now. Am interested in what will happen to Truman. Am more particularly interested in your views on the man. I'd surely like to talk over the present problems with you as you have good common sense ideas.

I haven't seen much of the Island as yet because of my job mainly and also the roads. Did get over to the big city which is about as far as from L.J. to Holbrook Lake.

For two days we were really busy, but yesterday and today have been really slow. That's the way it goes. I've had quite a few interesting cases and believe I have learned a little bit. Especially about the colored boys. They aggravate me sometimes, for some of them put on a big act. I've had several that are working on ships that required emergency removal from the ships. When we get them they are on a stretcher and after careful examination can find nothing wrong. They fool the pursers, who are first aid men, and get sent ashore to get out of work. One of them had even had morphine for his imaginary pain. It's good experience. They all have had bad feet and have at one time or another had gonorrhea.

Almost the end of July and have been here two months. There have been lots of changes.

Till Later,

All my love, Bill

*   *   *

Letter No. 95

Friday July 27,1945

Dear Tom and Bill:

Feeling a little tired tonight after our trip to Pueblo I probably will not write much of a letter but just say "Hi, kids". There was a nice cool breeze today and had it not been for that guess I would really have been pooched. We got back about six, Aunt Fan did not get in to see the doctor as soon as she does some times so were delayed a while. I got my glasses straightened and bought what curtains I could find for the middle bed room. They have a little blue dot in them and that is not the color scheme I would like for there but there was no all white nor any other color so-.

When we got home found two letters from you, Bill and that was wonderful being that Dad got one at the office this morning before we started to Pueblo and he on his trip. The last of the two that came this afternoon you wrote on sunday and here it is just Friday. Can you realize it that they can come so far in that short time. The other two were of the 18th and 20th but even that is good. Glad that sometimes you get our letters in eight days too. Am glad that Colliers and Time get there but sorry that the good old daily disappointment has not reached you. Will call the paper and check on the address.

Glad that your camp is improving right along and especially that you now have a shower. That must really add a lot to your comfort when it is so hot and sticky. Perhaps it cooled off a little after the rain you had. We heard over the radio a report that the planes did not get off on their bombing because of bad weather over Okinawa so guess that was the time.

If your first picture is as good as Tom's one and only was I think it is good and I know it is fun or at least it would be for me.

Glad that you told me about getting what candy and gum you need so will not send that but how about the raisins? And the little cans of minced ham and cheese? I am sending a box tomorrow and got some nuts to put in for Jane said that Dean used to like the nuts about best of anything she sent. There has not been any further news of Dean and now I think they wont hear unless they do after the war for if he got out of the plane safely he is probably on a Jap island and wont get off till the Japs surrender.

With the red cross men and the white officers and men there are ten of you white chaps in the company according to the way it adds up if my figuring is correct. Being so far from the gold braid is one pleasant feature about the whole thing I gather. I knew that you would get a kick out of the colored boys.

Well Mass in nice little chapel and a fried chicken dinner afterward must have seemed just like a Sunday in La Junta. Am glad the chow is picking up.

Thought that we might have another letter from you, Tom today but tomorrow may be the day. Or perhaps you are enroute to your next place? The twins did not come in today for Nellies mail is right where I left it, unopened so they are either off on some jaunt or the road is not passable.

Will go now and mail these and hope that before long we will be saying to each other "It is all over with the Japs".

Lots of love

*   *   *

Letter No. 96

Saturday July 28, 1945

Dear Bill and Tom:

Sure glad to get your letter this Morning, Tom and glad that you did not leave before for now I think that perhaps you have had a letter from me by this time. Tho perhaps it is a bit slow just sitting and waiting for your orders to come along. Have not talked to the Cransons but just suppose that Walter left today, and no doubt will be catching up with you, and can give you the high lights of La Junta news since your leaving here.

Glad you found the Burbanks agreeable people and hope if you get a date with the daughter it will be a happy occasion. I am going to write to them tomorrow and thank them for your invitation and hospitality. Tho I really think they were the fortunate ones. I would liked to have been in their place very much, having you around.

Dad will take care of buying the bond for you when he gets back next week and this is the Sisk address.

Mr. Fred Sisk
4711 Sec. Blvd.
Detroit, Mich.

That Sec. is really second in case I didnot make it clear.

Hope that bad toenail(It was black, Bill and about to come off when he was home) did come off so that you can join the boys in their golf these nice warm days.

Pat Casey's address is 1915 Grand, I think. She was here one day after we got home from Denver and felt very badly that you did not call again that night before you left for she said she had just gone down town for a little while and sat the rest of the evening on the edge of her chair waiting for you to call back. I told her you would be writing to her for you had asked me what her address was and she said "Even Grand Ave would get me for the same postman has been bring mail to us for year" so if that is not just the right number it is near enough.

Saw Frank Leonard in the store in Pueblo yesterday and he said they were so sorry that they did not get to see you while you were here. Ed and Bob had finally gotten together in the hawaiian islands where they both are just now. Bob tho is over on Hilo and Ed is on Oahu. Ed will not be going back to combat either they think but Bob will be there when the Marines make another invasion, but the CO said it would not be in August.

Dad will see Morris Bloom and tell him to send the trousers to you, T.

Nellie is with us this evening and will be going on home in the morning, she says. She had letters from Ginny who is still on the quest. Mary just went back to her ranch. She thinks that while the weather is so hot she will go up and stay a week or so with the Farthings where it is nice and cool.

Wonder how many fish Dad is catching today and if his face is sunburned. I bet not for my guess is that they probably spent about a half hour in the fishing boat.

Talked to Manual this morning, Fan being down town when he called and found out that there was a pretty good rain at the head of Stage and made water in some of the reservours up there and a little water at the head of Iron Canyon but very little rain at the ranch house. He wanted the vet to go out as he had found a cow that had died a short time before. Now we are anxious to hear what the vet thought when he examined it.

*   *   *

7/29/45

Dear Mother & Dad,

Today have been on this Island for 8 weeks. It has gone much faster than I had anticipated.

This morning I got to Mass in time for Confession and Communion. They are going to start having Mass here in the camp this afternoon; so hardly have to go anywhere for anything now. It has sprinkled a little today—Just enough to keep it cool.

I did my own laundry the other day and find I've got that total tale gray. Fortunately the greens we wear don't show it very much. The native laundresses didn't work out very well.

Honey, about the canned food—you don't need to send any more as we get lots of canned food. I can see the reason for lots of points on canned goods now.

I got a Tribune of June 1—Thats the first one I've received. Just got back from Mass—twice today.

I got the letter from Jess Humphries and the picture. The picture looks quite familiar. That was nice that you got to see Dud and family.

Was glad to see you know how we do our sterilizing. The autoclave is run by kerosene, but works very well. The radio in the sick bay is somewhat inhibited by the two generators out side the door, but we hear every thing we want.

We keep our ambulance busy now and have a few at sick call, but that is all.

Till Later,

All my Love, Bill

*   *   *

7/30/45

Dear Mother & Dad,

I hope this reaches you in time to wish you many happy returns on your 27th Wedding anniversary. Perhaps by luck I'll be home to help you celebrate the next one. I surely have messed up on your anniversary in the past—Especially the Silver anniversary.

I've been out of the States 7 months. Most medical officers are sent back in 18 mo. If so, I'm 1/3 of the way through.

Today it is plenty warm, but I don't mind it as we can take it easy. I usually have a little siesta after chow.

This morning we had another of our big operations. He (the patient) was a bad actor—mentally deficient. Will try to get him out of the company. But for appearances sake we will wait till his circumcision heals up.

Have no other news; so shall close and again God Bless and Many more anniversaries to come that I can help celebrate. I'll remember the golden Anniversary—so help me.

All my Love, Bill

*   *   *

Letter No. 97

Monday, July 30, 1945

Dear Bill and Tom:

Last night about 8:30 the fishermen came along with lots of fish, really they had about 22 in all some real large and some small. we took two big ones and one small to the Sabins and we had on large one and a small one. I cooked the large one at noon, baked it, for us and the little one, Tom took over to Mrs. Lagerquist. She was in the office this morning and was telling him how much she liked fish, trout especially so that little one just filled the bill for her.

Walter called me yesterday morning, they were leaving on the 1:30 bus. I gather from what he said that he thinks now that he wants to go over seas again in a fighter or something where he is by himself. Guess Tom he wants to do all the flying as well as all the picture taking. You see Bill sometimes that little brother of yours (may be wise) and not let Walter at the controls. Guess like all of us we just feel better when we are doing it ourselves.

Saw Pat going by yesterday, Tom and told her that you said that you were going to write to her but she said that she had all ready had a letter from you. She is not going to leave till about the seventh.

Aunt Betty and I have the party for the little Walker lady all ready to go tomorrow night. We will have about 20 I think. Are taking them to the hotel for dinner and then to the Sabins to play bridge.

The Koshare kids are starting tomorrow on a trip up state, Denver, Boulder etc, I think that they are to be gone about five days. Mr. West did my hair this afternoon and I wanted to leave it to comb tomorrow but he said that one of the girls would have to do it for me for he would be gone so guess he is accompanying them.

I heard today that Paul Church is on his way home. Mary Fran did not think that he was coming this way so bet she is all excited. Marg will hardly leave the house lest Bud should call. the papers are rather contradictory about just when the 9th army hdqs will arrive but it will be before long.

Dad said that as soon as they arrived at Eagles Nest Friday they went to make reservations for a boat to fish and the best they could get was sunday morning at 11. He says the place has surely changed since we went thru there some years ago. There is a little village there now and a couple of hot gambling places. Said he saw one man lose $150. in an hour or so. the people up there are all texans. guess they have lots of money to spend and they is the only diversion there is so they make use of it. Dad seemed to be the hot fisherman of the party and of the 22 fish he caught eight.

Will go now and see if I can locate Naomi to invite her to the party. We had intended to give this in her honor too but have never been able to find her so had to go ahead without that plan being carried out.

*   *   *

Letter No. 98

July 31, 1945

Dear Tom and Bill:

Last night about 12:30 the telephone rang but strange as it may seem I did not feel the least bit alarmed and got up without bumping into anything and got the light lit and then answered the call. A voice said "this is a friend of yours did I get you out of bed." I said, "That does not matter if you are a friend of mine" and then he told me he was Dick Counley. He was on his way from the Phillipines to Ft. Logan and his discharge. He said that he is going to write you Bill and to give you both his best. Says that he is just going to enjoy himself for the next three months before he starts civilian life again, or rather work to promote a living in civilian life.

The Sabins had letters from Bud yesterday and he said that he would probably be home before they could answer any of the questions he asked so just to hold them till he could talk to them so he will probably be coming along. He sent some pictures and wrote quite a description of Deauville, the place where they are not near to La Havre where they will embark. He said that the hotel they are in is perfectly gorgeous. Deauville used to be one of the swankiest resorts in France and it was there that the Duke of Winsor and "Wally" met. Bud had had quite a trip with the major for about a week and saw a lot of Germany. He cant understand why the Germans were not satisfied with such a rich country and waged this war which brought so much of it to ruin.

We had a letter this morning from Aunt Hattie. She did not have any startling news but told of their garden and flowers and what they are doing these days. She said that Gene says he does get around out there in the Pacific and might get in your vicinity some time,Bill. Surely hope he does and that he knows he is near you if he does and can find you.

There was no other mail, no letters from either kid. But tomorrow will most likely be the day for that. Tomorrow is Colorado day so Dad will have a holiday and we will not have to get up early. His Spanish girl is doing fine in the office and tends to her knitting. She does not pay any attention to any one who comes in but goes right on with her work, some what different to Helen and some of the others. This is our guest list for tonight. Pink and Ann, the three Guthrie sisters, Clyde and Blanch Todd, Bet Morse, Rusty Sheridan of the paper, Susan Gardner and Shirley (Nancy is away), Carolyn Hahs, Barbara, Justine, Bess and me. Naomi Davis's husband is leaving Sunday so she is not even coming so it is a good thing that we went on without waiting to see if we could honor her too at this time.

Suppose that you will be seeing Walter today, Tom, so perhaps you will get the low down on the home town. Ruth Draper bought the Klug house up the street that the Driscolls were looking at, so that the watch-maker in their store would have a place to live. He was not going to stay for he could not find a thing for rent. The Klugs bought Mrs. Bradish's house on Raton, about 305, so it is change all the time. I dont know what Mrs. B. intends to do but perhaps is going to Amarillo to live with the Shields.

Will bathe now and then fix a bouquet for the table for tonight. I have the flowers, bought from Mrs. Rupp but must arrange then in a bowl.

*　　*　　*

8/1/45

Dear Dad & Mother,

I was surely glad to hear that Tom is going to stay in the states. Hope Bud gets home and gets Stateside duty.

We've been having our little rain today. It clears up, rains abruptly, gets cloudy, stops raining abruptly, then suddenly clears off. This has happened about six times today. I don't mind at all however I have a nice dry tent and bed.

I am now getting the pony addition of the Times. I got the last issue eight days after publication. I enjoyed it very much.

My latest work hasn't been going too well—I get too cocky—put a couple of stitches in Robbins one of the officers—and put them in too tight so had to take them out. Then a boy who got hit in the head didn't get up and around as I predicted—so sent him off to the hospital.

I don't believe I'll be doing any major surgery here for the hospital is too close now. Till Later,

All my Love, Bill

*　　*　　*

Letter No. 99

Wednesday Aug.1,1945

Dear Tom and Bill:

This afternoon I have spent trying to help Shirley get an apartment. We went to look at one in the basement at the chestnut House, 322 Santa Fe. which I think she will decide to take. At least it will be cool while the weather is so hot and the man said that as soon as there was a vacancy on the first floor she could move up there. I hope he is not deceiving her for when I was telling Justine about it just a little while later she said that he had told Rusty Sheridan that she could have the first larger one that was vacant. She is already living there and has for some time so would seem that she should have priority. These apartments are not furnished but perhaps we can find enough around here and at the Gardners to do for the time being.

There was no mail today so I know that when we do get some it will be a big bunch, probably several letters all the same day. Guess,you,Tom do not know any more than you have or we would have had word of it. Last night Betty Inge was telling me that a friend of hers from Rocky Ford, Johnson by name is on Okinawa and so she took your address,Bill to send to him. She said that he is stationed on the south end of the island and if my guess is near right you are in that vicinity too.

Last night when we went down to the hotel for our seven oclock dinner there did not seem to be any clouds in the sky but as we came out it was sprinkling and after we got in the cars it rained quite hard for a few minutes but had stopped by the time we got out to the Sabin house but like good old Colo is it was nice and cool the rest of the evening. We could not have picked a better one. The girls all seemed to have a nice time.

The Sabins had a letter from Bud today,evidently from La Havre for he said from where he was he could see the ships loading and that they were very busy so we think that they too were getting ready to leave. That was the 20th and mailed the 23rd.

Dont know whether Dad is to go to the poker club tonight or not but any I will have your letters ready to mail when I go down to get him as soon as he calls me from the Elks Club.

Shirley read me a very interesting letter from Ed telling about a trip he had down to an underground factory. He told of the immensity in terms of miles and hundreds of feet etc. The tunnel leading down to it was 20 ft high and 50 ft wide. He said that he had walked six miles and he did not see many of the rooms. He spoke of some of the rooms being 600 ft long. The Germans were working it with slave labor just 24 hours before they surrendered so everything was there just as they had left it.

Last nights paper told of the announcement of the approaching marriage of Harold Herndon, I will send the clipping to you, Bill.

Dad just phoned so will close now.

*   *   *

Thursday Aug.2,1945

Letter no.100

Dear Bill and Tom:

This was the day for mail and we got a letter from each of you. Guess from the fact that you have been having a relief from the dust,Bill there is a rainy spell going on over there, and a plenty since you would gladly give us a share of it. Am glad that you had such a good dinner over with Dr. Lockwood and cold Beer too. That is really a treat I guess. Guess if you and your ambulance is kept busy with the work for every body around it helps to pass the time for you. It was good that you met the doctor who knew Joe Cowgill. Hope you do run into him and Gene Rourke, from the destroyer, Benson.

We were glad to hear, Tom that you have been enjoying life playing golf and other things. That Enyart boy from Ordway who is there is some relation to Mrs. Potter or rather I believe to Mrs. Potters husband who has been dead quite a long while. I bet the four of you had fun on that three days in Sioux City where there were not so many fellows and no lines to sweat out. The Burbanks are right in there pitching for you evidently and it must have been nice to ride over the country and see what it is like since you have no chance to fly over it. Glad too that you have had some mail and that the doctor finally cut most of that toe nail which must have just been hanging by a thread off.

Suppose by this time Walter has arrived and has told you all there is to tell about the La Junta base. I really dont know much yet. There was supposed to be something start up out there the first but I have not heard and there dont seem to be any more fellows in town yet. It would be great if you fellows came to it.

Last nights paper said that Custis Green is home which is very good news for it took him so long after he was liberated.

Shirley had a letter from Hay this morning telling her to get a place big enough for them too and they would be here next Tuesday or Wednesday. There is just not a thing so she, on my advise went ahead and took the little apartment that she looked at yesterday and they will just have to stay here till they can get their house. Dad thinks it will take just a month since the owners are returning to live in it themselves.

Dad bought a jersey cow for Aunt Fan yesterday from R.P. Lewis and now he is to bring her in to the vets place so they can test her for bangs disease. She is just a heifer, her first calf and only about five days old, that is the calf, I mean. So they are not sure how much milk she will give but enough, I am sure for Aunt F. The calf is a pure jersey heifer so I know Aunt F. will want to keep it and she likes to have the calf on the cow so that if she does not get milked occasionally it does not hurt her.

The Postdam conference is over and the dope given out but still we do not know what they did about Japan. Russia wants her own sweet time make that announcement I think. I dont think that it will be too long anyway.

Here is a picture,Bill of what the new Mennonite hospital will look like. Bet if that is built soon the Sisters wont want to try one here too.

*　　*　　*

8/3/45

Dear Mother & Dad,

Today is a nice rainy day—the most we've had since I've been here—thats saying quite a bit. I don't mind much now as have a dry bed, tent and clothes. The sick bay is not too wet except where it blows in the doors. The big difficulty is the mud.

I got a letter the other day of May 14. Some get held up. It contained the article about Jim Philpott's coming wedding. I first met him when I was a freshman at Boulder. He came to med school and was a class or two behind me. He's a good boy. You surely have a good memory mother—being able to pick out those names in the Post. I enjoy hearing about the boys. Also got the clipping of Capt. Nafe and Sylvan Benke.

Our water system does contain drinking water, However we have solved the heat of it, by putting a pitcher of water in the company's reefer. The have a big reefer to keep the fresh meat etc. that they get. We also keep some of our drugs in it. We have some penicillin, but haven't used a great deal of it. Our sick bay is designed to remain in our tent. It would surely be great to get a quonset hut, with a concrete deck. We are fairly permanently set, but this type of dispensary is designed to be easily moved. I'd surely dislike to leave the good tent we now have. One of the fellows has had to move 3 times.

In this kind of weather the only efficient vehicle is the ambulance. The Jeep is hard to start and won't run as well in the mud.

Till Later,

All my Love, Bill

*   *   *

Letter No. 101

Friday Aug.3,1945

Dear Tom and Bill:

Two letters came from you Bill today one written to the house on July 24, and the other to the office on the 27, which is suppose over here is the 28th or at least that is the way people have it figured out for us. Mrs. Sheridan was born in the Phillipines and she says that her grand mother had the cable telling of her birth the day before she was born.

You must have some harbor facilities where you are since you seem to do quite a little evacuating of patients from ships but you also said that you had been over to the big city which is evidently about seven miles from where you are as you spoke of its being about the distance that it is to Holbrook from here, so now I think that it is not Naha but one of the others in that vicinity and my guess would be (1) Itoman, (2) Koya, (3) Shuri. Perhaps you can say which guess 1,2, or three is right. Also perhaps NOB is at Naha. When I was talking to Dick the other night I said that you were on Okinawa and he said "How do you know" so I told him but that you had never said so but he thought my guess was right.

Am sorry that you had to give up the typewriter for I know it must have saved you time as well as making your reports look better. So you cancelled another big operation. The other day at Rotary Dad was talking to Dr. Johnston and told him that you were making Jews out of the colored boys over there and he got quite a kick out of it.

Yes we here in LaJunta have really had a lot of rain in July and another one last night but at the ranch it is very dry right around the house but there was a good rain last night too at the heads of the canyons and at Stage so most of the reservoirs on the prairies have water in them and at Stage so most of the reservoirs on the prairies have water in them and that helps a lot. My you are quite swanky to have sheets and the weathers cool enough to sleep under one. I have not done much better than that here in cool Colorado. So the colored boys try to put on a show of illness to get out of work well I guess it is quite a stunt even with the white soldiers too. There were some out here at this hospital even. One fellow was in there a long time because he was mad about something and said that he was sick and just would not work.

That issue of Time, the ninth which reached you on the 24th made pretty good time and so brought you pretty well up on the latest news.

I spent most of the afternoon either at the dentist or watching Eddie while Shirley got the things down to her apartment. There was big stuff enough in the attic of the garage belonging to the Opera house apts and the studio couch in the basement to fix her up pretty well. Ofcourse she will have a lot of little thing to get but that will be fun for her.

The canteloupe this year are to be quite late and they say it will be a couple of weeks before we have home grown ones on the market. Same with the watermelons and it is when it is hot they taste so good.

This is a humid evening like those on Okinawa I think. Saw Mrs. Inman at Zellers with Dorothy's two little boys and the littlest one is the very image Bob and they say has actions like him too.

Every one asks me if we have heard where you are to be sent Tom, they all seem so interested.

Will go now and mail these letters.

*   *   *

8/5/45

Dear Mother & Dad,

A little respite from the rain today. The ground dries out rather rapidly fortunately. It is surely hard to keep the deck clean in such weather.

I got another issue of Collier's yesterday which I really enjoy. Today is Sunday, but haven't been to Mass as yet. Have been invited out to a ship for a big Sunday dinner by a doctor for whom we evacuated a patient this morning. May not be able to make it as have several needs for me around here. (Indispensable?) Went out to a dinner last night to a CB officers mess. They get lots of fresh food off the ship. Dr. Wilson who has been with me since Hueneme is setting up a dispensary about 4-5 miles from here. He invited me down for dinner this evening.

Have been taking warts and moles off the officers. They have asked for it. The mail is again getting slow; so will probably get a bunch all at once one of these days. The mail will probably go pretty good yet for awhile till they get a more advanced place where they'll have preference.

All my Love, Bill

*   *   *

Letter No. 102

Monday Aug.6th, 1945

Dear Bill and Tom:

Writing that date makes me think that about 27 years ago your Dad took unto himself a bride and it was a good old hot day even worse than this has been. There was a good rain last night over much of the eastern slope of the state so there is a good north breeze today. Around Castle Rock and again about Fountain the radio says that there was considerable damage to crops. We have not heard from the ranch since but Fan called just before and said that there were lots of heavy clouds in the southwest and our rain here came from that direction so we think that they should have had a good rain. dad went to Stage as he no doubt told you and was delighted to see how well the two year olds looked and how good the pasture is there tho not so good at the head of Bent. And really at the ranch where they have been most in need as Aunt Fan says there is not much for the milk cows and the horses to eat around there.

I have been a working girl today helping to compare abstracts and "my maid"(Mrs. Garlington) had the lunch ready for us at twelve when we got home. Think that we will go out and have our supper or maybe I will find something we like since I am home about three thirty. Lela had to stop comparing in order to get the "take off".

We have great news today for Bud is in New York so the Sabins will be very busy now getting ready to receive him in a few days or a week. Now Bill when we hear that you are in San Francisco again that will really make the tears run down my old cheeks, you know how I always have to weep a little when I am terribly happy. And I hope it will be not so long. Maybe a few of these new bombs which they are giving the Japs will have the right effect.

Dad just phoned me that he had had a wire from Marian saying that Marsden will go thru tomorrow eve on the chief. Am glad she wired us so we can go see him, and get the latest dope on where he is to be and when she will go along. Aunt Gertrude was upset when the schools out there let her out for next year but I guess it is better they did for now she can follow him about.

Lea went to Ft. Logan today and when he returns he will be "Mr." Garlington. He does not know just what he will do but till he does they will be here in La Junta. He can go to Civil Service or take a job with the Santa Fe for a while but think that he favors the first as it is more in line with he will want indefinitely. Hay is his problem for she wants to stay in La Junta if at all possible. Shirley is down scrubbing her apartment today getting ready to move in but they still want to get something where they can all be together.

Ed does not know just what they are to do with him. He says that their 93rd is to be broken up for many have points enough for discharge, so he may go to the Pacific or be kept on there.

Hay kept Eddie this afternoon while Shirley is working on her apartment and now has taken him out for a ride in his cart and will go down and meet his mother.

This is my night at the USO and since Marg has had the news I know she will want to hold me to the arrangement we had the last time that she went then if I would go this time so I must be on deck. Will make some hamburgers for the supper so it will get done quickly.

*   *   *

8/7/45

Dear Mother & Dad,

When we have the sun it doesn't take too long for things to dry out-, but our daily rain soon puts everything in its previous shape. It probably isn't much hotter here than in L.J. It's not nearly as hot as Missouri. The nights cool off well. It is a lot like Hawaii.

Yesterday I got six letters and a Time. That's the way it goes, none for a few days and then several. I was interested to learn the first hand dope of Tom's that Churchill was not likely to win the election, and he didn't.

The Lopez girl Marguerite I believe should be good help in the office if she is like Rita.

Hope that Dr. Cooper gets the hospital. That would surely be a lot of fun helping getting it going. I would surely like to have gone fishing with Dad. He did all right as far as the fishing goes.

Am getting the stamps and everything. About the packages—Mother It's a lot of trouble for you—and takes such a heck of a long time to get here. But I assure you that anything you send will be used gratefully to good advantage. The other night we had some of the canned meat on crackers with cold bee—It really hit the spot. We now get a case of beer and a case of coke a month.

Cokes are a lot harder to get than beer. Last night I had 3 cold cokes—Boy they really hit the spot. We have been playing catch with a soft ball. It is good exercise. Haven't been swimming much lately.

Today they have the ration of cokes and beer 3 each per man. This will be twice a week. I got a beer from one of the mates. Will have to return the favor.

Not much other news today.

All my love, Bill

*　　*　　*

Letter No. 104.

Tuesday Aug. 7, 1945

Dear Bill and Tom:

There has been quite a little excitement today for we went to meet Marsden at the train and when it came in we waited for him to get off of the car that Marian had told us he would be on but no one got off and we never did see him. I think that Marqin must have made a mistake and meant that he would leave there on Tuesday so we will try again tomorrow and if that is not it then I guess we will just have to give them a "cussin".

While we were waiting there we saw them using one of those little cars like they have in cities for dragging the baggage about. You see we are now quite citified.

We had some other callers just before going to the train and hardly recognized them at first for it has been quite a little while since we have seen them and when we did it was not for very long. The boy got his wings out here at this base and was from Kahoka. He was in Italy flying a B-25 and is now on his way to Santa Monica for re-assignment taking his family(wife and boy one year old) along.

I worked again today and Leila and I got two big abstracts all compared. In the morning we will get an another long one that just came in but Dad says that is not all, for there are a bunch that are waiting comparison.

Shirley and Hazel are going to stay at the apartment for the first time tonight. Hazel has gone down to the house to beg some dishes from the Harms(they are not really using hers at all so it is quite satisfactory) and as soon as I get your letters ready will go by and pick her up and take them down. We had company. Shirleys folks came by. They are now on their way to California for sure. Before they left Aunt Betty and Justine came by so I am a little late with the writing. The latter pair went over to see bobby who has been sick for a few days. Dr. Davis says that it sounds like flu. Hope he feels fine by the time that his daddy gets here.

Will stop now and go get the Garlingtons fixed for the night.

Aunt Fan had a pretty good rain at the ranch on Sunday afternoon and now if she just gets one more.

Aunt Mayme is in Idaho Springs with her family this week.

*   *   *

Letter No. 104

Wednesday Aug.8, 1945

Dear Bill and Tom:

While we wait for Shirley and Hay to come back from the store so that we can go get a little supper somewhere I will write a little for this is church night and would like to have my letters ready so could mail them for Dad is going to poker club and cant mail them later. We went down to the train again tonight but there was no sign of Mardsden so now we give up and will wait and see what they say about it.

When I went down to the dentist this afternoon I met Bud McClusky and Stu Danford on the street both here for thirty days.

We had quite a visit and both were wishing Tom that they could have seen you but told me to tell you "hello" both.

So Russia is at war with Japan and they have already felt the effect of the atomic bomb so do hope that the answer comes very quickly which I surely think will happen.

Stopped to see how Bobby is today and found that he is much better, no fever but looks a little droopy yet.

We had another big rain last night, about .50 inches. and at Swink they say there was 2 1/2 inches, also a cloud burst at Thatcher.

I spent several hours at the court house with Delia comparing today and we got along fine and will go again in the morning.

Mr. Jones of the Pen Drug store was down today talking to the owners of the Opera House Pharmacy about taking on the job of manager here. It looks like probably it will be the thing they decide to do but will not do anything till Bud gets here so he can have a say in it as he has not had any voice yet. Mrs. Lagerquist wants Mr. Jones for they are very close friends.

The people at Hively house have been sanding their floors at night. So last night it was near midnight when they quit and about that time the wind, rain lightening and thunder began and lasted for an hour or more so I did not have such a good nights sleep altho it was lovely and cool.

Got your letter, Tom today. It had been missent to Campo, wherever that is so was delayed. Sure glad that you and Weaver got together again after about a year of being separated. Hope the trip to Shannandoha did not fall thru. I remember that you and he had planned to visit his home there when you went to Lincoln and then he was sent to California instead. I will hunt up the golf balls and send them if I find any.

I heard today that John O'Hare is on Okinawa, too. It seems like there are quite a few from here out there.

This seems to exhaust the news supply for this eve so shall close and russle up a little gossip for tomorrow.

*   *   *

8/9/45

Dear Mother & Dad,

Heard good news this morning and surely hope it is true—that Russia Declared War on Japan. That would really help bring a more rapid close of this war.

You are right—there were 10 white fellows but now just 9 as one of the red cross men has left. I've been with these boys so long—that when a company of white army boys were over for chow last night they looked sort of peculiar.

There were rumors that we might leave here and go to another part of the island, but it is entirely rumor so far.

Received the clippings you sent from the Post and naturally enjoyed them.

More good rumors about Japan this morning. Hope something comes of it.

There are also rumors that an officers club will soon be set up not too far away for us. Many of the CB's already have theirs.

My watch has surely run good. This weather hasn't been too good for it, but has run without a hitch. The hard part is keeping a band for it.

Enjoyed the report of Dad's prowess as a fisherman.

What about T. and this Pat.

*   *   *

Letter No. 105

Thursday Aug.9, 1945

Dear Tom and Bill:

Today brought a letter from each of you, yours Bill written the 30th,ten days, not bad and Tom, yours just yesterday fore noon for the stamp on it is timed 11:30 A.M.

Was glad that you, Tom said that you have Fred's address for now I will inclose the bond for "Chucker" which we had had for several days but I did not have his address neither did any of the family in La Junta so last night I wrote Aunt Nell to send it on to me but as you have it will send the bond in the letter.

We got out the Ellington booklet and found the pictures or Skukis, Shlusher, and RL Smith and do remember them all. It is strange that you come together again after over a year. Bet there was quite a little talk especially since you all had the same instructor. Wonder if any of them knew where he is now. And I think that the picture of a girl which I found on the bed in the basement is the one that came down with Smith's girl and you dated.

I am surely sorry that I cant find but one golf ball I sent it to you this afternoon. I am sure that there were three or four that I kept out of those I had gathered up to send to Bill but I cant find them. Did you use them when you were home? Hay thinks that maybe Lea will have some he can let me have when he gets back from Denver. Shirley went up this morning for she had to get her things from Bonnies since Bonny is moving into an apartment and she and Lea will come home tomorrow. Grandma is taking care of Eddie and I think that she is pretty tired tonight.

Bet you, Clegg and John have a fine time in Shanandoha. Suppose he will be there for his 30 day leave but you expect to be back Sunday or Monday so will probably not get this letter till you get back.

Senator Johnston is going to get a lot of other fellow's votes too I believe if he gets them to cut down the army and let the surplus out but I dont think that it is going to be done. However now it looks as if the war will be short even if the poor foolish Japs fight it out till the last. I dont think,Bill you will have to serve out the 18 months that you say is customary for medics. I think that you have over half of your time in right now and surely hope my guess is a good one.

You are a bit rough on those poor colored boys making Jews out of so many and this one was a little mentally deficient so hope you succeed in getting him out.

You bet I hope that you both can be present next year to celebrate our wedding anniversary.

Have been trying to get some books that I think that you would like to read, Bill to send to you but so far have not had much luck. Did not send a package last week or so far this week. Wish that I could send something that you want but am not sure what that would be.

Just talked to Aunt Fan. She says that things look pretty good out there now for there was a good rain Sunday and there have been little showers nearly every evening since. I am glad for it was pretty bare and dry around the ranch.

The vet got the report on her cow which was negative for bangs disease so she can use the milk now. She is not giving much milk yet but is pretty thin. After the grass greens up and they give her some grain no doubt she will do better

*   *   *

Letter No. 106

Friday Aug.10, 1945

Dear Bill and Tom:

My what news there has been today except that as yet the Allies have not digested it all so that they can decide what answer to make. We all hope and pray that it will be the very end. Now that it seems close it seems hard to realize that it could ever end. The news of Japans acceptance of the Potsdam ultimatum was the first thing that we heard this morning when we turned the radio on at 7:30. Then it had not been received by any of the Allied heads so all day we have waited rather breathlessly for that confirmation and on the 5:30 broadcast this eve it came. You see Bill I was right last night when I wrote that I had the feeling you are more than half way your over-seas experience for if peace comes now it surely wont take longer than that to get you home.

Just talked to Aunt Betty and found out that Bud is at Ft. Logan and will be home tomorrow night. And now if this darned war is over he wont have to go on to the Pacific which is really grand.

Uncle Earl was in Trinidad and saw Aunt Nell who told him that they have sold their house. He said that Aunt N. seemed quite upset about it but that they dont give it up till February so they can have Christmas there anyway.

Lea and Shirley have not yet arrived from Denver so we had our sandwitch and Hay phoned me that she was going to go over to the little eating joint(one that has started up in the filling station that use to be on the corner next to Kleins store) and get hers for they may no come till nine oclock.

I read in the paper last night that there was much rejoicing on Okinawa yesterday over the fact that Russia had entered the war so I bet with the news today there is real celebrating and that will it be when it is final.

There was quite a piece in last nights Democrat about Lt.Col. James Taylor's being decorated for unusual bravery in rescuing some natives who had been overcome in a mine shaft in which there was great danger of gas fumes. He went in at his own risk and pulled one of them out.

Aunt Fan sold some of the older horses from the ranch today to Fattz so the boys brought them in today. They rode some of the ones they were selling and then Alex brought the truck in to take back the boys and saddles etc. He brought me some eggs for which I was grateful for they are getting hard to get. Dad said that this morning about nine some of the fellows went in to the Kit Carson for breakfast but that there was no meat on any kind and not any eggs so they had oatmeal and toast.

Bobby seems to be fine again so will be full of pep to greet his Dad tomorrow eve. I asked him what would be the first thing that he would say to his Dad and he said" Hello"

I saw by the paper the other eve that Dwane Atwill is married and Bill Zellers told me this morning that she is here.

Will close now and by the time I write again,Monday no doubt we will know if the war is over or whether it will be a little longer yet. My bet is that it is over.

*   *   *

8/11/45

Dear Mother & Dad,

T'was surely good news that the Japs would accept the surrender terms providing they could keep the Emperor Intact. I hope that something comes of it and we don't have to keep up the war. Maybe we'll all be back home sooner than we expected but I am keeping my fingers crossed. Even if the war ends now, I doubt I will get home before my 18 months are up.

The other day a gasoline drum caught on fire and one of the boys had a few bad burns. He didn't want to go to the hospital; so we are keeping him. We are trying out all of our skills on him. He is coming along very well. We have had several good cases as I have told you, but no exotic tropical diseases. We have stopped taking ataerine for malaria prophylaxis, we still have no malaria. We injected all sprained ankles, sore feet, and backs with novacaine. I don't know whether it cures them or not, but it surely cuts down on the number of them we get as most of the boys don't like needles.

Did I tell you Davidson the pharmacist mate at the Marine Hospital is planning on going to medical school. He seems quite serious about it.

Hope when I write the next letter the war will be over.

Love, Bill

*   *   *

August 13, 1945

Dear Mother and Dad,

Boy I sure hope that this surrender goes through. Looks pretty good so far and think the Japs will ok it. It surely will be grand if it does happen, for Bud might be in the States and won't need him out here.

I had a letter from Woody yesterday. He has tried twice to get down to see me, but because of the roads hasn't made it. Wally Gist was here, but has left. He was with the Marines. I was up to the hospital the other day and ran into a fellow by the name of Walt Mack, who I knew at Boulder. His home is in Pueblo. He'd heard from Charlie Fisher who is now at Mayo's. The Fishers have a child now. The Cowgills are now expecting. Adele lost a baby while he was interning; so hope this works out ok.

My roommate Chief Bridges has been out 18 months, and is hoping to get back before Christmas to see his little wife whom I feel I must know by now. He is trying to get a commission. He was a track man in school and came in under Tunney's program. Most of those of those fellows have their commissions by now.

I got the clippings of the airplane crash in New York. And, also, the note of Harold H's coming wedding. It has been a long time since I have seen him. I never thought he'd be a preacher. Also, got the stamps just fine. 'Til later,

Love, Bill

*   *   *

Letter No. 106

Monday Aug.13, 1945

Dear Tom and Bill:

When I wrote you on Friday I thought that surely when I wrote today it would be after V-J day but still we wait for the good news which I feel will surely come soon.

I am writing this to you Tom as well as Bill tho you told me this after noon not to write till we would get your new address but I will hold the letters and send them to you then. If I dont do that I will omit some of the important news,perhaps thinking that because I had written it to Bill I had also told you.

You see,Bill we had a talk with your brother this afternoon and now know that he will go down to Victoria,Kansas tomorrow if he did not go this afternoon. He thinks that he is to instruct on B-29s but first he will have to learn a little about it himself. I imagine that before he does that Togo and his clique will decide they do not like the taste of the Automic bombs. At least Tom you are moving a little nearer us which is better than getting farther away. It was good to hear that "resonant" voice of yours.

We had your letter of the 8th,Bill in todays mail and seems that the other doctors on the island are very nice to you or else pity your need of good food since for in that one letter you told of three invitations you had had. Will Dr. Wilson have better food at his dispensary than you have at yours or is it just the change that is good. So the officers are trusting you to take off their warts. Hope that you get good results. Are the warts a condition which arises from living on Okinawa or did they always have them and the Nave just sent all the "warty" officers there?

Johnny got home for a short visit Saturday afternoon and left at noon Sunday. That made it possible for the Sabin family to all be together Saturday eve as Bud arrived about four that afternoon. Marg,Bud and Bobby were here yesterday afternoon but I did not have much of a visit for Bobby thought my job was to play with him. Bud took him to the farm this morning and they rode horseback so guess they are having a lot of fun together.

Dad is going to a drug store meeting in a few minutes so will close so he can mail you letter Bill.

*   *   *

Letter No. 107-Victory Letter

Tuesday Aug. 13 1945

Dear Tom and Bill:

How can I sit still long enough to write but it is the only way I have to throw my arms around you while the tears of joy run down my cheeks. I know how you wish you could be here to celebrate this with all the folks at home. La Junta now at 6:15 has just roused up and the fire whistle, the Santa Fe whistles, all little whistles there are in town and most every car horn are wild and going full blast. I wonder if you Tom are in Sioux Falls or Victoria. Here all shipments were cancelled at five last night and so we thought that perhaps your change was also. And you Bill way off in Okinawa. Well it is just a little more so out there I imagine for the fellows there most of them know what war really is. I dont see how I can ever sleep this night that we have so longed for for nearly four years. We, the Rourke family has so much to be thankful for, with three, no with Dud it is four of our boys home and you, Billy boy and Eugene coming one of these days.

The neighbors just came over and want us to come over and have a drink. You know that is just not quite your mothers way of being truly happy and all I can think of is to thank God that you are all right and it is over. Anyway we cant find Dad just now so I told them that as soon as we found him we

Gosh the boys came back and by force took me over to their house and then went on a search for Dad. Found him after he had been over to Woodbridges and brought him over and now we are home thank goodness for if they could have kept us there we would have been drunk too for they are going all the way. The Garlingtons are back now and so think we can keep away from them for a while I hope.

We are going down town in a few minutes to mail these letters and see what is going on down there. The Garlingtons said that when they were there Mrs. Leroy and a great bunch of kids were riding around on the fire truck and tooting the siren. Oh this much is sure this will be a night to remember for some people and for some they cant remember.

Will write again tomorrow so for now ta-ta.

*   *   *

The Pacific—
after the War

August, 1945 – June, 1946

Letter No. 110

Thursday Aug. 15, 1945

Dear Tom and Bill:

I am sure that you will see a big change in the writing of this machine for Lea did a job today cleaning it up and putting on new ribbon etc. I have known for along while that it needed some such work but I really did not know much about how to do it.

The Garlingtons are to get their house this week end for Mr. Harms is sick in the east and as it will be a long while till he is able to come back they decided to give it up now. Their daughter who has been there will take Shirleys apartment and she and Eddie will go up with the "Pop and Mom" as she calls Hay and Lea. If you should be coming home by any chance this week end, Tom they will go down there so as to leave your room ready for you. For some reason Dad has it in his noodle that you might get a little leave to come home.

Manual was in a little while ago and says that both Monday and Tuesday nights they had good rains at the ranch, with the canyons all running big so that "other big rain has come" so guess all is set for a good grassy winter. It is good that it has come early enough that the grass will cure up well before frost. Guess Aunt Fan will go out tomorrow since she has learned that the road is passable.

I have not written you since V-J day and perhaps you may think that the soldiers next door were too eloquent in their persuasion and I was not in fit shape the next day to write but such is not the case. They did come over here later and still thought that every one should have good strong drinks so most of the one they fixed up for me went down the sewer when no one was looking. One of the wives got pretty sleepy so the had to leave before Bud, Marg, Mac and May came along also Ted Hartman and Reuben Inge. they did not stay long either for they had promised to make other calls. We got to bed about 11:30 but I was wide awake so did not sleep till about three AM. Yesterday we all made a holiday and the Garlics and us played contract all afternoon.

Fan and Dad went to Pueblo today and both of them came home tired for the stores were not open and so they were sitting around the clinic or standing on the street from 11 till about three. We think that we can play a little cards when I get this letter written anyway. Hay and I did the Sisson laundry too today so we are not just as fresh as daisies this eve either. The long whites will probably call us early.

Dad said that one surely could see the evidence of the raising of the gasoline rationing by the numbers of cars on the road between here and Pueblo. Usually there are very few but today there were many.

Guess this is the news for today so will close now and more tomorrow.

*   *   *

8/15/45

Dear Mother & Dad,

Today the word is practically certain of the surrender of Japan as Pres. Truman announced it himself. That of course is surely grand news. It surely makes me want to get home quicker, but I doubt that my tour of duty outside the continental limits is shortened any. The victory was prematurely celebrated the other day and hope that it is more sanely enjoyed today. It falls on the day of the beer ration which is good for the boys.

It looks as though we may be in this same location for some time yet; so we are improving it a little. They are putting eaves on the dispensary today which will give us more shade and air. We have had to put the side flaps up and down every time it stops and starts raining which is quite frequently.

Hope that Sabin is home for the chances are good that he won't have to stay long in the army now. Had a very sweet note from Aunt Betty thanking for the cards. Also heard from Ginnie Sisk. Hope Ole T gets good duty—Is he still at Sioux Falls. This will just about wind up the air Field in L.J.

We are ahead of you in time. When we are going to bed it is morning in Colo of the same day. When we get up you are going to bed the night before. Your intuition isnt very good for once. Fairly close but not it.

Not much other news for the Present so shall close.

All my love, Bill

*   *   *

8/16/45

Dear Mother & Dad,

We are still joyed at the turn of the war. When the war in Europe ended I was at sea and this one in Okinawa. The only thing that could make me celebrate the day more would be to celebrate it with you.

Both our vehicles—Jeep and ambulance are running quite smoothly now. The jeep had been under the weather. The clutch and Brake worked simultaneously. That is when you put in the clutch to back the brake went on and vice versa. However a good grease job did the trick and they now work loosely and independently.

Do we have a chateau now for a dispensary. It looks like a real summer resort. We have shade over the water barrel, too. Another new addition to the sick bay is a telephone.

I received your letter of Aug. 5, Dad, in 7 days—That is about the quickest yet.

I joined the officers Club when I was at NOB the other day which cost me $50 so I wrote a check. I dont see what good it was to join as the only thing you get is a whiskey ration of a bottle a week. The only time you can draw it is after 5:30 P.M. and I don't like to come back after dark. I'll get the $50 bucks back anyway.

Haven't much other news until later,

All my Love, Bill

*   *   *

Letter No. 111

Friday Aug, 17 1945

Dear Tom and Bill:

Three letters came from you,Bill today and the last one was written the day that the Japs first accepted the Postdam peace terms. From the tone of that letter you were quite pleased and so now that the war is over I know that you must really be more than thrilled as every one is. In San Francisco they continued the celebrating so long that it became a riot that the police had a time breaking up. I am enclosing a clipping from the Post about it. Too bad people get so crazy rather than being just sanely thankful for such a great benefit as peace.

We also had a letter from Gene and from some things he said we judge that he was in the vicinity of Okinawa when he wrote it and I think that he was in hopes of seeing you Bill. Hope that by this time he has realized that hope and you have gotten together. He said that he had not gotten ashore yet to see you but that you have as good duty as there is in those parts. He hoped that his "swell doctor" and you could meet.

Was so glad Bill that you told me that you enjoyed the canned meats on crackers for tomorrow I will get another box off to you. I had sort of given up that maybe it was not worth while but since it "really hit the spot" there will be one on the way every week. I am just sorry that I have let two weeks elapse without sending one. I had planned to send you this week A.J. Cronin's new book for they say that it is good but when Dad went to Pueblo Wednesday where he was to purchase it the stores were all closed (they were still celebrating) V-J day.

I was also glad to hear that the weather is not as hot as Missouri and that the nights cool off well.

I had a letter today from Miss Rogers in Albuquerque who told me about the son of Dr. Ralph Mendelson. I am sure that you will remember my telling you about this man who graduated from high school here in the same class that I did and after the last war was doctor to the king of Siam. This son of his is on Okinawa, a doctor who she says they sent over there right out of med school without internship, taking care evidently of the natives for his picture was in the Time some time ago with a bunch of native women around him. I did not know at the time that he was some one I knew anything about and the fact that his name was Berg did not make any impression on me but I thought at the time that I would send the clipping to you and Dad thinks that I did. Isnt that strange?

Hope the rumors of the officers club come true so that you will have some where to loaf a bit.

There was no letter from you,Tom today so we think that you have nothing to report but even so we have sort of been thinking that there is not so much for you to do there and that maybe you might be making us a little visit. Just wishful thinking I suppose.

We had our supper out at the country club and now are home and grandma is trying to put Eddie to sleep. His teeth seem to hurt him and so he is a little cross and wakeful.

Hope your badly burned boy is still coming along fine since he wanted to stay with you instead of the hospital.

Fan went to the ranch today and while we were out at the country club Aunt Mayme was here and left me a plant that she evidently had brought from Idaho Springs but we did not get to see her for she went right on to her ranch. Must stop now.

*   *   *

8/18/45

Dear Mother & Dad,

Have seen a good many of the fellows that I knew at Hueneme. Last night I went up to the officers Club and met two of them. I drove them up to where they are camped and then drove back here—it was quite a jeep trip all together.

They had a letter from you as of July 2. I had been wondering why Justine was home and now I know.

Also ran into several other fellows I've known along the line; so had a good time for my first evening out. Today is Sunday and am going up to see Walsh and have Sunday dinner with him. The Jeep is always giving us a little trouble—For real transportation we rely on the ambulance. Last night had to get the brake fluid replenish and this morning we had difficulty starting it. However the boys are good mechanics and keep it functioning.

They have a barber here in the company. These people are interesting and have characteristics that I find quite amazing. The barber insists on putting a very luscious smelling oil on my hair and tries to part and comb it which is impossible. There is always a small gathering around his establishment overflowing with the entertaining humor of these people. Most of them are very easy to get along with and are nearly always happy. Most of them are just like children however and lack very much education.

They are lazy some of them—One boy is lazy with his bowels which sometimes don't move for a month. We gave him about 9 enemas yesterday and were still getting fecal return. They are very appreciative, especially those you can help.

Today the Japs are to go to Manila. I'll be glad when we have our troops in Tokyo. As for the navy—I'll have to get married to get out of this business—but no one to marry.

Not much other news,

All my Love, Bill

*   *   *

8/18/45

Dear Mother & Dad,

I received your letter of 8/10 yesterday—only 7 days—also letter of 8/9. You were surely right in your prediction. Was surely glad to hear that Bud is home. The news surely is great—We heard the first announcement about 8:00 PM and you in the morning of the same day—

I was glad to hear of ole Dick Counley again. He is to be discharge. That's fine. The marines are much more strict about censorship than anyone else.

I have evidently not yet received the letter that Tom was moved from the sound of the last letter. Sorry that you sent me all the golf balls for I've not had a chance to use them.

There is lots of scuttlebutt about the point system for the navy. The last one I heard would give me only 4 more years that I'd have to remain in the navy. No one knows.

I guess I really am a little rough on the boys—Will probably have to change my tactics for a civilian practice.

I was surprise to hear that the Sisks had sold their house. What are their plans now.

We have been having good chow lately—pork, mutton, beef—I think I had lost a little weight but have quickly picked it up with our chow now.

Not much more news now. Till Later

All my love

*   *   *

8/20/45

Dear Mother & Dad,

Yesterday I had lunch with Walsh. Then went over to see Woody Brown and fortunately caught him at home. His outfit has a swell camp site on a hill over looking the ocean with pine trees and rocks. Up north it is much prettier. They don't have much difficulty with mud. I then picked up Walsh and we all had dinner with Woody. That's the best mess I've had on the Island. The CB's do things up right.

On the way back Walsh and I stopped to see the fellows we knew at Hueneme. It was a pleasant Sunday afternoon. On returning found they had brought me 3 letters from you. One contained a clipping of the picture of the Mennonite Hospital. Hope they still plan to put in a Sisters hospital. Also the note about Dads fishing prowess. Also enjoyed the clipping about Dengue Fever. I've had a few cases I thought might be Dengue, but they weren't very severe. I wondered what happened to the address on one of the letters then learned that the post office filled it in. Too bad you missed Marsdon. Hope that the work in the Abstract Company is caught up. Even had you working— eh Mother. I'll bet Dad would like to keep you there all of the time.

Today the Japs are in Manila and soon be occupying Japan, I hope. Not much other news. Till Later

All my love, Bill

*   *   *

Bob McClusky is in the state & Bob Panter is back too.

Letter No. 112

Monday Aug.20, 1945

Dear Bill and Tom:

This morning we had two letters one from Bill and the other our first from Tom since you have been at Victoria. From the fact that you had had only one letter since you have been there and that evidently one that was forwarded from Sioux Falls, you have not received the letters I have been sending just to the Walker Field so am glad now to have a little better address. In case you do not have it Bill it is

248th B.U.

W.A.A.F.

Victoria, Kansas

We were glad too to learn that you have been assigned as adjutant as permanent party even tho it is not a very good and no good towns close it is better than some island out in the Pacific,Ill bet. The job with regular hours will help a lot to pass the time and keep you from being bored. Eight to five are just bankers hours.

The size of the B-29 that you went out to look at is like a story some told me today about a fellow asking a pilot of a B-29 how he liked it and he said "It is just like sitting on my front porch and flying my house." We wonder what kind of a plane you flew on the trip which you made taking those officers to Chicago and Lansing. It must have been a thrill to land at the field where you first entered a little cub plane. Too bad that you did not get to see the instructor that you had had there.

Reading your letter again I find that you had gotten the first letter that I had sent to you at Victoria.

When you wrote your letter Bill you had just one day to wait for that big news that the war is over for it was dated the 13th. But I guess that was sunday out there so it was really two days after that that it came. No I dont think that Bud will be going out of the states now but he says that he believes that it may be a year before he gets his discharge.

Too bad that the roads and the mud interfere with the visits you and Woody might have together but it seems to me that there is not so much rain in the fall and winter according to the Geographic article. And Charlie Fisher is at Mayos? He should get some where in this world if he is ambitious. Seems to me I knew that they have a child but did not know that the Cowgills are expecting.

Hope your Chief Bridges gets home for Christmas and also that he gets his commission for I know that most of the fellows who went in in Tunny's deal did.

Did I tell you that Eleanor is working at the Elk Horn Cafe and that she has bought a little house in west La Junta. She has just heard once from Dick since he was here.

I go to the USO tonight and Dad is going down and play a little at the club. He sort of lost out yesterday by our going to Stage Canyon.

The Garlingtons are in their house but as yet are not very well straightened up. It is quite a mess as yet and there is a good deal of cleaning they have to do.

Will go now and do my patriotic duty. Mr. Malouff is talking to Dad and is asking all about the two of you.

*   *   *

Letter No. 113

Tuesday Aug. 21, 1945

Dear Tom and Bill:

This has been a regular Okinawa day, I guess for it has rained about every half hour since about midnight last night. Guess there has really been a lot of water fall for the rivers, Both Picketwire and Arkansas are pretty high. I talked to Aunt Fan this morning and it had evidently rained out there about as it had here. It makes the cattle people pretty happy but the farmers are not so pleased for this sort of weather is not good for most of the local crops, onions, melons, tomatos etc. The first cantaloupes were at Zellers this morning and I got just one for I fear they are a little overanxious to get them on the market and so have not let them ripen enough. Can tell better when I cut this one.

The temperature has gone down today to 58 so we are nice and cool. It did not seem to get so cool till this morning for it was so very still till about six and then a little breeze sprang up. There was no lightening either with this rain.

Just talked to Aunt Betty. Justine had a letter from John yesterday in which he said they had asked the cadets down there how many of them wished to continue their training and when a very few said they wished to go on the training program was discontinued and so he said he would be home soon so we suppose that he means that he will be discharged. But the Pueblo paper this morning said that the B-29 training there would continue at full speed so guess that type is to go on so your field,Tom will probably be kept going at least till Feb. when you said that it would close.

Can you imagine what Dad just did? Made a fire in the fireplace and it surely feels good. Tomorrow we will probably be roasting again. We can have a nice quiet evening by the fire side all to our selves.

Just read in last nights paper (I did not read it yesterday) that Patsy McCune (Pat) was married last summer a year ago but the family has just announced it now. Why I dont know. Some fellow she met at the Uni of Ohio.

Since it was rainy today Mrs. Stone and I did not wash but cleaned the house instead so now I can sit in the midst of a lot of cleanliness and the whole thing is in readiness for the poker club tomorrow night and Dad can have them anywhere he wants to, in the living room, dining room or the basement.

Aunt Fans light plant is sort of on the bum and she cannot get anyone to fix it before next week so we may have to go out so Dad can look it over and see if he can find anything wrong. Of course if we would hear that T. might be coming home we would not go out. Hey, T. any chance?

Guess I will go now and fix some hot soup for our bit of supper. I should have made some drop cakes, taking advantage of the cool to make a fire in the oven. Maybe I had better go do that.

*   *   *

8/22/45

Dear Mother & Dad,

Both of our Red Cross men have moved away from here, because of lack of business. They had collected two chickens while they were here which they have left behind. They each lay an egg almost every day. They aren't exactly beautiful chickens—one a white one and the other brown. The brown one is in the setting mood, but is still laying eggs. Perhaps I'll assume the responsibility of seeing they get food and water. If someone doesn't I'm sure one of the boys in the camp will soon be having a chicken dinner. We don't keep them cooped up and they hang around very well.

Dr. Whitaker of a C.B. outfit I'm taking care of down here was down yesterday. He has about a month & a half to go. He is a good egg—He interned at Iowa Univ.

Our business is surely slow these days. The other night we had a drunk; so its getting just like Stateside duty. I think I'm a little free with the needles which doesn't appeal to the colored boys.

They moved the movie from here so I haven't seen a show in some time. We don't have far to go to see several different ones, but I just haven't bothered about it.

Not much other news for the present,

All my love, Bill

*   *   *

Wednesday Aug.22, 1945

Dear Bill and Tom:

Lelia and I have been comparing today and just finished for this time and in the morning will begin again so now I am home and while everything is quiet will write a little to you tho there is not much news except weather and even that subject is rather dull today being neither cold or hot sunny or cloudy, windy or still. I think however we can now say that we have had fire every day of the year since we set the furnace up this morning and the heat felt good. There is terrible weeping and woeing among the farmers and if the sun does not come out bright and warm soon they threaten we will not be enjoying cants this year, so whether we like hot days or not we do hope they will come along.

There was no mail this morning and so I have been watching for the mail man this afternoon as he might bring something.

This day was set aside by the Bishop as the official day of Thanksgiving in the Catholic church so we started off with High Mass at seven this morning and there will be services this eve. There will be choir practice this eve after church so I will be busy while the poker bunch assemble. As yet do not know whether they will play up here or down stairs but no matter I must clean the front porch before the time of their arrival and wash up what few dishes I made with my lunch at noon.

There were two adds in the paper the last few nights for washing machines for sale so I have been out this afternoon chasing them up but did not have much luck, for one place could not find anyone home and the other the machine had been sold. I have thought for a long while that with another machine to do the rinsing while one does the washing I could get thru in about half the time and so not mind the laundry at all. Then too Aunt Mayme had asked me to watch the adds for she would like to get one for Olive. However no doubt they are some more of the things that will soon be on the market again and maybe I can have a new one to wash with and this old one for the rinsing. Mrs.

Stone will have to do it by herself tomorrow for I am going to work in the morning again.

Saw Bud when I was coming home at noon on his way to Rotary. I bet they made him make a speech and gave him a big welcome home.

The mail just arrived but only a little note from "Annie" Walker. She said to tell T. and Bill "Hello" so hello.

I also just called Mrs. Cranson to learn that Walter is at home since Sunday morning at 3:30 on a little leave to relieve the home situation as his father is having quite a little asthma and the boys are getting their stock ready for the fair. She said that Lea is feeling a little better since that knee is draining. Has a good appetite and looks better.

Bonnie Basinger is substituting at the USO for the asst. director till school begins and was on the job for the first time Monday eve when I was down. Poor child was hobbling around on crutches. She had just stepped down wrong from their two door steps but had twisted the ankle and torn the ligaments. She said it tired her so much to walk on the crutches and so was not doing much but sitting and trying to learn by experience (there is no one there now to show her) what is to be done and how. Mr. Harms is not back and dont know just when he will be so the place is more or less running along by itself for all we have is our volunteer help, ladies like me and some good men like Mr. Humphries.

I too learned today for the first time that Marguerite has a baby nine months old. Her husband is in the Pacific. Lelia told me this morning that he just met her on the street one evening when she had her arms full and begged to be allowed to help her home and from that time on would have it not other way but that she would marry him. She told him the several reasons why she could not, being Spanish and he white, being a Catholic and he not but none of them were a reason as far as he was concerned so he became a convert. His folks in Alabama seem to be very fond or her and want her to come

Here I had all kinds of interruptions. Father Bertrand came then it was time to go for Dad and I had just finished straightening

the room downstairs and sweeping the front porch when Aunt Nell
and Mrs. Monroe came on their way to Trinidad from Marys where
they have been since Sunday. So after fixing Dad a bit to eat and
doing the dishes it is now time for church so I will have to run along
and write more tomorrow. Just learned that Johnnie Moore had
been out to see Ginny on his way to Guam.

*   *   *

Letter No. 115

Thursday Aug.23, 1945

Dear Tom and Bill:

This morning Dad got a letter from you,Bill at the office which
you had written on the 16th and then when the mail man came
there was another written on the 15th which was the 14th over
here so was V-J day, and by now you should have the letter that I
wrote to you boys that eve just after we had the good news. It still
seems as if those Japs are not just too willing to give up their arms
and last night I read that the Chinese think that the Japs are storing
some of their weapons away in underground secret places but I
think that old McArthur should know them well enough that he will
be able to keep one jump ahead of them in their treachery.

I am glad,Bill that you now have eaves on the dispensary so you
can keep the flaps up even when it is raining and so be more
comfortable.

Guess from what you say that the membership in the officers
club will not be any great benefit to you as you cant even get the
bottle of whisky that it entitles to you but maybe you will be that
much better off. And when you get over to NOB you at least can sit
down there and rest a few minutes with a feeling that "I belong
here".

Bill cant you make the Navy feel that you are greatly in need of
more schooling and so they should send you back to get busy on it. I
imagine now that the war is over the censorship will be lifted so

that you can say just where you are located so I am going to stop guessing for you say that my last one was not so good but of this we're now are sure that you are on that end of the Island and so we are "pretty warm" in our surmises.

Yes Ginny and Johnnie Moore got to celebrate V-J day together in San Francisco. Aunt Nell said they came near being caught in that mob and that by the time they got home Ginnies stocking were shreds from firecracker scorches.

Yes bill I finally have that time business sort of straightened out in my mind so now when I am going to bed I think of you as getting out and around about your next days business,operating etc.

Aunt Mayme was in at noon so ate dinner with us. She says that the country now is just beautiful and green and water everywhere. She had had a letter from dud telling her that the prominent funeral had gone off very well. The services were in Idaho springs and the burial in a moseleum (I have tried to find that word in the dictionary,but cant and I really do not know how to spell it) in Denver, the first funeral of that kind that he had ever even helped with so he had been a bit nervous about it.

Yesterday aunt Fan had a letter from one of the Murray boys in Denver telling her about his mother,Cousin Kate, whom we had thought perhaps died some time ago for the last that we had heard months ago she was very low and not expected to live but just days. She evidently survived that spell but on Memorial day fell and broke her arm and shoulder, was recovering from that and a short time ago fell again and broke her hip so now is in Mercy hospital just waiting till the end, but to the surprise of everyone seeming to recover again. She is nearly 90 years old but certainly must have a very strong constitution.

Saw by the paper night before last that Monroe is due in the states this week. I ordered your paper sent to you Tom so you should start getting it very soon. I surely wish that you could get it,Bill even if it was old when it came but maybe if there are not so many over seas from now on there will be a better chance of its getting through.

Yesterday I went over to the library to get Mrs. Steel, the librarian, to recommend some books that I could buy to send to you,Bill and found out that she will get them for me and allow me the discount which she gets for the library. She says that she has always done that for the members of the library board. She had an extra copy of "The Green Years" by A.J. Cronin so let me have it and I will send it to you this week and then can send others as she gets them.

We had our first home grown canteloupe this morning but did not think that it was much better than the shipped in ones that we have had. I guess all the damp weather seems to lessen the sugar content in the things which ripen about this time of year. They say that the beats will not have so much sugar because of the excessive moisture.

Mr. Horning is trying again to sell the house over here and is asking $18,000.00 for it. He had a nibble the other day but guess the fellow thought that was a little more than it is worth.

Must go to Dr. Klob and since it is a grand day told Dad I would walk down and drive home with him at five as my appointment is four so I had better start on it now being about 3:30.

*   *   *

8/24/45

Dear Mother and Dad,

Last night I went up to Brown Beach, and saw a stage show with Kay Kyser. It was really crowded—just like the States. The ride back was beautiful as the ole moon was shining.

We turned in our points the other day for the navy system. 1/2 point for each year of age, 1/2 point for each month of active duty, and 10 points for a dependent. I've got 21 points and it only takes 49 to be discharged or released to inactive duty. I figure by this method I can get out in Sept 1949. Guess I'd better get married; for that would cut off almost two years—who shall I marry.

Surely wish I could find some fertile eggs. Poor ole hen—put some unfertile ones under her. It would really be fun to hatch some little chicks.

Our mail is now going—I don't know where—We have quite a time trying to find it. This is such a little outfit no one knows where we are. Haven't much other news for the present—Till later,

All my Love, Bill

*   *   *

Letter No. 116

Friday Aug.24, 1945

Dear Bill and Tom:

Guess the farmers are happier today for the sun has been out hot and bright ever since about 8o'clock this morning when the fog which was hanging over like California cleared up. That has been a strange thing this summer, we have had so many cloudy mornings and clearing later in the day when usually no matter how rainy it is in the evening we can depend on the sun coming up bright and shining the next morning, guess the Automic bomb must have changed the weather at least there was much such speculation of that till the weather man made a statement in the papers refuting any such idea. So now we dont know just who to blame. Poor President Roosevelt cant be responsible and Eleanor has kept very much in her corner since she retired from the white House.

I have "The Green Years" packed up and will mail to you,Bill when I go down to get Dad at five. I wonder how long it will take it to go to you. I read some of it last night, to where I left the book marker (my shopping list) and liked it so now will get it out of the Library and finish it. The box was too large so I stuck Democrats around it to fill up the box.

Had a letter from Aunt Kathryn Lee today and it is one series of woes, Wilbur has been on the sick list treating for ulcers which he thinks he does not have, Marion and Dorothy have worms (quiet now for they dont seem to want it known) and Johnnie is having shots for hay fever which he has been having pretty badly. Isnt that a mess?

You will probably not have letters for a couple of days now for Dad and I are going out to the ranch tomorrow and back Sunday afternoon so he may not get his Sunday morning writing done.

Justine had not heard any more from John about coming home so guess he is just "sweating it out" down there and I bet it is just that when he is so anxious to be with his little wife.

Last night the telephone rang and when I took down the receiver I knew that it was along distance call so thought it would be T. but central asked for Mrs. Charles J. Sisk and when I told her she was in Trinidad I heard a very familiar voice say "will I could not get her in Trinidad so thought she might be in La Junta" and I called right out "Oh Fred" and then realized that he could not talk to me so I said to central "Maybe he would want to talk to me" but heard him say he thought he would try Trinidad again. Now I am wondering if he had news of a discharge but I bet Nellie dont write us for ages as she usually does, so I will just have to keep right on wondering.

We are anxious to hear how you and your job got along,Tom for when you last wrote you were to start the next day. Maybe will get some word tomorrow.

*   *   *

8/27/45

Dear Dad & Mother,

Had a big week-end Saturday afternoon Dr. Rankin, who I have been with since we left the States, Grannis, and Casey came down. Had an infected hand to open so Rankin gave the anesthetic and I opened it. We then all went out to the Island where Rankin is stationed. It is really a lovely place. The best place to swim around here. It is nice and green. He has a good set-up. Now has another Doctor on the island so perhaps he'll get to come over and see me more often.

I got the package mother sent with raisins in it. That was really a clever means of sending them and they arrived in perfect condition. Enjoyed the news papers and the story from the Sat. Eve. Post. Hope that the conclusion is forthcoming.

Also received a bunch of the L.J. Tribune Democrats. Saw where George Brumfield was killed here a month after his wife died leaving an infant son.

Surely nice to realize the war is over. Sounds as though they really celebrated in the states. They had more casualties that night (when they first announced it) than on a good many nights. Crazy idiots started shooting all the guns. We had to get in our own fox holes.

Sounds like a good deal to get a manager for the Drug store. Hope it works out. Not much other news for to present. All my love, Bill

*   *   *

Letter 117

Monday Aug.27, 1945

Dear Tom and Bill:

There is so much to tell you today and so many letters from you to comment on that this should be really a good letter.

First we got back from the ranch yesterday eve about six after a nice trip, especially so since everything out there looks so very fine, green as a lawn and the grass already heading out. When Dad was out that way just three weeks ago it was pretty bare and the calves especially were not at all good but now they are as fat as butter. The cattle were all lying around the many holes of water in tall grass and looking very contented with full stomachs and water without traveling any distance. We saw the boys handling some of the broncos some very pretty horses but did not ride any for the gnats and flies drive the horses as well as the people nearly crazy. We will go out this fall and do that.

Now for the letters. We had yours, Tom on Saturday written at your desk in your own little office in the orderly room and even your writing shows that you have a desk to write on. I have decided that you and Aunt Fan write much alike for I picked up an envelope of yours and at first glance thought it was her writing.

I seems that you would be getting out if you were still a second Lieut. but have not points enough for a first. Well if they keep you on that job I think that it will be very good experience for you and you can go to Boulder when the right time comes. If you went right now maybe there would not be many of the fellows back anyway so later might be better. On the other hand if you went before the rest get there you might be a sort of lone wolf with all the pretty little freshies.

I know you would like a car and I dont blame you a bit but your logic is very good. That a used good car is hard to find now and they will not be worth much when the new ones get on the market. That is something you just have to work out all by your lonesome. If a person got a good break at a car that some one had to sell which was not already too well up on mileage then it might be all right.

Bud Lane has not gone to work yet and dont think he intends to til his three months are up if he can keep out of it.

Today we had three letters from you Bill. One of the 18, one more of the 18, and one of the 20th. Yes we were hearing the news of the wars end at 7:30 AM and you about 8PM of the same day. I finally have it clear in my mind so now know just about what you are doing at any time of the day. For I know that you are sleeping. We like to hear about your good chow these days, pork, mutton beef etc and glad that you are gaining weight.

Your trip up to the officers club to see two of your Hueneme friends must have done you a lot of good for the tone of you letter was very cheery. Strange that they had that letter from me to you of July 2. How long had it been there?

Yes if you were here you would not have me tell you what is wrong (right I should say) with Justine. She was over here this morning washing her hair in our nice soft water and is getting quite a tummy on her. John's name was on the last list of those getting their discharges so he will be home to stay in from "one week to six weeks" he says. I am so glad that they can now get settled when he gets something to do before the baby comes which they expect in January.

I knew Bill that being like your Dad in some things you would get a kick out of those colored boys and your description of the one who cuts your hair and his humor was interesting. Also about their laziness especially the one who is too lazy to have a bowel movement and you had to give him nine enemas and still did not have him cleaned out. I bet he wont let things go so long again.

It wont be long now till our troops are in Tokyo if the typhoon slows up pretty quick. There has been a bad wind in the gulf,too between Corpus Christy and Galveston.

Well,Bill I dont think that you can get married over there unless you take a little dark girl for I have not heard you mention any wacs,or waves or even nurses so guess there are just not any white women over there.

Am glad that you got to see Woody finally and that he has a pretty camp site in the pines. Seeing him with Walsh and then visiting the other boys that you knew it Hueneme must have been very pleasant.

This morning we had a letter from aunt Nell telling us the news that Fred had for her the other night when he was trying to get her and called here. He is to go to the Pacific. He will have two weeks furlough and then report to Camp Meade for a years assignment to the Pacific so you may be seeing him one of these days,Bill. Jean will go to Ann Arbor during his absence. Aunt Nell is quite upset but think she should not be so much so since the fighting is over and it will be quite an experience for him. Had a little note from Gene with a copy of an item which was printed in their paper about a Trinidad woman getting her tank filled up on the day rationing was off and as she drove out of the fill station the tank couldn't stand the strain and went to pieces.

Bob McClusky is home. Was on his way to the Pacific but at Panama the war ended so they were sent home instead. H e said that they would have given him his discharge at Ft. Logan if he would have taken it but he wanted to get his 30 days and then told them he would decide.

Think that is all the news for today so will close now for I have to have my hair combed as I had it set this morning and may have to sit under the dryer for a little while.

*   *   *

Letter No. 118

Tuesday Aug.28, 1945

Dear Bill and Tom:

Since Dad and I have been called to attend a meeting for consideration of the proposed hospital and we think we had better be there to protect ourselves(otherwise we might find ourselves giving a half million or something) I will write a little now before Dad comes.

Mrs. Stone and I did the laundry this morning and got along so fine that we were all thru at eleven and she had gone home. guess I am getting faster in my old age or maybe dirtier and so less clothes to wash.

This morning when I went to church at 7:30 the temperature was 58, really cool for this time of the year. The days seem warm but not really so when the high is about 90.

We had another letter from brother, Bill this afternoon of the 22nd. and a letter from Aunt Gertrude. Marian is going back to Chicago with Marsden who flew out to California. They will drive but do not expect to come this way but by way of Salt Lake City and north. Bane is going to live with Gerturde while Marian is away,in Marian's house. They seem to think that will be a good arrangement for Bane drives more than Gertrude so they can get out more. They have an apartment in Chicago for which they have to pay $108.00 a month. Isnt that just dreadful for evidently it is not such a grand affair or in so very good location. Gertrude said they would try to find something else when Marian gets there.

We heard over the radio at noon that there is 15 inches of water in Houston from the typhoon. I wonder if it got into the Rice Hotel. It must be one sweet mess down there.

Tom, your brother has gone into the chicken business in Okinawa with two hens which furnish an egg or two daily. It seems they belonged to some Red Cross men who have left and didnot take the poor chickens along. where do you keep them at night? As I take it they are just around in the day time.

I judge that Dr. Whitaker is your boss but is to leave the island in another month or so.

What on earth did the drunk find to drink so much of that he had to be taken care of by the doctor?

From the fact the Red Cross men have gone and that the movie has been taken away it begins to look to us that your company may be getting ready to break up. Am glad that there still are several close enough that you can see a picture when the mood strikes you.

There has been a world of activity in the air around here today and right over head like it use to be. Sounded like they were coming right through the roof several times. They are fighter planes. It seems that there are lots of fellows coming in here these days but no one seems to know just why or what.

Roy Oberling who has been in Okinawa is home now. He is in the Navy but has been with the Marines as a Corpsman or something. Think that we will try to see him and learn a little more about the island. He was in that same part that you are,Bill I think for he landed first on the north but there was not much doing there so they were sent down south to relieve some of those who had been doing so much down there.

Will close now and fix the supper for the old man and me.

*   *   *

8/29/45

Dear Mother & Dad,

The radio this morning states that we have landed troops in the Tokyo area which really sounds good. Can hardly wait to get home.

I got the package of books the other day. They really came fast. I've already made use of them. We have needed them quite a bit. I hope I won't waste as much time now. The new books you got in Denver from Jess is just what we needed for many of our problems. I got the box with raisins, etc. the day before. The raisins were in good shape.

Do you remember my speaking of a boy by the Name of Edmondson. There were two of them. The older Bob was in my class at Boulder. The younger Bill was in the class behind me in Med School. He interned at the US Naval Hospital in San Diego. Shortly after he started his internship he got pneumonia and died. He was a very intelligent boy.

Enjoyed the D.P. in the box with the books. What can I make out of the Eagle Brand. My tent mate Tommy Bridges was disappointed as he doesn't like raisins, but he ate some last night.

Last night we candled the eggs we have under the setting hen and as we suspected—no luck. Fresh eggs are awfully scarce and rosters even been more so.

Not much other news today.

All my love, Bill

*   *   *

Letter No. 119

Wednesday Aug. 29,1945

Dear Tom and Bill:

Soon it will be three months since the day that Bill landed in Okinawa and T landed at Bangor,a day to remember in many ways no doubt for each of you as well as your dad and mother.

There was no mail today but a letter from Robinson to you Tom which I will send on tonight. I note that he is in Las Vegas,Nev. and I hope that Dorothy is with him as no doubt she is.

I cut a clipping from the Post today about Bob Truscott's wedding which I am sending to you tonight Bill. Also one about the woman in Pueblo that the chickens picked to death. Just as a warning,Doc not to let the two hens live in the house with you.

Aunt Mayme was in this afternoon and visited me while Jack went with a man who was returning Bud's mare to the farm. She(the mare) has been sojourning at the Farthing ranch on her "honeymoon" like "Falla" did once.

At the meeting last night most everyone seemed to think that there was not much (about $300,000.00) in the way of building a Sisters hospital here and officers were chosen to start the ball rolling. I dont feel too optimistic about it for I dont think that the other doctors in town favor the idea and perhaps that will influence many people who otherwise would think it a good thing for the town and would help out financially. Henry Klein,pres.; Maurice Dawson,vice-pres; Sophie Ruegg,Sec; and Mr. Stoffel Treasurer were the officers elected. They are a good bunch to do it if it can be done, and we should soon know for the Sisters want an answer soon for if they dont get one here they have other places in view.

Bobby Boulton and her husband were killed in a car accident in California. Their nine month old baby who was with them was unhurt. They will be buried here and the baby will be with the Boultons for the present at least.

Dad saw Bob MacClusky at Rotary today and he was wishing that he could see you,Tom. Guess it was in San Antonio that you last saw each other.

Bud Lane told Dad yesterday that he would go to work about the first as they would not let him stay out of it any longer, the railroad really need men right now very much. Jackie has a bicycle now and has been going thru the throes of learning to ride it.

Nellie wrote Aunt Mayme that perhaps she and Charles would rent a house here and live down here till he is retired. Guess she would like to have Jean and the baby come and stay with them while Fred is away so maybe that has something to do with the idea.

Church night. That reminds me that Paul Church and Mary Fran have been down visiting the Inges while he is home on his 30 day leave.

*   *   *

Letter No. 120

Thursday Aug. 30,1945.

Dear Bill and Tom:

Supper is over(rolls and boiled eggs), Dad is reading the evening paper and Fannie is playing solitaire so I will write to my boys, and comment on the very good letter that we had from you,Tom today. Tho you had no good news of when you might expect to get a discharge we were interested to hear about the Saturday evening you had with the date from Russel "the gal wasn't bad" said your brother so he thinks he may get another date with her.

So you dont like the B-17 as well as the B-24 since your trip to Chicago in one but then you did not fly it, so that may make a difference too.

Since so many are leaving that field and it might be possible that they would send you some where else it would be nice if that some place happened to be LJAAF. If that could come to pass then we would not care too much how long it was before you would get that discharge. Yes I imagined that in this one thing, the matter of a discharge, Clegg will beat you since he is just a second. Oh well it wont be so much difference so I still think I'd take the first.

Hope you follow that hunch to go see a doctor about your eyes for it doesnot pay to fool along with them when a change of glasses of just the use of the ones you should have around somewhere might help in reading so as not to strain them.

Had a letter from Virginia Winchell today and it was mostly trying to persuade us that now that the gas is plentiful we should drive back to New York. She mentioned that Julia is to come back to school the first of November but did not say that they would be bringing her out. However I think that I will make the counter suggestion that they do that instead of our going back there(we have no intention of doing it any way). she said that Bill is coming to St. Louis if the world series is there so that would be just on their way. Julia has the same job that she had last year but with a raise in pay. V. said that she does not like to work too well but that she does like to buy new clothes with the money. She is in the map department.

Made a pan of rolls for Marg and bud but when I called they were going out to dinner so I sent them over to the rest of the Guthries. Because Aunt Fan came in today was the reason of the bread making and I would pick the hottest day we have had now for quite a little while. Last night the low was 68 and the night before it was 58., so that is quite a difference.

Aunt Mayme told me that she is going to bring me some sausage tomorrow from a hog of theirs which they had butchered so in return I thought that it would be nice if I had Mrs. Raney bake a cake for her and Jack as I know that Mary does not do very much fancy cooking, it seemed like a fair exchange to me.

Am glad Tom that you are not getting the paper and all the local gossip.

*   *   *

Letter No. 121

Aug.31, 1945

Dear Tom and Bill:

This is one of those days when there seems to be little to write about so I will just converse with you for a while. At noon when Aunt Fan and I were listening to the radio we heard that the army will release about 4000 doctors in the near future since they are so badly needed in civilian life so ofcourse my thought was "the navy better do likewise". Well perhaps something will happen to make them give it some thought in the right direction. At least it is a nice thought to have and hold. Even in Fred case perhaps they will not be over there as long as it now seems. In Europe where they now have over a million men it will soon be reduced to 400,000 thousand. I wonder if Ed will be one of those lucky ones who gets to come back. I am sure Ham Lambert will be out in at least six months.

Dad went to the first meeting of the Quarter Back club at noon today as he wanted to see that the new coach is like. There will be a game here two weeks from tonight. Went over to the young Sabins this fore noon to take them some fresh bread as I had promised. When I got to the door Bobbie came bursting out with the announcement that "Mummie is sick" so I went in rather cautiously to find her on the davenporte his imaginary patient. According to the game she had been hurt in a car and was just generally sick all around and had to be bandaged from head to foot etc. Bud had been out to the farm early this morning to take Dr. Hudspeth to see the mare that is about to be confined, the one that lost her colt the last time but he thinks that she will get along all right this time.

Aunt Betty and Justine should be home tonight if they were able to get all the shopping done that they had lined up for themselves. I gave them a bit to do for me as I want something to knit for the Little Lloyd and could not find any thing here.

All that I have to show for this long days work is a clean stove and it does not show but just the same I know that it is no longer greasy and will enjoy cooking on it a little more.

We are going over to fix the altars in the morning for I have an appointment with Dr. Klob in the afternoon. I hope Mrs. Baldridge likes the idea for I think that I would rather do it every time in the morning as it is not so hot in the church at that time. I do not have any flowers this year to use but she thought that she could find some at least for tomorrow. Next week I will get some from Mrs. Rupp. I see by the calendar that there are five Saturdays in September this year which is hard on us ladies. It seems that there have been for ever so long, too.

Supper over: Dad is going down to meet with the boys in regard to the drug store so I will get these letters ready for him to mail. Just heard over the radio that the points for officers of the air corps now will be the same as for enlisted men, 44 they said. Just rumor I suppose.

*   *   *

9/1/45

Dear Mother & Dad,

Our troops are now in Japan. Boy that's good to hear. It would surely be good to be home for Christmas, but the chances for that are nil. Our mail hasn't been very good the last week—Everythings tied up elsewhere I guess.

We now have 3 patients in our Sick Bay—none of them are very sick. It's the most we have had at once. We put some coral in front of the sick bay where all the trucks for the camp go leaving big water and mud holes. It has helped a lot.

Today is pay day so may go up and draw a little as I am down to only $3. It will be the first Ive drawn since April. Have been on this Island now 3 mo. and have seen a lot of changes.

Went to the show last night and the sky was clear as a bell. Fortunately we were dubious so we took our raincoats. It rained like mad, but we sat through the whole thing and looked like a bunch of wet hens, afterwards. The show was hardly worth it, but we are still fairly young.

Not much other news for the present till later,

All my Love, Bill

*   *   *

9/2/45

Dear Mother & Dad,

Had opportunity yesterday for a good deal which I accepted. It will be a good thing if it goes through, but I'm keeping my fingers crossed. It isn't going home. It pays not to get into trouble and polish the apple a bit. It's about the only news I've got and can't tell you much about it yet.

Had several letters yesterday from—you, Tom, Ginnie, and Marion. Mail is still just a little slow.

In one of the books was a letter I received from you while I was at the Marine Hospital. It was fun to read it again.

Am Glad Tom is again not too far from home, but imagine he has had enough of Kansas. The Warts I've removed from the officers are just good ole USA warts, Removed in Okinawa.

I got a letter you wrote May 28, explaining more of Ginnie & George. It only had a 3¢ stamp on it thus the delay.

Haven't seen Gene Rourke. I'm not easy to find on this Island, for I'm not in a very big outfit.

Our boy with the burns is practically well. The boy with the infected hand is also well, except that he's got the hives now after we'd discharged him as cured.

The plans for the Catholic hospital really sounds like it's coming along. The Hal Harrisons are really coming along with their family.

Have not much other news for the present. Until later,

All my Love Bill

*   *   *

Letter No. 122

Monday Sept. 3,1945

Dear Tom and Bill:

This is Labor Day and if you call being at the USO labor then I have done the day justice for I was there from 10 till one this AM. But now I do not have to go tonight for I got a girl to go for me. Neither the director or assistant are here now so every one is sort of pinch hitting. Bonnie Basinger is doing the job for the lady supervisor (on her vacation) and a man from Denver for Mr. Harms but of course neither is very familiar with things there so have to depend on the volunteers quite a little.

I fried Dad and me a piece of meat, warmed some spuds and opened a can of peas and called it our dinner. He is a good sport and never complains however bad I treat him. Guess that is the reason I try to do my best most of the time.

There was no mail delivery today but when Dad went to the PO this morning there was a letter from you, Bill in the office box. It was written the 27, 26th here, that was a week ago Sunday,yesterday so came along in eight days. That must have been a good week end and it sounded as if you meant the two days but dont suppose that you could have been away from your post over night, that you spent with Dr. Rankin and the other two doctors on the island where he is stationed. Some one said that the paper this morning said that now you could tell any and all that you wish and if that is so we can soon know all about you and your friends and where you all are etc.

I have sent so many boxes with raisens in them so I am not sure just which one you received bu t am so glad that the raisens were in edible shape. How did I send them? You said that it was clever. Tell me for soon we will be getting packages for Christmas ready and any and all suggestions will be very welcome. I think you should get the rest of the story for I put the rest in another box that I sent the following week. That too I did not know whether it was a good idea for thought that perhaps it would be difficult to follow the pages, loose like they have to be. Am glad that some of the home papers have come to you so now maybe since they have found you more will arrive and you do get some news from them that I do not think to write you. About that Broomfield boy, for instance, I did not know that you knew him, I didn't, so did not think to mention his being killed over there.

John Lloyd arrived last night and soon will go on to Ft. Logan and his discharge. I dont know what his plans are or if he has any. His Dad had wanted him to locate in Denver but now it seems that his Dad thinks that he will locate in Wichita so suppose he will want John to do likewise. dont think that Justine would be very anxious to settle in Kansas. Margaret had all the Sabin family to dinner last night, celebrating Bud's birthday so I have not seen any of them since but Dad saw John at the Elks this morning.

Bud and aunt fan drove to Stage Canyon Saturday afternoon so had a good visit together as well as seeing the country in all its splendor, grass and water every where. Bud has a two year old colt that he wants to have broken to ride so since the boys at the ranch are now doing some of that kind of work guess when they bring in the jersey sow this week they will take the filly out and handle her with the others that they are breaking.

Aunt Betty was just here and says that John is going to Denver tomorrow.

That surely must have been a wild night when the news of the wars end first came to Okinawa that sent you to your fox holes, we did not know that you had such things, but if you did not need them against the Japs am glad you had them to use when the American boys went crazy. It seems as if those in authority could have stopped the shooting of the guns etc. It is such a shame that so many had to lose their lives in such a useless way. There were pictures of it in the

Life magazine and told how the flak they shot up came down thru the tents and killed boys.

Tiburcio's boy came this afternoon and mowed the grass, the first time in a couple of weeks and it had gotten solong that Dad and I had made up our minds to do the job ourselves this eve after it got cool but now we dont have to. However I think that I will go out and rake up a little wild grass that they did not do too good and maybe when he gets here he will help me carry out the debris at least, so will close now and go put on my slaks.

*   *   *

Letter No. 124

Tuesday Sept.4, 1945

Dear Bill and Tom:

Mrs. Morse just called me to invite me to a shower party for Barbara Kendall next Tuesday eve, a week from today, a dinner at the Kit Carson. Her fiancee arrives about Thursday next week and they will be married soon there after for he has only about two weeks furlough. I imagine that it will be just a quiet wedding since they still have heard nothing from Dean. I hope that I can get a party for her in some time but dont know till I talk to Jane.

We had a letter from each of you today. Tom's written on the 30 and mailed the next day but because of the two holidays we did not get it till today. It was a long letter, three pages. Glad to hear that you got your radio all set up and going. guess it is as well to wait now for a new address for Jean to send the bond. My understanding of Fred's assignment is that it reads for "one year" so maybe that is all they will keep him. We have been hearing a lot about keeping up the draft and that is one of the talking points for keeping it going so that new ones can replace those who are over seas in the occupation army and they will not have to stay so long.

Yes, Tom it is a bit hard to picture you as a stern diciplinarian but just the same I bet you can be when they irk you some and if that is your job you will do it. You will have a big pay roll to be responsible for, $20,000,00 is quite a sum of money. Do the guards go along with you to get it? guess you will have to be having some more hay fever shots next spring if it is going to be bothering you like that. Glad it held off till you are about out of the army anyway.

You have done well saving all that money. Aunt Betty told me that John and Justine have not saved a thing. Do not even have their car paid for but ofcourse two of them to keep and moving around so much one can see why.

John and Justine went to Denver today and he will get his discharge then they will visit a few days with Mr. and Mrs. Lloyd after which she will come on home and he will go down to Kansas to see his mother and other relatives. Traveling around like that is not so good for her right now so she will not attempt it.

Your letter Bill sounded like you had had really a good evening when you went to see the stage show with Kay Kayser in it and rode home in the beautiful moon light. That sounded a little romantic. Was there a good looking nurse along by any chance? Better find one and get those extra points in for discharge so that it will just be 1947 instead of 1949 when they let you out. Phooy you will be here in a year and maybe much less, I say.

This morning I went to the store for milk and cream but it had not come so this afternoon I went back but it had all been sold. I called Dad and asked him to get some down town but all he could get was milk, no cream. Dont know what has happened to the cows all of a sudden but all the milk men have cut off the store to about half of what they were getting. We are going out to Ted Hartman's for he told Dad he would give him a pint. It is good that we will soon have our own for they brought the old jersey in today. she will be fresh in a couple of weeks and then they can have all their old milk and cream and see if we care.

Bill that is a sort of mean trick to play on the poor old hen to put unfertile eggs under her for she will just keep on sitting on them till they get so smelly that you have to break it all up. wish I could send you some good ones so that you could have your little "chicken business" but dont see how it could be done. Could you not borrow a rooster from some of the native for a little while or maybe your could find some big bird eggs for her to sit on.

We hear that now all censorship has been lifted so the letters you write from now on will be more of a pleasure to you for you wont have to consider carefully what you are putting in them.

Glad Tom that your paper seems to be getting there and you for one in the family far away do know what is taking place in this burg.

Will go now and get our cream and mail these little letters.

*   *   *

9/5/45

Dear Mother & Dad,

Today I had my last (I hope) look at the Island. Things had surely changed in the three months I'd been there. When we arrived you could see them shelling from battleships and army artillery into the very place where I shortly later set up the dispensary. It has been good and interesting experience. I really have enjoyed it.

Today we are at sea. What an improvement in this ship and the one we came here on. There are only our components about 20 men on it. It is not meant for troops so they give us just about the same as the merchant crew. Rankin and I have a separate room with two real bunks with bedspreads on them. The chow is like eating out at a Restaurant in S.F.

We get new gear for our components—that is different gear. I wish we could have just taken what we had. The ambulance looks H_. The Jeep appears even worse than the one I had. We are short on a few things, but we've learn what to do and the how isn't very hard. We asked for it so can't complain.

Dr. Walsh is also on the ship—he is in another similar component. He had quite a time getting the Dog aboard. We put it in a pillow case tied it and then put him on top of the cargo in a net. He was then swung from the barge to the ship. Quite an experience for a dog.

The purser on this ship was at the Marine Hospital While I was interning, and we remember one another. He was one of the fellows taking the training they had for pursers.

That is about the news for tonight.

All my Love, Bill

*   *   *

Letter No. 125 1945

Wednesday Sept. 5, 1945

Dear Tom and Bill:

Rotary day so had not seen Dad all day till just this minute when he came home so now before I get a good start on your letters I must go listen to the news with him and also hear if there was anything new under the sun down town today.

Well the news and supper over, neither one was exciting so will now get on with the writing.

Bud was on the program at Rotary today and Dad says made a good talk, just telling his experiences etc. We have all felt quite a little excited today about the 45 points business for men who have been over seas, as of May 8th,1945. Bud had just 45 at that time so we hope he will be one of the lucky ones who do not have to return again on the other side of the water. Dad says that he and Marg took bobby to the fair today. I think that I was about to talk Dad in to taking me but then I remembered that I had promised to take care of the snack bar at the USO tomorrow afternoon so I guess I cant accept his pressing invitation.

Bud's little mare arrived at the ranch without any trouble after they finally got her into the truck. She had never been handled any so did not lead and they just sort of pulled and pushed till they got her in. In the endeavor she got quite a bad cut across her nose but Manual stopped at the Vets on the way out and he took a couple of stitches in it so that it would not leave a scar but the boys do not want to do anything with her till it gets healed up a little for fear it would break open again.

The girls choir is progressing very well in spite of the fact that they are not very regular in attendance but we hope that will not be the case when school is going and the weather is a little cooler.

Mr. Horning is putting oil in his furnace this winter and also wants to put in a water softener. So just before supper I went out to change the water and he nailed me to ask me questions about the old water softener that aunt Mayme had had over there and how satisfactory it was. He figures that the oil will cost him double what the coal did but with him being away so much he figures it will be much more satisfactory. Frances is still in California. We miss little Bobby a lot running around in the yard and playing with the dog,Topsy.

Tomorrow Dad can live all day at the Elks for I will be at the church in the morning fixing the Altars for first Friday and at the USO in the afternoon, but I will take care of his appetite needs at noon anyway and in the evening I will write my daily letter to you, guys.

*   *   *

Letter No. 126

Thursday Sept. 6,1945.

Dear Bill and Tom:

My strenuous day is now over and I can relax and do something pleasant for a change. I even had a guest for dinner this noon, just Mary Farthing but as usual she could not stay(very sorry indeed) to help me with the dishes. She was taking her boys to the fair this afternoon so of course had to get going. She had come home from Trinidad Tuesday but I had not seen her since till today. She says now that Aunt Nell thinks that Fred is to go to europe for his year over seas. I should think that would be much more pleasant, quite like a year of travel since the bullets dont fly any more there.

Dad's girls went to the fair this afternoon so he kept the shop open but said that there was practically no business. The court house was the only place that shut up shop today. Quite different than in the old days when the town would be like a deserted village on Watermelon day.

Aunt Betty and I will have our party for Barbara on Monday eve at the hotel. Will have about three tables of bridge and dinner. It will not be a shower for the other one is and the Kendalls thought that was plenty of that kind. Dean brought his son-in-law to be in to meet me at the USO this afternoon. The boy had just arrived from Arizona via the bus so was quite apologetic about his appearance, which I thought was slick. He is very nice to talk to but is not so very good looking, principally because he has one bad eye. I dont know whether he is blind in it or whether it is sort of like Mac's but it is much more noticeable than Mac's.

Poor Mrs. Stone is having quite a time to get moved for the transfer men keep promising her to move her and then dont come so she cant come again tomorrow to help me with the cleaning so we will just live in the dirt another week. I really would not take a prize for my house keeping this week. I have spent three mornings either at the church or at the USO, one morning I had a headache so did nothing and now this afternoon at the USO again so you can see how my time has been utilized. Guess Bessie and I will have to go shopping tomorrow afternoon for the prizes etc for the party so there goes another day. It is a good thing that I have not planned to do very much canning of fruits for I just could not get it done this way.

Well the Driscolls will soon be all fixed up in the old Bradish house on Raton, 814, for they paid for it yesterday and you cant guess who bought the lovely place they had in Rocky Ford. The Merrifields. The son-in-law is going in with Mr. Merrifield in the manufacturing of his patented sacker and they will all live together.

Guess these little bits of local gossip will hold you for another day so I will sign off now.

*   *   *

Letter No. 127

Friday Sept. 7,1945

Dear Tom and Bill:

Big letter day today, one from each direction both of which were most welcome. Bill's written the 29th and Toms the 4th which in each case was very good time. I guess air mail does not help coming this way at least from Victoria. I have been sending them that way air mail but dont know that it is much quicker either. Can you tell me,Tom or have you been able to notice any difference.

Am glad Bill that you got the medical books which we sent for we fear that by the time they would reach there you might be on your way to some other place and glad to know that they come in handy. We think that those books were about six weeks in transit for I mailed them the 17th of July just after we had come home from Denver after Tom left for Sioux Falls.

Yes I remember the boy, Bill Edmonsen and was sorry to hear that he had died from pneumonia after he had started his internship at San Diego.

If I did not tell you,Bill what the Eagle Brand milk is for I am very sorry. I had carmelized it by boiling it about three hours. Different people have told me that then it is just a good carmel candy so just open the can and EAT. I hope that it is still all right but after such a long time it might be moldy or something. If you have the facilities for boiling it and like it I could send you some with out first boiling and maybe it would go better. Please advise. I am sorry I cant send something else than raisins since your tent-mate does not like them but dried fruits are very hard to find. Perhaps if the package I am sending tomorrow goes thru all right he will like it better for I am trying to send you a birthday cake, a little angle food, as I did the other one packed in pop corn.

Your letter had the money orders for the $200.00 in it Tom and Dad duly took it down to deposit for you. You are surely the rich man but all that money will be very handy when you start back to school.

I will send your winter uniforms next week for I would hardly have time to get them out by noon tomorrow. Yes I too wish that the things you sent from England would come for I fear they may all be rotted by now.

So Walt is going to take unto himself a wife. I think that is fine since they seem to be so terribly much in love. Will they be married before he gets his discharge?

We had another interesting bit of news this morning, a card from Aunt Nell telling us that Fred had called the night before and that now he does not have to go over seas. He has just 46 points and Bud 45 so the army is really nice to us setting it right at that particular place.

Eleanor Willett was here this morning and telling me that Dick is now at Pratt Kansas and the first thing he does is to ask her to send him some money. I cant understand why he cant get along on what he makes.

Saw Roy Black as I was wending my way to the store this morning and had a little visit with him. He said to tell you Tom that he thinks that he will be out in about two weeks, around the 25th. I asked him what he wanted to do then and he said "Well I have hoped that Tom and I could go to school together".

Dad was talking to Mr. Doyle yesterday and he was telling him that John Lewis is teaching in Germany so guess it will be a while before he is coming this was. Roy also mentioned that the Jackson boy is still in Germany and thinks he will be for quite a while, his work seems to be some sort of specialty.

The weather. It has really been fally today and comfortably cool with that sort of hazyness in the air which usually accompanies the autumn. I wonder if we are not likely to have early frost this year.

Just heard big Jack calling little Jack and he said something that had a familiar ring like this "I have called you three times now

COME HOME" I made me laugh for I can remember times like that myself.

Bud Lane now comes home all grimy and dirty but I bet it seems good to be at work again.

Dad just announced that there is to be another of those long drawn out Drug store meetings about a manager. Yes, Tom Fred Jones did live here about the same time the Nobles did and belonged to our night club then. At one time they lived over at Aunt Maymes and remember when you and Bill used to play Mitt.

Will stop now for one very good reason I Just cant think of any thing else to write.

*   *   *

Letter No. 128

Monday Sept. 10, 1945

Dear Bill and Tom:

This morning we started the furnace for a little while and did it feel good for the temperature was 48 on the porch. The radio said 43 in Denver but they always seem to get the best of us at least over the radio.

Your letter, Bill written a week ago Saturday Sept. 1, came this morning and I agree with you it would be very very good if you could be home by Christmas but we do not even dare to think like that for the hope is so slim even for Tom there is nothing for sure. Just the same there is no cost to hoping so we will keep right on but remember that there is no disappointment when our hopes are dashed.

Three patients in your sick bay must have seemed quite full and imagine putting coral in the driveway instead of gravel of which I suppose there is none, but just the same it sounds rather swanky to me.

Was at Pomps this morning and he said they had had a letter from junior and he too spoke of going to the show(Kay Kayser) and sitting there in the rain so maybe it was the same night. He has now gone to Japan but when in the island he was on the very southern most tip.

Just after we had had dinner this noon and were listening to the radio who should appear at the door but Aunt Nell and Uncle Charles, can you imagine. They were just driving around this nice day and wanted to go out to see Marys fine horse,so they did not even sit down. Aunt N. says that Fred and Jean did not get the house they thought that they had in Ann Arbor,fortunately so are still at the apartment they previously had in Detroit. So you can send the bond to "Chucker" now,Tom.

Bud leaves for Ft. Logan Friday but it is not quite so bad since he thinks he will not have to go over again and my be discharged within a year.

Also at noon Mrs. McKellar called me. The first time that I have heard from her since you boys came back from England. she wanted to know what I knew about discharges. Said that Klegg wanted to be out for the fall quarter and that he wanted to go back to school with you. Are you taking all these fellows to Boulder with you,Tom? The Uni should give you a discount on your tuition. she says that Klegg is flying but she could not tell what or why so dont know much more than I did before about it but I did understand her to say that Klegg is writing to you today.

A rather important looking letter from one Lt. Hosttetter from India came this morning with "Please forward" on it so Dad has already done so,Tom so you should get it soon and maybe some day dreams it will cause will help to cheer the weary hours.

How about Betty,Bill? She should be about to get thru her training now it seems to me. And I saw by the paper that the Cadet Nurse program is to be discontinued.

Aunt Mayme was in this morning in fact had just left when the Sisks came along. Next week she and Jack are going down to Texas where they got her horse "Fred Bailey" to see if they can purchase two mares of the same strain. It seems that that is the only way to continue the real strain. To mate him to a mare of his own breed and she thinks it would be worth it to get these mares even tho they cost money.

She had had a letter from Dud telling her about a funeral he had had with burial in Crown Hill in Denver. That is two of those in the last few weeks. He also told her that he had an ambulance case(maternity) and fortunately the girls sister was along for just before they got to the city limits the baby was born.

Mrs. Lambert was telling me Saturday that Ham had written that he and Ed are in communication and think they have a plan worked out to meet. Ed is still rather unassigned so dont know if he is to be occupation or not but guess he is rather suspicious he is. Little Eddie is getting cuter every day. We were there Sat. eve and played bridge with Hay and Lea while Shirley went to the Gardners. Eddie did not go to bed till about 9:30 but just crawled around and was as good as gold then when he got sleepy Hay put him in bed and rubbed his back a little while and he was off to sleep without a murmer. They took him to the show one night that we went with them and he just watched like an old man and then when he got sleepy went off to slumber land and not a sound out of him. He liked the Koshare show too. they took him there and said he had a fine time.

Have to go now and run out to aunt Bettys so we can fix the flowers for the tables for tonight.

*   *   *

Letter No. 129

Tuesday Sept. 11,1945

Dear Tom and Bill:

My company has just left. Oh, you dont know who it was? Well Monroe, Betty and baby Lance. He got back a couple of weeks ago but they just came down here now. He is, like Bud thrilled with the fact that he now will not have to go over seas again. He has about 69

points. The baby is very blond, blue eyed and husky about the same
age as the Garlington baby, in fact just a few days younger. He is
bigger than Eddie but not as cute or maybe it is just that I have seen
more of Eddie.

The party last night went o ff very fine. Bet Morse and Jane
Kendall had high and second high. Lucille Klinker does not play
contract a lot so made me stay by her side the entire evening and
together we did pertty well. the wedding comes off a week from
Thursday in Pueblo and they leave from there for his station, Lake
Field, via Mesa Verda, Grand Canyon etc. The party tonight will be
much bigger for it is an old lady party as well as girl party. We just
had the girls last night, 12 of them.

I just read in the Alumnus which came today that Donald Haley
who taught music here at about the time you boys were in school
had been killed by being thrown from a horse at Colorado Springs in
July. Do you remember him.

Am starting a little sweater like the one I will make for Justine, in
some white yearn that I have on hand so that when I make hers I
wont have to rip out or spend so long on it that it is all dirty by the
time that I get it done. You see I will learn on this one but I hope that
it will be good enough that I can give it to some one, if the need
arises.

I got all your things together, Tom and will put them, I think in
an old suit case that Bill brought from San Francisco last fall with
some of his clothes but which is not very much, I think that it was a
cast off, if I remember rightly that he picked up, so if you want to
throw it away it will be well and good. I may have to send your caps
in a separate box so that they wont be crushed.

Mrs. Hunter called Dad at noon today for permission to buy a
step ladder which consent Dad gave right away but evidently Mrs.
H. had a speech all ready to give in order to persuade him so she had
to give it in spite of the fact that if and when he got a word in he kept
assuring her that she could make the purchase. I really had to laugh
at him for he was so bored listening to all the details of reasons why
he should allow her to get the little ladder etc. I guess she felt that

she had really made her talk clinching and patted herself on the back that she got her way.

We hear there are to be several changes in business locations down town in the near future. The Needhams have to move to let in the Nehi, the Modern Foods have to go somewhere else for McKenzie,who owns that building is going to use all that space to put in a larger stock of furniture, refrigerators, stoves etc., Mallouf is putting in some kind of a store where the cadet club was but I cant remember what it is to be and I think that there were some others that I dont recall just now.

Just talked to Aunt Betty to ask if I could stop for her tonight and she said that Justine will be home tonight John got his discharge yesterday so he is an ordinary civilian now.

I found a little hole in one pair of "pinks" so will go draw it together before I put them in the box, they are dirty but guess you can get them cleaned there as well as here and then they wont have to be pressed again.

*   *   *

Letter No. 130

Wednesday Sept. 12,1945

Dear Bill and Tom:

Well,Bill you really did have news for us this time and am going to send the letter to you Tom in stead of trying to explain it here. Please send it back to me so I can keep it with the others. the only thing that I dont like about it is having to wait so long for mail again. We are so anxious to know just what the deal is but from the tone of your letter we think that it must promise to be interesting at least. We judge that you will be in Japan for Dad talked to Mr. Bloom and he says that Ben was shot down there. I cant remember the name of the place, those queer names get me all mixed up for they are so much alike.

The address you gave Bill had a little more on it on the envelope so perhaps you too had better but it on Tom. It is g-10 Comp 24. You seemed in a hurry and some what excited when you wrote that letter so perhaps you just left it off like I evidently did when I wrote you that letter last May 28 and just put three cents on so it was delayed so much that you have just now received it.

Am glad Bill that since it will be some time till you again get mail that you had several letters before you left. I wonder just what you meant when you said that it pays "to polish the apple a bit" Did the big boss sort of like you and that is the reason that you had this chance.

Am glad that you told us about the boy with the burns and the one with the infected hand being well for we have often wondered how they got along.

Too bad that you and Gene have not been ale to get together but he may still be around out there for a while and yet there could be a chance. I will send aunt Hattie your new address right away.

Tom when I was fixing the hole in the pinks I felt something in one of the pockets and found a 50 cent piece in there but I did not disturb it so you had better get it out before you send them to the cleaners. I will send you the bill of lading in this letter. it is cool enough here today to wear heavy clothes with pleasure.

These little old fighter planes they have out here now do a lot more buzzing over us than any we have ever had and so fast you can hardly get your eyes on them. Lucile Houghton told us the other night that all they do with them is get in their flying time. That there is just nothing going on out there, but there are lots more fellows than there have ever been.

I have to go over to the library at five for a special meeting to pass on the budget so it can go to the council tonight. After supper there is church and choir practice for me and Dad goes to the poker club. aunt Fan came in today and so suppose that she will accompany me to church. She and Dad are going to Pueblo tomorrow, so Dr. Lassen can give Dads ear another treatment. It has not bothered him much since the last one.

* * *

Letter No. 131

Friday Sept. 13, 1945

Dear Tom and Bill:

Guess I had better be writing you a little letter now,3:30, for Dad just phoned and invited(well he asked if I wanted to go) me to the football game tonight for I will be busy later and I did not get a letter off to you yesterday. With cleaning the bedding and one other closet,Mrs. Stone helping, and then the rotary picnic I just did not get one done. Oh yes I did one other thing too yesterday afternoon I went down and selected me a pretty blue dress for new outfit for fall. Now I must get a hat and think that will fix me up for a while and not caring too much for shopping I am very glad if that will be all the effort I have to put in on that type of thing.

When getting the dress I learned from Mrs. Woodruff that Tommy is in the hospital with paralysis of the face. When I told her about your bombardier having had the same thing happen to him evidently from the same cause she felt much better. I am wondering if that wont mean that he may get to come home as he has never been home since he went over there, over three years ago and has not had any furlough since.

We had lots of fun at the picnic and as usual Mac was the clown of the party. They had a feed and then a watermelon bust and bon-fire on the lake shore with singing etc and then went in to the pavilion and danced. We took Hay and lea and they seemed to enjoy it too. guess we all ate something that did not agree too well for Dad and I, both of them and Marg whom I saw at the store this morning have been making frequent trips to see Mrs. Jones.

Bud left at about seven this morning with Al Miller. Was glad that he had a chance to drive up rather than the train and with congenial company. They could talk over the city business on the way. Marg said that bobby took his Daddy's leaving pretty hard but ofcourse it does not last long with one of those tender years. He had

had a swell time last night. He was all dressed up in western style and looked cute as the mischief.

Saw Paul Church there(Mary Fran Meyhews husband in case you dont remember) and he asked about both of you boys. He thinks that he will have to go to the Pacific for he is a Lt. Col and when they get that high they move around pretty much.

Doris Simons, Mary Frans cousin who went to that place in Lower Calif with us from San Diego that time is going to be married and her mother is a house mother for the Delta Gammas at Arizona U. this winter. The son,the doctor in the navy has been assigned to seas duty again on the Pennsylvania. Surgeon in charge I think she told me but it could have been ass't.

Marg Larsen is in love with Arizona U. so her mother told us last night. She expects to see Mrs Simons when she is there a little longer.

Mrs. Guthrie has gone to Oregon to see John Guthrie (his wife lives there and he is to be in the states only about three weeks they thought that he would hardly have time to come down here too) but will stay only three days there for bill is due to arrive here most any time now. Am not sure whether he is to go on or not but suppose he is for most of the officers seem to be doing it. We have heard that is the reason they are keeping the GIs in so that there will be men for all these high ups to "officer" and of course they want their present pay to keep on as long as possible but it wont when we return to peacetime levels and many of them are reduced in rating.

We had two births in the family yesterday. the old jersey gave birth to a fine bull calf and Buds mare had a filly colt. The Hartmans are going to have the calf and the daughter Jean wants to raise it for her 4-H(I pretty nearly said 4F) club calf but he Dad says that since he knows that he will have to do the feeding it is his. I imagine he will weaken however.

Monroe was over yesterday and borrowed a tennis racket so that he and Betty could play. He says that if he can get a fellowship when the war is over he is going to the Uni. of Arkansas and get his masters degree and then either teach or get a music store someplace,anyplace just so it is not colorado. He seems to want to get away from all the family and associations. Queer duck that fellow.

This is all that I think of just now but will leave it in the typewriter and maybe think of something else that I want to add.

Dad has no news but I recall that I have not told you that Mrs. Irby died last night after being very sick all summer and more or less so for a long time. She had cancer.

Were glad to get your letter,Tom yesterday which you wrote Monday, and because the proposed change in the discharge of officers in the air corps seemed to have given you a little bit of mooding I enclose a clipping which sort of disaggrees with that report of 85 points for first Lts. and I hope will sort of cheer you up a bit.

So Walt was home last week again but the rascal does not let us know of his presence. And he is to be married this week end. If going up with him would lessen your chances of coming home for a weekend I hope that you let him go alone and find someone else to stand up with him.

Will close now as we must go to the game about 7:30.

*   *   *

9/14/45

Dear Mother & Dad,

The censorship is over. I learned for sure the other day so I can tell you that I am today on Saipan. We arrived early yesterday morning about 4 A.M in the rain on an open boat with all our gear and no place to sleep. We grabbed what gear we needed and found enough sacks at the airbase (naval) where we still are.

As usual no one knew what was to happen to us. We are supposed to be as I understand on our way to Iwo Jima to prepare for our next assignment. They found a ship bound for Iwo which could take our cargo, but not us. They sent the boat with the cargo and most of our personal baggage out to this other ship. We luckily got it back last night—I was really fortunate as I'm not missing anything yet.

Now that the censorship is lifted I can tell you a little more about where I was. We were stationed at Yonabaru, Okinawa which is on the Southeastern side near the southern portion of Buckner Bay. There really wasn't much to tell of Okinawa that I haven't told—or perhaps you may think of something you would like to know that doesn't come to my mind at the present.

Mr. Boles, a Lt. Comdr. who is the administrative assistant of the Senior Medical officers of Okinawa came on the same ship with us—the Santa Monica. When this new Job came up he offered it to me and since it sounded pretty good and would get away from Okinawa I took it. I don't know where we will eventually wind up, but maybe Japan, China, Formosa, or Korea.

We hit Saipan at the rainy season, but fortunately it is practically all coral and there isn't any mud. It is really like civilization after Okinawa. We are living in a quonset hut. Have running water and a toilet that flushes. How long we'll be here I don't know. Am not looking forward to Iwo for I doubt that it is as pleasant as Okinawa or that it is much more built up. Saipan is really a big base. Has all been built in less than a year. On the way to Okinawa we stopped at Eniwetok—didn't get ashore and at Ulithi which is really a big place as far as the navy goes. Went ashore there to Mog. Mog is the Fleet Recreation Island. Had dinner that night on the Air Craft carrier Shangri La. Have seen lots of fleet units here and there.

With the latest point system I'll be able to get out of the navy in 1951. Until Later,

All my love, Bill

*   *   *

9/15/45

Dear Mother & Dad,

As yet no means of proceeding upon our journey have appeared and we are making ourselves at home at the air base. One of the boys that was in the barracks is from Colo. and was at C.U. the year ahead of me. We talked over the good ole Boulder days. Night before we found the big officers club and there ran into a fellow we knew at Pearl Harbor.

Dr. Weber told me before I came into the navy that it was a proposition of "hurry and wait". That is surely the truth. It doesn't irritate me as much as it used to. And now I just relax and enjoy the waiting and hurry only as fast as it is convenient.

Today the sun has come out and it is really nice—only a little hot. Perhaps we will get a swim this afternoon. Last night we went to a movie which I'd seen before. There is one thing I don't like about being out here is the difficulty in getting clothes clean. I practically always have to do it myself because of which all my clothes assumed a permanent gray tinge. It will be great to have lots of clean, starched, and pressed clothes.

Not much other news—

All my love, Bill

*   *   *

9/16/45

Dear Mother & Dad,

A lot has happened in our outlook since my last letter yesterday. Our trip to Iwo Jima has been cancelled. We were destined for duty on one of the Island around there, but it was called off, and now what will happen to us is a matter of conjecture.

In the meantime however we ran into a dream set up. We are to stay here with the military Gov't Hospital here. The quarters are next to the beach which is really a beautiful beach with crystal clear water. Good food—the best out here and quarters better than any BOQ in the States. It is rather a small group of officers, but they have a small officers mess and club. It would take a lot of money for a tourist to find a place like this. I'd like to spend the rest of my tour right here, but of course that will probably not occur. They have some navy nurses at this hospital and other women close by. All of the work is done by the natives.

We are to start to work tomorrow, but won't mind a bit. Till Later,

All my loves, Bill

P.S. I don't know when we will get mail,. Had better use the address on the envelope.

*   *   *

Letter No. 132

Monday Sept. 17,1945

Dear Tom and Bill:

It surely was good to hear your voice last night and how near we came to missing it. You see, Bill we had a telephone visit with your brother about 8:30. About five we went down to the Garlingtons to have some of the watermelon that we had brought back from the rotary picnic last Thursday(gosh it was good, wish both of you could have had some with us. It was so big that six of us had great big pieces out of just half of it.). so we sat around there for none of us wanted any supper but for some unknown reason about seven Dad and I decided that we should come home altho they wanted us to stay and play cards. When we got here I took down the receiver to call a number and central said to me "Is this 250" When I said yes, she told me that long distance had been trying to get us and had made several attempts. I asked if long distance could tell us who it was and so on but she said no so I just took a chance and called for Tom Sisson at the Officers Club at Walker Army Air Field and it was not long till the voice of brother,Tom answered. I have been wondering why you did not give us ring some night as you are not usually very busy evidently. Have wondered if the trip to California which you said was a probability came off today. Have thought about it all day and if by this time you are trying to get hold of some of the relatives out there.

During our conversation Tom told us of accidently running into George Spar,Lt.Col.,at the officers club last evening and having a long gab fest with him over the old times.

We had a surprise visit during the afternoon yesterday from the Leonards. Ed was with them home on leave from the Pacific and his air plane carrier, the name of which I dont remember. He still has about thirty days and they are going to drive around to see the rest of the boys at least all but Bob for he is still with the Marines over in your region,Bill. Charles and his wife and baby are now in Topeka, George is at San Angelo so in one trip they expect to see both of them. Ed is still the sort of odd boy that he has always been but seems even taller than before. He is really big.

Saturday bud phoned Marg that he would be in Denver and on pass till today so she and Gerry Woodbridge went off to the city,leaving here about 5:30. It has sort of burned me up because she did not take poor little bobby along and they did take the little Judy Woodbridge. Marg is so darned afraid that Bobby is going to be exposed to something or other that she keeps him like a hot house plant. there has been quite a little infantile in Denver so I suppose that is the reason.

Aunt Fan is having the house at the ranch stuccoed. It will cost in the neighbor hood of $1000.00 but we will think that it is worth it for then it will not have to have a plastering job every year or so and wont it look ritsy. She seems all thrilled about it for they guarantee it will stick and that is the reason that she has never done it before for it seemed to have no satisfaction back of that kind of work.

That Dad of yours is getting to be more of a fibber all the time. I just cant depend on him at all. for instance this morning I was going to the USO and would not be home till one oclock so told him that if he would come down there I would make him a sandwitch but he refused saying that he would get him something to eat and ofcourse I supposed that he would go to the Kit Carson. So when he brought the car back to me there at one I asked him if he had had a good lunch and he assured me he had. then when I got home what do I find? Tracks. Yes the dirty dishes of a shredded wheat and a glass of milk so now I have hash cooking so I can stuff it down him this evening, the raskel.

I hope Tom that if you get a move when the Air Technical Service command takes over next month they see fit to move you here. The Lt. Burton next door is leaving,got his discharge and asked me why you did not ask for a transfer to this field since it is in the same command as you are in. He says they try to place the boys as near home as possible.

Am glad that you are finding the job interesting for at least that helps and indicates that you are learning something. Lea says that there is lots of responsibility to it for just as you said it is up to you to make decisions when the higher officer is not on hand.

I am going out by the Sabin house on my way to get Dad for I have not seen Justine since she got home from Denver, and have not more than waved my hand at Bessie for ever so long and as Aunt Fan left some peaches here for me to give to them will kill two birds with one stone, and take them out. Also I must give Bessie a check for my half of the party we had before it gets so old that I dont remember that I owe her.

*   *   *

8/18/45

Dear Mother & Dad,

Have been doing a few physicals on some of the prisoners returned from Japan and it has been fairly interesting. A few of them show real evidence of malnutrition and avitaminosis, and can sure stand some of those vitamin pills. They have interesting stories to tell. Most of the ones I've seen have been captured on Wake Island or Guam. A few from Hong Kong.

This afternoon Rankin and I did two autopsies. It's been about a year since I've done anything like that. They have some good cases among the civilians here. I've seen disease I never expected ever to see. They are supposed to have a few cases of leprosy and will have to see them soon. One of the Doctors here practiced in Canon City—His name is Wyatt, I believe—He has a son in the C.U. Med School.

We have maid service, Laundry, and just everything. We wear greys all the time and even have to be in uniform for dinner (Long trousers) and the Club.

Am writing you from the Club looking out on the beach and harbor

Would surely like to get some mail. Dont forget my new address.—G-10 Comp24. USN Milt Govt. Hosp. 202 Navy # 3245.

Till Later,

All my Love, Bill

*   *   *

9/23/45

Dear Mother & Dad,

I am now working here at the hospital. I don't have a definite job, but help on a couple of medical wards Two Tb. and female Medicine. It is more like being a Medical officer. It surely is a change from my usual medical duties in the navy.

We've been here a week now and hope it continues for some time. We don't have to work very hard and really have a good place to live and recreate. Last night they had a dance at the club. The women are pretty scarce and I was dateless. I did get to dance several times by cutting-in. I enjoyed myself any way. These women out here are really independent as far as dates go and I don't think I'm very apt to go to all the trouble it takes to get a date; for there aren't many I've seen that would be worth it.

We usually see a show in the evenings. Right now I am listening to the radio which has some very good programs. Till later,

All my Love,

Bill

*   *   *

Letter No. 133

Tuesday Sept.18,1945

Dear Bill and Tom:

This morning another letter came from you,Bill which you had written on the ship on the way to your new station and so we have it figured out that it was mailed after you had landed so perhaps it wont be so long till we get one after your arrival there and hope that by that time the censorship has been lifted out there. This letter was censored and the date is blurred on the envelope but inside the

5th. All censorship was lifted according to the papers and radio on Sept. 3rd but guess they just dont learn about things way out there so quickly.

We hear that McArthur now says that all he needs for the occupation of Japan is 200,000 men so that ought to mean that a lot of them will get to come home for there must be many more than that over there, but guess that does not apply to the Navy any way.

Sorry that you did not fare so well in the gear supplied you for this set up but maybe it will do. Perhaps you will have better roads over there. Must have been nice to find that you had known the purser when he was taking his training at Marine Hospital, or at least that you each remembered seeing the other there. Guess the ship was a merchant ship from what you say and that there were just about 20 of you on this particular trip. Glad that it was a better set up than the other trip but not being so long it would not have mattered so much. Yes now that it is over I guess it was good experience. Especially seeing the shelling going on from the ships and the army artillery where you so soon set up your dispensary. From reading over old letters I find that it was about three weeks from the time that you first set foot on that Island till you went over to the place that you had your dispensary, the place under fire when you landed there. So can realize that there was just nothing there at first. Ed Leonard told us Sunday that he had landed on Okinawa twice once, at least before the bombing and said that then Naha was a nice little city of about 200,000 with street cars etc. but the next time he saw it it was not to be seen.

We surely are wondering if you, Tom went to Calif. yesterday but think that when and if John L. gets in today as Justine thought that he would he will know for he probably stopped to see you.

We had a guest for dinner. Mac came up and ate with us. May went to Denver with Mary Lou when she went to enter D.U. so is away. He and Dad sort of took a little vacation and stayed here visiting till about two oclock, so I was a little late getting things cleared up and the dishes washed. I thought that by this time I would have all the ironing done but really have hardly made a start at it. It is really the easiest thing I do,to put it off, much easier than doing it but it catches up with me finally and I just have to take myself in hand and stay with it till I finish.

*   *   *

Letter No. 134

Wednesday Sept. 19,1945

Dear Tom and Bill:

Guess this will be short and sweet for having been in the house all day and not even having had one single telephone call I am really devoid of news. I have not even listened to the radio. I did go get Mrs. Stone this morning and took her home at noon and in Aunt Nellie's car. It was very nice that she left it here just at this time for Art Needham finally decided to work on our clutch so it has been in the shop since yesterday morning. Sure hope he gets that grabbing out of it and since he is putting in a new something or other guess it should do the job.

Have not talked to the Sabins today so dont know whether John got in last night or not but since Teeny was expecting him I doubt that he disappointed her.

Did I tell you that I am knitting a little jacket for the off spring. At least just now I am learning on some other yarn so that I will do a good job when I start on the pretty blue that is here.

These days now are just perfect like fall days are in Colorado and wish that we could all take a nice trip to Missouri or someplace but without you two it would not be much fun. That is something we have in store for us and we hope that it wont be too long either.

Bud went thru here night before last and was able to let his family know so that they got to see him. He should be getting to Ft. Bragg about tomorrow I should think but if he was on a troop train guess it might be longer.

Mariam Manning called up last night to know your address,Tom for she said that there was a boy there at their house whose home was in Hayes and that he would write to his family to look you up. Dad asked her if he had any sisters and she said that he has. So maybe something will develop from it. Who knows?

We are looking for another letter from the Pacific now pretty quick,about the last of this week so we figure that you probably landed about two weeks ago then.

Am going down now to have my new dress fitted and altered so that I will have it to wear when our bridge club meets some time soon. They wanted to meet this Friday night but I objected for there is a football game and I knew the men would all want to go and ofcourse I have to go to keep Dad company.

Hay and Lea are going down to Amarillo to see Aunt Bessie Garlington and other relatives and friends. Mrs. G. had a cataract removed about two months ago and is with the relatives down there. Shirley and the baby will not go but stay and keep the home fires burning.

*   *   *

Letter No. 135

Friday,Sept.21,1945

Dear Tom and Bill:

According to the date this is the first day of fall and we should be getting a storm and indeed there might be one in store for us for there is a warm wind from the south that seems rather ominous and the sky is a little overcast at times. Last night I again slept with just a thin cotton blanket after having had to use three light wool ones so we may expect a change of some sort, I think.

I did not write yesterday for I got busier in the afternoon than I thought I would be and too had company for a little while,John and Justine. John reported that he had stopped to see you Tom and was greatly disappointed to find that you had gone to California. Said that he had left a note for you and so by this time you no doubt have received it. He said you were not to be back till Wednesday so you must have had quite a little time in Cali. and we are very anxious to know where you went and whom you saw, if any of the relatives. We are looking for a letter tomorrow if you wrote after you got back.

We were very much surprised this morning on receiving another letter from you,Bill that you were on Saipan and headed for Iwo Jima with the eventual destination most anywhere over there, China,Fermosa,Japan or somewhere. I dont see why they brought you way back to mid Pacific just to take you back over there again,but then I just dont understand the army and Navy ways, period.

Am glad that now the censorship is lifted and you can tell us anything that you like. Was glad to know that I was not too far off in my guess of you location on Okinawa but I cant find Yonabaru, on my maps but know just about where it is since you say that it is near the southern portion of Buckner Bay.

I know Tom you will be interested in reading this letter when you have a chance to come home some weekend so will not try to tell you all the content

As I have told you Aunt Fan is having the house stuccoed at the ranch and now the question will be what color to make it. Dad thinks dirt color so it wont get dirty and Aunt Nell said "NO,no,white" so poor Fanny will have a time to suit everyone. Guess she will just have to suit herself.

Last nights paper had the account of Walters wedding and said that they are now here visiting his family but we have not see or heard a word form any of them. It was evidently a big wedding and maybe you missed something by not going,Tom but we are glad you did not if it would have lessened your chances of coming home some weekend. We can hardly wait for that to happen.

The twins arrived this noon and took off for Trinidad in about an hour. Mayme bought not two mares but four. One of them, so the twins say has been a greatly sought after little filly but the owner would not sell to any of the previous buyers but quote "Because Mary was a woman and would be more loving to the pet they let her have her". You know all that sort of conversation etc.

Marjorie Larson Has pledged Kappa at Arizona. Emily Ann Hoyt is now home and can see very well with her new cornea. It was taken from a man who had to have his eye removed from some other cause so could no longer use it himself. Doesn't it seem sort of uncanny but how wonderful? She was to see Pink one evening and Pink said that she sat there and read the paper without her glasses on.

Do hope,Bill that all this running all over the Pacific wont make your mail too,too long in getting to you but know that it will surely slow it up a lot. I will keep writing however and when it does catch you it will swamp you. It is sure good to not have to think of Kamakazi planes and mines any more.

Had a letter from Gene yesterday and he inclosed a memoranda of the entire log of the Benson with all her engagements etc and the waters where she had been and all. He said that transportation etc had made it impossible to see you,Bill even tho he had been in your territory.

I wonder,Bill if you were able to take all you medical books with you this time and radio etc. Oh,yes and where was NOB on Okinawa.
Later—

We finally found Yonabaru also Owi Jima and everything but bet when your next letter comes to us your destination will be something entirely different for I dont believe they know just what they want to do with you. We heard tonight that McArthur says it will not be necessary to occupy Japan longer than six months so maybe there will be some of the fellows coming this way ere long.

Dad says to ask you if you are still attached to the Colored Company.

*   *   *

Letter No. 136

Monday Sept. 24,1945.

Dear Bill and Tom:

I know that the sojourner will not get this letter for a little while but will include him just the same. You see,Bill Tom has been grounded out in Los Angeles (I think however you had best not mention it to the family out there lest they think that he left on schedule,thursday AM) so is not at this station in Kansas. Not a bad deal to be grounded there. What if it had been some spot like La Junta, I did not say La Junta, I said like La Junta. To some of the other boys I think it would be terrible to be grounded in La Junta. Evidently,too he has been making the most of his time for Dad had a wire from him a little while ago asking that he wire money for he was broke. From that we judge he has not been "mooching" on the relatives so they no doubt think he has left.

Well we are glad that you have had a chance to do a little spending for a change.Oh here are the twins.

My, what a surprise. Charles was with them and going to stay at the ranch all night, can you imagine such frivolity. Olives sister called this noon to tell me that Olive and Judy would be down either tonight or tomorrow so guess Mary will be in again tomorrow to get them, or at least see them. Nell and Chas plan to go home tomorrow.

John Lynch, a fellow who used to have an electric shop here and who has come back to open up again was going out to the ranch this afternoon to see what he could do for Aunt Fans plant but guess he got lost for he had never shown up when she called a little while ago. Her plant will not charge so when she runs the batteries down she will be without lights. Naturally she saves it as much as possible so does not use the radio at all and misses it very much, cant hear her daily sob programes etc.

Had my hair set this morning and am going down not to have it combed so will finish this letter later and maybe Dad will have something else of interest for me to add.

The Jetts who have lived next door now for a long while may be going back to their ranch and if they do will tell me in time so that I can give Justine the cue and she can have first run at Mr. Horning for it. Just hope something comes of it for they are anxious to get located. John was to go down to take to Lloyd Larsen this afternoon and then if that was not promising would go to Santa Fe to see about where there seems to be an opening to see about it.

My paper just wont stay right maybe it is me.

Supper over. Dad says that Mutt called her folks from Raton last night. She and Roscoe were on their way to Ft. Logan for his discharge. Dont know what other plans they had.

Aunt Mayme says that she was offered $4000, for her Fred Bailey horse. Guess she paid $1000 for him but she did not want to sell now. Her new mares cost her for all four about $2500 so that was not as bad as I thought from what she said about this one being so very high priced. Dad found out thru Mac who made the arrangements for her payments of them.

Had a letter from the Lyons from Lincoln today. the folks who had invited you did the dinner you had to leave before you got, Tom. They have heard from her cousin who has been a POW in Japan since the fall of the Phillipines. He will be home by Thanksgiving.

Bobbie and Marg came over at that place.

Bob and I had fun in the "little room" (that is what he calls the basement room) and got out some of your old toys. One game where you run a marble around and it drops into holes with numbers on them. Ofcourse the count did not mean anything except that he was beating me all the time. If I said I beat you that time he would say "No you didn't" so my score just could not be very good.

We will mail these now and come back in time for the news.

*   *   *

9/25/45

Dear Mother & Dad,

Tomorrow I have the duty so should best drop you a line this evening. I probably wont be very busy, but may. There are surely

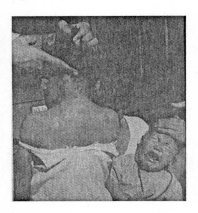

a lot of interesting cases in the hospital. There is an awful lot of tuberculosis on this island which is probably true of most of these islands. I have been doing some of the pneumothorax on the TB pts. We had a little girl with Tb of the larynx who was having an awfully hard time breathing so are going to give her another air passage tomorrow (Tracheostomy). About half of the patients have yaws which is a very rare bird in the states. They have six lepers which we observed the other day—the first I've ever seen. Would surely like to stay here, but imagine it won't be too long that we get word to move somewhere else. Would surely like to get some letters and perhaps I shall in another week.

Today had my hair cut by a Jap barber. It was a novelty for a barber shop as the barbers weren't Chatterboxes—mainly because they don't understand much English.

Until Later,

All my love, Bill

*   *   *

Letter No. 136

Tuesday Sept. 25,1945

Dear Tom and Bill:

After laboring most of the day I will now sit rest and write. Mrs. Stone and I did the laundry this morning and this afternoon when I went to take the things in they were just damp enough to iron well so instead of folding them I just ironed some so should not have a very big day for tomorrow. But I now feel the effect of keeping on the go for quite some time. I did try to take a little rest just after I got the dishes washed but there was a lot of noise next door for they are putting in Mr. Hornings water softener and the plumbers were working right out side of the windows, so I did not stay down very long.

Jackie Lacy seems to be having a party, I suppose it is his birthday,on their lawn and there are about a dozen kids his size over there and Bud is helping Madeline with the entertainment.

I did not tell you, Tom that we have had letter from both Aunts, Gertrude and Kathryn telling about your visit. It seemed to impress them that you seemed glad to see them. Of course they said all kinds of nice things about you but dont want to swell you up too much so wont repeat them. We wonder if you are still grounded or if you are back in Kansas by this time.

I think that we are more anxious now than ever to hear from you,Bill for we are so curious to know where you are going. Dr. Weber and wife are here. He told Dad that your assignment with the See Bees was a good one and that there are many could be not so pleasant. He too said nice things about you but you can guess what they were since he was talking to your father. June has had an operation which connects some nerves to her glass so that she has pretty good control of it, so Pomp was telling me yesterday. She had been in there to have her hair done so had to let him see the scar but she wears her hair sort of down over it so that it does not show,he says but that she is very conscious of it as yet. She says that she thinks Dr. W. would like to settle here again.

On my way to the store a little while ago I met Mrs. Larson, Roy Black's aunt who told me that Roy got home Saturday, a civilian. He does not know yet what he is going to do. His mother rather favors his staying here and working but tho she does not say anything, Mrs. Larson thinks that he should go back to school.

Mr. Lynch the man who was going out to the ranch to see about Aunt Fans light plant started twice yesterday but did not get there so this afternoon Dad went out with him. They are not back yet so must have had quite a little work to do on it.

The twins and "Charlie" came by this noon on their way to Rocky Ford with a double purpose in mind, to get some meat that Mary had butchered up there and to see Judy and Olive who are with her sister up there. The Sisks were going right on to Trinidad and I imagine if they could come Olive and Judy will be with Mary when she and Jack come back.

The work at the office is piling up again so I may have to go down and get them straightened out soon. Dad said Dick told him there were 35 abstracts on the shelf.

The leaves are starting to fall and some people are burning them this evening so it really does seem like winter is not far off.

Dad got home so we had our supper and now are ready to go mail these letters and settle for the evening.

*   *   *

Letter No. 137

Wednesday Sept. 26,1945

Dear Bill and Tom:

It is now five thirty and so will just have time for a little letter to you before Dad comes home, and as it is church night want to have it ready to mail as I go. I think that Dad will be going to the poker club for Mac is in Denver and that makes a vacancy for which Dad is the official substitute.

We had your letter,Bill of the 15th, today and tho very glad to get were surprised again to hear that you were still at Saipan but since you have developed the right attitude toward those waits and can go ahead and enjoy yourself were not disappointed. Glad that you made contact with a former CU boy for tho he was a year ahead of you there he could talk the same language, "Boulder". With access to a good officers club,shows,toilets with running water etc perhaps you can forget the fact that your clothes do not look very well after your own laundering. As I ironed this afternoon I wished that I could do a few for you so that you would feel respectable again. Well maybe I can fore too, too long we hope.

Lee Cranson died this morning and tho I have not yet been over there we did send some roses to the house with sympathy card. I suppose that if Walter had gone back to Kansas he will come on home for the funeral. While I feel very sorry for the family it would be a cruel thought to wish the poor boy back to endure more of such hopeless suffering.

Hay and Lee are still at Amarillo and having a fine time,so Shirley told me last night when I talked to her. She said that Ed is still not very happy at having to stay in Germany but since they now say that all those who have had two years of army life will be discharged in November (just another rumor,I think) she is hopeful that he will be home by Christmas. She said that little Eddie has been cross for he has some more teeth coming thru.

Will crotchet for a little while now and see if Dad has anything new when he comes and then finish.

Well Dad had these little bits. Vernon Konkel was at Rotary today. He is to report on the west coast.

Dr. Johnston introduced Dr. by saying "The best D—doctor in the Navy" and Dad said he wanted to get up and challenge that statement by saying "Now,here, I have a son in the Navy" but guess he knew they would fine him if he did so kept quiet.

*   *   *

Letter No.138

Thursday Sept.27,1945.

Dear Tom and Bill:

How I wish I could send this by special plane, bill so that you could have some mail real soon but it ought not to be too long till it gets to you now that I have a sort of permanent address for you. What a perfect setup. If it were only for the duration of your stay in the Navy you would be in clover,and for your benefit,Tom I quote from his letter. "Quarters better than any BOQ in the states,good food,the best out here" also a swell officers club all on a pretty beach with crystal clear water. You see Tom the trip to Iwo Jima was called off and they are to stay with the Military Gov't there at least for the present. There are nurses there and also other white women and maid service with laundry and all and from the sad tone of the condition of his clothes in the letter we had yesterday I am inclined to think that that is the best feature of all. Not so, Brother?

Now if we could just know for sure where you are tonight Tom there would be nothing for us to wonder about, but I sort of guess that you are back in Victoria and that we will have a letter tomorrow.

We are having another spell of cold weather and it about 42 this eve so perhaps before morning the damage to the tomatoes and all will have been done but as it is cloudy this eve with just a little moisture falling there is a chance the frost will not come.

You boys dont know it so I am now telling you that you and your mother gave your Dad a poker table for his birthday. I had quite a time keeping it concealed till today for it is rather large but put it way back in the northwest basement room and got by nicely. This morning I dressed it out still packed as it came from the Denver Dry Goods Co. almost to the door down there and put a greeting on it and then asked Dad if he would go down as there was something wrong with my curtain stretchers. When he got to the foot of the stairs it just blocked his way and he had to see it. I think he was a little surprised for once.And the first thing he said was "I dont need a poker table". Well if he does not use it enough to get the moneys worth out of it guess I will have to take up the game, for one could not play bridge on it, that is sure with all the holes it has right in front of each player for the chips.

Roy Black came over to see me this eve and to find out when you would be home,Tom. I told him that perhaps you might come next week end, that would be about the sixth of Oct. How about it? He said to tell you that he is going to work till next spring and start back to school then and that you had better wait for him.

Roscoe is here now and was in to see Dad this afternoon. He sure wished they could have met up with you out in Las Angeles,Tom for they were still there when you arrived out there.

Hazel Brown is off duty at the office for she has a strep infection in her nose and is feeling pretty bum for the are giving her sulpha. Dad says the abstracting will run over $800. this month.

Aunt Fan came in today and she and Bessie Sabin will go to Pueblo tomorrow.

Bill's new address,Tom is

William R. Sisson, Lt.(jg)MC-USNR
G 10 Comp 24
USN Military Gov't.Hospital #202
Navy#3245, %FPO San Francisco, Calif.

*   *   *

Letter No. 139 1945.

Friday Sept.28,1945

Dear Bill and Tom:

Your letter,Tom arrived today airmail from Los Angeles and hope that we will hear from you via telephone tonight from Kansas with the news of what your orders of Oct. 3,mean. We hope that you are to go to Separation Center and from what all the other boys think of your possibilities it must be that. Both Roscoe and Roy Black cant understand why you have not already been on the list.

We are glad that you had such a swell time for the week you have been grounded out in California and I dont blame you much for not letting the relatives know that you were still there when you had such a bunch to help you do the town. Twenty was quite a party, and there are a lot of things about the sojourn there we will like to know but no doubt we will be seeing you fore long and then can have it all first hand, and then I will relay it on to you,Bill.

It has been cold as the dickens for this time of year all day today, about 45. I have not been out much, went to the funeral this afternoon. Saw that Walter and Margaret Ann were there, I did not go out to the cemetery but about froze just going over to Dads office afterward.

Bill,Dad thinks that you should be taking some pictures and says that if you want him to he can get you film at the drug store but is not sure what your camera takes, so let us know what you need. Guess your wants are rather well taken care of now but I will send you a box once in a while anyway,as Toms says "Just for the heck of it".

I think that our new neighbors on the north of us are about to move in for the transfer men were there with a load of furniture this afternoon. Mrs. Hollis has been quite sick this summer so guess that is the reason they have not moved before. It will be nice to see lights over there again at nights.

Lea came up last eve and helped Dad take out the cooler. He was going to do it himself last Saturday afternoon but I objected so he waited till Lea was home and could help him. Lea starts to work out at the base next Monday.

Have looked over the letters that you no doubt have missed, Bill in your move but which you will eventually probably get but these are some of the bits that seem to me you would like to know without waiting longer.

Barbara Kendall married a week ago. John Lloyd is discharged but has not yet decided what he will do. they are here yet. Bud nor Fred will not go over seas again. bud is at Ft. Bragg.

Aunt Fan is having the ranch house stuccoed, white. Walter Cranson is married.

Rumor says this is now a Separation center as of orders today. Maybe Tom they will send you here. guess that is the news for now.

*   *   *

9/30/45

Dear Mother & Dad,

Yesterday I got about a dozen letters learning you knew I'd left Okinawa. By now you no doubt have learned of the good deal I now have on Saipan. It has lasted for 2 weeks and am surely in hopes it will last for a long time. If it were to last the rest of the time I am to be overseas it won't have been a waste of time. We have really good cases. They can't speak English and don't always want something. You can do anything you want for whether it's good or bad they appreciate it. I hope they don't decide to send me to Truck or someplace. There is a G-10 that has been here a little longer than we have and they are going to Yap.

Enjoyed the article about Bob Truscott's marriage. The girl had been in Sweden through most of the War; as I remember the last I heard from Truscott. Would surely like to be home for the football games. I'll bet it is nice now at home. I was really in a hurry when I left Okinawa. Learned about it at noon 9/4 and left to board the ship at 9:30 9/5. We had to get out orders, pay accounts, And records before we left and everything was about 10 miles apart.

Today I am O.D. Have a good case in a POW that has me puzzled, this is more like being a doctor here. I hope Tom and Bud soon have an opportunity to get out of the Army.

I believe that's about all the news to date. Until Later

All my love, Bill

*   *   *

10/4/45

Dear Mother & Dad,

Today I received your letter of 10/28/45 which was a week ago tomorrow. It was the first letter I've received since you learned of my present address. They have been taking a lot of the mail by ship so I imagine that this one came by plane and therefore why it arrived before the others.

Last night I went to a play given by an army outfit here "George Washington Slept Here." It was very enjoyable.

I got the negatives of the pictures I took on Okinawa developed and when I get some paper I'll get some prints made. Some of them look like they'll make pictures. I still have several rolls of film left.

The work is still swell. I work on the tuberculosis wards—male and female medicine. I also do about all of the pneumothoraces—and what ever else I can think of. I very seldom leave the hospital for there isn't anything else here that you could want that isn't right at hand.

Rankin and I asked the Senior Med. Officer of the Island if we could stay here for awhile—I hope so. Probably what will happen now is that we are shoved off to some forlorn rock I never heard of.

It is a good feeling to come to Saipan from Okinawa. Always before I was an absolute Neophyte. This way—though I've had less time—they at least can't go bragging about all the things they've been through without some comment from myself.

Hope Tom gets his discharge soon. Glad Bud & Fred won't have to do more overseas duty. Good that Johnny Lloyd is out.

Till Later all my Love

*   *   *

10/7/45

Dear Mother & Dad,

We had quite a rain here the other day and with quite a wind which blew it into these Tropical Quonsets making everything wet. It blew quite a few trees down. We've had quite a bit of rain, but this morning it was clear and hot.

I received several of your letters. I brought all my books with me, but don't know how long they will last as the mold really gets into them. NOB was about 7-10 miles North of Yonabaru on the bay. They finally got a semblance of a road down to the coast before I left. I'm not attached to the colored boys now, they got a relief for me in G-10, Comp 62—I guess they're still there. The Captain has gone to Guam and may find out something of our future.

They had a dance last night at the officers Club. Walsh meet a nurse and fixed Rankin and I up with one girl. Rankin didn't seem very interested so I spent most of the time with her. It was a good party.

Surely Hope Tom gets to the Separation Center and is out before Thanksgiving.

As I write this I'm listening to the World series. They have two broadcasts of it. One at 4:00 AM. and a rebroadcast at 1:00 P.M. I'm listening to the rebroadcast. I already know that Detroit is going to win this game. The radio is working ok.

It is a beautiful afternoon; so think I'll get a little sun.

All my Love, Bill.

*   *   *

10/12/45

Dear Mother & Dad,

It is good to be closer to Medicine again. Last night we went to the meeting of the Saipan Medical Society at an army hospital and they gave a very interesting series of talks on chest wounds. Afterwards they had Beer and Sandwiches. I guess none of the Doctors I know are here as I didn't see any at the meeting.

I haven't heard from little Betty for a long time. Last I heard she was to spend the last 6 mo. of her training in the USPHS, but where I don't know.

Just heard over the radio of the big storm on Okinawa. Glad that I'd left. We had a few samples of wind while I was there but nothing like what they got this time.

Ole Tom is home all done with the army today I hope. I know he'll be perfectly satisfied at home. Johnny and Justine next door would really be fine.

My duty is rather complicated—and has been all along. I was never attached to the Sea Bees. I was under the Staff of the Senior Medical officers with the object to setup dispensaries like ours where we might be needed. As it turned out we were quickly forgotten by the Staff medical office—except for Mr. Boles who arrange our present situation. It just so happened that where they sent me there was part of a CB battalion without a Med. Officer at the Camp. In addition to this outfit (12th special C.B.'s—Stevedore Battalion). There were two base Companies—both colored (as well as most of the 12th Sp C.B.). The Base Companies have about 250 men and are really just labor companies. They both did stevedoring at Yonabaru. We lived with and set up the dispensary in the camp of the Base Company # 32. I guess we took care of about 800-1000 men. This is fairly complicated and I never did understand it, but to make it even more complicated. The two base Companies were attached to 12th special N.C.B. We lived like See Bees without most of their advantages.

The mail is coming along pretty well now. I am getting your letters in about 8 days. Mail on Okinawa was a tough proposition because nobody knew where we were or what we were attached to but I think we did pretty well.

I now have the Women's Medical Ward all to myself, practically—I am supposed to be under another Doctor but he has left the whole thing to me which fine. I do some of the Tb. work—all of the neumos. Will get another Job when the Executive Officer leaves—at the Charan Kanoa Dispensary, but still will have plenty of time to do what I like. I learn something everyday.

Till Later,

All my Love, Bill

*   *   *

10/14/45

Dear Mother & Dad,

A peaceful Saturday afternoon and Sunday and now before dinner and our evening movie, I'll write a note. This afternoon we listened to the Army-Michigan football game. They also broadcast the Navy game, but was swimming during it.

We went Church this morning. Dr. Wyatt is a good Catholic and sees that I get to mass. Four of the nurses are also Catholic so we all go together.

I have accumulated two Jap rifles since I've been here with no effort on my part. Now I don't know what to do with them.

I received a letter from Dad yesterday written a week ago today. It took only six days. That's pretty fast. Usually it takes about 8 days.

We went to the show tonight. It was pretty good. All the theaters are open air and we were blessed with a rain. We've learned the peculiarities however and take our rain coats.

Not much other news. Till Later

All my Love, Bill

*   *   *

Monday Oct. 15,1945

Dear Bill:

You have fared pretty well I think these last few days and with a big long letter from your brother on Saturday and Dads yesterday but I have not written you since we had your letter of the fourth so will now comment on it.

We are so glad that you had had one letter of recent date and maybe now they will reach you a little quicker. The one of the 28th which you had had that day was the first one I had written with your present address so maybe that is the reason that you got in such a hurry.

We had been a little puzzled about just what you were doing for we did not understand what a "pneumothoraces" are but after consulting the dictionary I think that it is the prose collapsing the lung, am I right? If that is what it is my understanding is that that is quite a delicate trick.

I surely hope that the Senior Med Officer can see "eye to eye" with you on the deal of your staying on Saipan. We saw by tonights paper that Paul Needham is now on Okinawa.

The little clipping about the "tie-breaker" business does not tell you how smart your brother is for he tied with Kent McCauley on all but the Rocky Ford-La Junta score and on that he gave them one touchdown. Last Friday they had it again a Quarter-back Club meeting and we hear that he tied with one of the assistant coaches for the low again. They have a kitty a dime a piece so he should realize about $1.50 out of it.

Tommy is now a hard working man at the office, reading writing insurance (know you envy him that?) and some other things. He was really busy today.

I think that now we have really learned how to spell "Saipan" but it took quite a while. We would look it up and I would forget again when I went to write it.

I had a couple of good breaks today. I thought that I would have to go to the USO twice, this morning for myself again tonight for

Marg for with Bud home I did not think that she would want to go down. Yesterday after noon they called me from the USO and said that this being Mrs. McKenzies birthday and due to the fact that her daughter wanted to give her a surprise at she wanted them to ask her to be hostess down there so that they so she could get the luncheon ready with out her knowing it so she went in my place. Then this afternoon Marg called and said that Bud and Bill Guthrie were going to Legion tonight so she and Ag, Bill's wife would go down so that I did not need to.

Ham Lambert called his mother from the east coast yesterday morning and will be home in about a week.

Roy Black is here and think that he and Tom are waiting for this letter before they take off for the show or something I had better sign off and let them get on their way.

*   *   *

Tuesday Oct.16,1945

Dear Bill:

I got the paper in the machine before supper but that is as far as I got for these hungry men were crying for food. Then I had to let down the brothers brown slacks at least let the cuffs down and press them. He bought a snazzy new sport coat in Denver last week and it just came today. It is a sort of yellowish tan so of course had to have brown slacks to accompany it. It has real broad shoulders and is long at least on the long boy it comes down where it should and now so many of his clothes lack that feature. I dont know whether he grew in the army but all his clothes seem a little snug on him. Even around the waist. As shirts are hard to get he has fished down into your supply of white ones but I think that they are a little tight in the neck for him. Guess I will have to set the buttons over a little on them. You have so many white ones that I think there will be an ample supply for you even after he has taken a few for himself.

Dad had tom writing an abstract this afternoon or rather copying one and said that he did a nice job on it. If the ceiling on the sales of houses goes into effect as they are now talking of it will sort of stop this continual exchange of property which will not be so good for the abstractors.

J.B. Morehead Jr. is here now on leave after being out in the Pacific for quite a while. Dad was telling him that your big worry now is that you will be sent to some island like Truk. And he said that you would be very fortunate in his opinion if you were sent there for he knew a fellow who had been stationed there are he described it as a very nice place.

Bud,Bill G. and John L. went duck hunting this afternoon. Dad did not know where they went so I cant tell you either. Mrs. Guthrie says that Bud and Bill play cribbage by the hour. It is so grand that they are both here together. It makes quite a house full for Mrs. G. but she says she does not mind and if once in a while the confusion gets on her nerves she goes off into her room and after a little rest is fine again. Of course she is very happy to have them all there together.

Mrs. Stone helped me do the washing this morning but I sent her home as soon as I could for she was feeling miserable with cold. She should not have come at all but insisted that she was not going to give in to it but by the time that she went home I think she had changed her mind for she said that it would really feel good to get into bed.

The neighbors are all out in front these days raking the leaves that are falling fast. You know how ours are always a bit later than the others around,being different kind of trees so I only joined the pack for a little while. We thought last eve that the city was getting ready to clean them out of the gutters so we all ran out and got busy and then they went off and did not pick them up. Guess they were just getting the street ready to put some more oil on it and it surely does need that. The city now has most of the streets in pretty good shape for they have been working on them all the summer.

Nellie and Fanny are coming in tomorrow but want to go by the way of stage canyon and see the steers that are in the Colard place. Dad is taking Hugh Ford out to see them tomorrow afternoon and another man a little later in the week I guess unless Hugh gives him so much he cant refuse. Mr. Kitch has already offered him 12 1/4 cents for them which is a pretty good price. Think Tom is now all fixed up and ready to take this to mail so will close for this time.

*   *   *

Wednesday Oct.17,1945

Dear Bill:

This mornings mail brought a letter from you of the 7th so it must have been about ten day coming over here. Any we were very glad to get it and know that you too had had several letters from home and that you answered all my questions about Okinawa.

The weather that you spoke of must have just preceded the one on Okinawa that did so much damage. Are the tropical quansets not as rain resistant as others for you said that everything got wet. I bet that was a mess. Seems funny that it can be so hot there when the days here are so perfect and the nights so chilly. Well you will soon be out of the states ten months so if the duration of your stay is to be 18 months then you have done more than half of it and we can begin to count the days off till you will be coming home.

Glad that some one gets you fixed up with a date once in a while even if you have to share her with Rankin but he was a good egg to have let you have most of the time with her. You did not say that she was big and fat,tall and slim, short and dumpy (like your maw) or beautifully willowy. Red head, platinum blonde brunette or lovely to look at How about it?

Just between you and me, I dont like these little sheets of paper Pop got it for me at "our drug store" so guess it was all that they had.

Keeps me changing too often and when they get near the bottom they slip.

Aunt Nell was telling me today(she and Aunt Fan came in from the ranch and she went on to Trinidad this afternoon) that Tom's old sweetie, Peggy Walker is to be married again. Her husband Tommy Thompson was killed in england.

Gee I hope the Captain is successful in finding out at Guam something about your set up in the future. Maybe it would add to your happiness and maybe it would be just as well if you did not know but at least it would settle the question for you.

Wish that I could send you something in which to keep your books in so that they would be dry and not mold. Perhaps I can think of some way in which it could be done. I will put on my thinking cap.

Aunt Nell actually says that the steers look fine and that they should for they are standing in all kinds of good grass and right at the pond of water. They should be gaining a little weight all the time now. Dad is out there with Mr. Ford to look at them this afternoon.

Just had an interruption. Tom and Bob McCluskey(Mr. Bob as of two days) just came in and announced that they were going out to ride horse back. Tom had an invitation to the Nu Phi Mu, whatever that is, dance at Harmony hall this eve but he did not at all interested in going. Guess he does not know them very well.

I got into giving a party all of a sudden today. This morning Aunt Betty called to invite me to lunch tomorrow at the Kit Carson for Mrs. Davis's sister-in-law who is visiting here, and before I knew it I was helping her to give the party, and it fell to me to call Mrs. Frey at the hotel for reservations and that was when the bad blow fell for her good cook has left and so she is serving only breakfast and dinner now. Well Aunt B. had already asked the guests to lunch so there was nothing left to do but get it ourselves. She is having it out there and fixing the table etc. and I am to do the cooking, that is the all the cooking which we cant get Mrs. Raney to do for us but we are only having nine so it wont hurt me any.

Well Dad just came home. Sold the steers at 12 1/2 cents, 1/4¢ higher than his other bid so they will be delivering them next Monday.

Guess they go to California or somewhere like o that, way off any way.

This is church night so I must go get the supper so we can get off in time. Dad is going to the poker club tonight so will be out late. dont know what T. will be doing.

*   *   *

10/18/45

Dear Mother, Dad, & Tom,

Not much new has happened since I last wrote to you. We are having beautiful weather on Saipan—At least it is hot. It is a lazy climate and I find it easy to loaf—Though I find that easy everywhere. The cases are still plentiful. We have 3 cases of tetanus in the hospital and strictly between us I am entirely at fault for one of them. I wonder if I'll ever be able to practice medicine.

I was interested to hear that Dr. Rowden was or is here. The hospital 39th Gen, is pretty well broken up now. I surely enjoy the clippings and think it was a wise thing to stop my subscription as I don't get very many of them especially when I change addresses and then they are very old.

I hope that I can enjoy your Christmas package here. I'm afraid the stores here aren't offering very many nice gifts for Christmas. They have sent in a dispatch asking that we be attached here at the hospital, and surely hope it goes through.

Glad that Bud is getting an additional 15 days. Too bad they don't let him out, as I doubt that he is doing too much. When his ten years are up he'll get out. I enjoyed the letter Tom was writting to Pat. I suppose he has the opportunity now to date her occasionally.

Well haven't much other news for the present. Til later

All my love, Bill

*   *   *

Friday,Oct.19,1945

Dear Bill:

Seems that you have been a little neglected for I did not get a letter off to you yesterday but will try to make up for it today and write you a good letter altho there is really no much new under the sun to tell you. It is just wait for the days to roll by till the time comes for you to come home and then we will all really begin to live again normally,it is just half normally now that Tom is here.

I told you in Wednesdays letter about the party that Aunt Betty and were having yesterday and that it had devolved on us to do all the work as the hotel is not serving lunches now. well I made rolls, jello salad, and meat loaf. That really seems like very little to do but it was enough to keep me hopping all day so when it was time to go to bridge club last night I was a little weary but that must have been just what the doctor ordered for me as I had a good score. I am sure my partners must have been the good ones for I was asleep most of the time.

Guess I have not told you that it is now decided that we go to Missouri early Tuesday morning and drive all the way thru in the one day. We will be gone about a week so the boss says.

Oh I forgot to tell you about Mrs. Davis's marvelous score last night,8600 in the four rounds that we play,six hands to a round. In one round she and Mr. McCartney made over 3000 and in two others she made over 2000 each. I never did play at the same table as she but guess she just made 700 rubbers over and over again. there is a game tonight with Manz(no that is not right, guess it is Las Animas) and since we seem to have the winning team I will go along with the boys. Bob McCluskey is going with us too so Tom announced.

Guess he will tell you all about the horse back ride they had the other evening but even so I will put in my bit. The two boys and Margaret Strain rode out to Hill Crest and had a sandwitch and then rode back by moonlight. If Tom had had a little lovely with him it could have quite romantic,I should say.

Aunt Fan brought the little saddle from the ranch in to Bobby when she came over and you should have seen how his eyes danced with glee over it. I have not heard yet how he got along when they tried it. He really loves to ride but ofcourse so far has ridden just around the corral with some one leading the horse and you may remember how much fun that is.

The chief reasons that we are now ready to take off on our trip is that, the part came for the apartment furnace and the other that the steers are sold. Those two things Dad had to see to before he could leave. Then too he was wishing that he could find some one for extra help in the office while he and Tom are both away and just now when he came in he tells me that it is all fixed and that Mutt is coming down for that week. So every thing seems to have worked out fine for us.

This morning when I moved the davenporte to clean under it one of the legs came off so now the two Toms are very busy trying to put it on again. Guess I was a little too husky today for I also knocked my mothers picture off the table and broke the glass all to pieces. It was a sort of decorated glass and I doubt that I will be able to get another one so pretty.

It (the davenporte) is all fixed. My what great guys I have around here.

Tom got his dollar and a half,in fact 55cents,at the quarterback club today for his good guess last week on the scores. the men seemed to think that he reads a lot on the teams but he says that it was pure luck, and not skill.

Will go cook a little food for the hungry pack so we will have lots of time to be in plenty of time for the kick off etc.

*   *   *

10/21/45

Dear Mother, Dad, & Tom,

Yesterday I was O.D. and was not too busy Thank God, for I developed a nasty cold—the first I've had since I've been here and since I was in San Francisco as a matter of fact.

They had a big party yesterday at the Club, but being OD I was not able to attend. They also had a party at the farm—where the natives go for quite a few things. It was too bad I was OD but having this cold wouldn't have enjoyed it very much. I am much better this evening.

I received the good letter Tom wrote today and really enjoyed it. Also the clipping—especially of the discharge of Lt. Tom Sisson. I'd surely like to be there following the local Football games. We listened to the Purdue—Ohio St. game today.

Haven't much other news from this end. Till Later,

All my love, Bill

*   *   *

10/24/45

Dear Mother & Dad,

Monday I got a bunch of back letters from you and I caught up on all the news. It took me quite a while to read it all. I hope the package with the book "The Green Years" follows me as I haven't received it. I'm glad Tom has been able to make use of a few of my clothes. He is perfectly welcome to any and all. I hope I won't need any white shirts for navy uniform when I get back.

I know Dad would get 12 1/2¢/lb for the steers and would not have been surprised if he gotten 13¢. Now comes the job of delivering. Last year I about wore myself out doing just that thing.* Last year about this time I was getting ready to join the navy. I had surely never heard of Okinawa then—now I have been and left there. This is now the longest I've ever been away from home.

In Tom's letter I surely enjoyed the Return address Mr. Thomas M. Sisson.

Last night we went down to the Navy Air Base to see a USO show which wasnt too Bad. Tonight Rankin and I are going to meet Walsh at the Fleet Officers Club. Walsh now has temporary duty with the marine—MP's of this Island. I am surely glad I didn't get that.

My field of activities is slowly expanding around here, but still have lots of free time. I now go to Chanan Kanoa every morning for 1 1/2 hours. Boy—I really see lots of interesting cases. Anything I see I want to examine more. (If a woman) I admit to the hospital to my ward.

Till Later,

All my Love, Bill

I got the stamps and airmail stickers—Thanks.

*driving yearling steers from Stage Canyon ranch to Ayer

*   *   *

10/27/45

Dear Mother, Dad & Tom,

When you think of me—think of me sitting on a sandy beach of a Tropical Isle enjoying the sun and water. Really lots of people would go a long way to find a place like this. Today is really sunny—Church in the open air is really hot. But the rest of the day will spent in trunks listening to the football games.

Last night Rankin and I went to see a play—"Junior Miss" a USO Show. It was better than most. The night I was OD, I was called over to where the Red Cross girls, Navy Nurses, and USO girls stay to see one of the USO girls. They are some lot. I guess I haven't been here long enough for they had no appeal to me. After that Rankin and I picked up the nurse who gets off work at 10PM and brought her over to the club for a beer and coke. She is a little Italian girl and very pleasant.

I am now the big gun in tuberculosis as I have the two Tb wards to myself now in addition to Female Medicine and the

Charan Kanoa dispensary. I did half a tonsillectomy the other day—while Dr. Adams helped. He is a good egg.

This noon I am going to eat with the CPO (Chief Petty Off). They say it is to be fried chicken.

Not much other news for the present all my Love, Bill

*　　*　　*

10/28/45

Dear Dad & Mother & Tom,

Just another short note today to answer a few letters. Today you are all in Missouri enjoying Uncle Murrays farm. How I'd like to be with you. One of your questions Dad in an earlier letter was whether or not I'd get back 6 mo. after the signing of the peace. Well I don't think so. I imagine I'll have to stay out here until my 18 mo. are up—About getting out—it takes 53 points for Doctors. I have 23 3/4. At that rate I'll get out in 1950. Therefore it just depends on breaks and when they lower the points enough or stop using the point system.

I have a good set up now.

Have enjoyed following the L.J. football team—they are surely doing all right for themselves.

You surely did all right with the steers. I wonder how much they weighed.

There are quite a few fellows around who have an acquaintance with Colo. Three went to the Jap Language school, one went to school at Boulder, another taught at Adams St. Teachers, and Dr. Wyatt who is a valley man.

Not much other news for the Present.

All my love, Bill

*　　*　　*

Tuesday Oct.30,1945

Dear Bill:

Home again. But we did have a little further difficulty today,just a flat tire which was pretty badly shot so that it left us without a spare the rest of the way home so "the boys" did not want to drive very fast (you know how mad that made me?) so it was about two before we got here. We found everything fine and two letters from you waiting for us which was a very good welcome indeed. Hope that all three cases of tetanus are doing fine and that you dont let that conscience of yours bother you too much. There is a higher will than ours and when we have not done things willfully then it is really not our fault, even tho we can see later how it might have been different.

Hope that you may see Dr. Rowden but would not be surprised if he left the island before you have that opportunity. Yes, I dont know why I have not long ago resorted to that way of getting the news to you but kept hoping that the papers would reach you a little better than they have.

Hope that your cold did not amount to much and you got rid of it soon. That hot climate should melt it out. Guess you are rather lucky that it is not summer while you are there but since you are pretty far south I guess there is not so much difference between winter and summer anyway. I notice on our globe that the day that you will pick up when you come home is called Meridian Day.

Aunt Fan tells us that in our absence she sold the cows. To Mr. Kitch so Dad does not have to worry about it. We might have staid a little longer if we had known that but it suits me as is. she also says that Johnny has bought the Adamack store so it looks as if they will really be settled here and that is mighty fine. Bud leaves in the morning for Memphis but do hope that the lowering of the points the first of Dec. lets him out. You will see in the clippings that I will send you tonight how many of the boys are getting out now. guess you and Ed Garlington will be among the later ones but in your case it is not bad if you stay there and are really getting experience for you will have to get that some where and there is perhaps a better place than in the states somewhere for there are so many different kinds of diseases.

Mrs. Slyvester just called me(Oh, ofcourse, I mean Mrs. Parhm) and asked me to sell bonds again and tomorrow would be the day but I begged off for tomorrow as I would like to get the laundry done and it is a big one, but next week I can have things arranged so can help out, this being the last one we will have.

Aunt Fan was very busy today when we arrived. She had made a cake and bread so I dont have much to worry about for the supper. However I think that I had better go down and get all the clothes sorted so I can get a good start at the washing in the morning so will close for this time.

*   *   *

10/31/45

Dear Mother & Dad & Tom,

Today is Halloween, but it is not celebrated by the kids as much as in the States—at least I've heard or seen no evidence of it. Tomorrow will be November and I'll have completed 10 mo overseas. I hope by the end of the next 10 mo. I'll be home and out of the Navy.

Nothing startling has happened around this place. Two of my Tb patients died right after I took over the ward and am expecting two more real soon. There is surely lots of tuberculosis here. It is hard to do anything with it as the natives so not understand. Saipan was a Japan Mandate since the first war and had Jap Medical Care. From what I can learn the Japs did nothing for the tuberculars. Now the old active people give it to the young children who quickly die—Of course there is an excess birth rate to maintain the Population.

There are 3 Jap doctors in Camp Susupe who run the dispensary. From what I've seen I think their medicine is quite inferior to ours. In the Hospital Japs Midwifes do the deliveries, except for the difficult ones when they call one of the Navy Doctors. Not much news today. Till later, Hope you enjoyed Mo.

All my Love, Bill

*   *   *

Thursday Nov.1,1945

Dear Bill:

Another month has appeared and that much nearer to the time which will be bringing you homeward and while I know that this experience is the very thing that you need and it is fine to be getting it there it will still be a very big thrill for us when white sails in the sunset are carrying you home. Gosh,I nearly waxed sentimental.

It seems that your brother is stealing one of your old flames for a date tonight, Ida Ordner is the favored one. It is hard for so many boys to scratch up enough girls for dates. Ham,Bob McClusky,Roy Balck and I dont know who else. Anyway it seems like old times to have the phone ringing and things doing around here.

Tom's clothes he shipped from England came today and most of it is dirty clothes so tomorrow I am going to get at them for I dont want to do them when I have a big wash of ordinary laundry. Aunt Fan brought a little from the ranch so we will do them too. You have not said much lately about your laundry situation so I presume that it is better and again you are able to have clean starched shirts.

The carpenter finally came this afternoon and has fixed the chicken house up in fine shape so that I can now get the hens in here and really set up a chicken business. It has cost me enough to buy a lot of eggs but sometimes they are hard to get and then anyway it is nice to have them fresh. I began to think that Mr. Sisson was going to have to do the job for me but now all he and Tom have to do is get the trash out of the yard and in to the ash pit, and fix up the nests. Well if they dont do it I can myself and maybe I am just a little too optimistic but I will smile my prettiest.

This was a Holy Day and I wonder if the good catholic doctor got you off to Mass this morning like I did Tom. I sort of hated to get him up for he and his gang were out to the dance last night and did not get in till about two this A.M. and so he was pretty sleepy I am sure but jumped out of bed when I called like a good little fellow.

Aunt Fan and I will go in the morning again for the poor souls and early,seven AM.

Think that I had better stop now for T. is to take this as he goes for Ida and I hear him out of the tub so had best be getting it addressed etc.

*   *   *

Friday Nov.2,1945

Dear Bill:

I am wondering how the game is coming along with Las Animas. Tommy went but Dad could not get away for dick was at home this afternoon as J.B. was leaving. Ham Lambert was to go with Tom but most of the other fellows had to work so could not accept his invitation. This is ofcourse the hardest game that the boys have as L.A. seems to be the only other team that amounts to very much this year.

Mildred Jenkins was telling me a little while ago that Don Hollis has left home and as yet they are not real sure where he has gone. They do know that he got a ticket on the bus for Oregon where they have relatives. They wired these relatives to let them know just as soon as he arrived there but as yet have had no word and like all mothers Mrs. Hollis is getting very nervous about it lest some mishap has befallen him on the way. Mr. H. like all Dads says "Oh, he is all right.Stop worrying." He had told Dad he would rake the leaves but now maybe Justine will have to get out the rake and go to work. On the other hand maybe we can find the Tiburcio kids and they will do it.

Thought we might get another letter from you today but no such good luck and now we will be looking for one on tomorrows mail.

Dr. Hansen and wife are here on his terminal /a leave. It seems that he contemplates locating in Philadelphia where he has an offer of some kind. Well that is one you wont have to combat when you set up your office here. Yes?

Poor Johnny had a set back in his business venture today for when Earl went over to the court house to look over the estate papers he found that her daughters still own half of the store and it seems that one of them does not want to sell. He had a stock of goods coming,a vault and a neon sign so if they cant straighten this tangle out he will go in in some other location which ofcourse would not be so good as an established place there which is really a very good location. Johnny says he will never do business with a woman again.

I am sending 'in this letter' two adds from the local paper, the first of which did burn the Drug Store company up a bit and you will see why. The second one shows the correction. that paper can make the mistakes.

I had heard that John Geiger is to be discharged but this morning at Mass I asked "Izzy" about it but she did not know it if it is true, so maybe it is just rumor.

Well deposited a lot of Englands soil down my sewer in the basement this morning when I did the laundry which T brought or rather sent home. I dont think much of the job they did over there on the clothes. They were a dirty bunch.

*   *   *

11/4/45

Dear Mother, Dad, & Tom,

I imagine you are all back in La Junta now. I was surely glad to hear that Uncle Murray looks well. How I'd liked to have been there with you all.

Today has been rather quiet and peaceful. I listened to the Navy Notre Dame game which Notre Dame should have won.

That was a tough break. This morning I went to Mass at the Navy Base. I arrived a little early and while waiting I sat at the base of the flag pole. Unobserved by me the Captain walked by (at least I didn't realize he was a Captain). I didn't salute and he gave me quite a lecture. Now I'm sure that the next time I see him I won't salute. This place is really getting stateside.

Last night had another party and believe it or not I got myself a date, with Miss Orlando the Italian girl. The Band was poor and she had to work till 10:00 p.m. But had a good, but short time.

Yesterday went sail-boating which is really fun as this is a nice lagoon between the beach and the Reef. They have several sail boats around. One Afternoon Rankin and I got out and the wind stopped. Rankin pulled the boat and me back. Till Later

All my Love, Bill

*   *   *

11/7/45

Dear Mother, Dad & Tom,

A year ago yesterday I reported to Oakknoll for Duty with the navy. I've surely put on a lot of miles since then.

I had a sad experience the other day. A baby died at the Charan Kanoa the night after I'd seen him in the clinic. An autopsy didn't show too much. You've surely got to keep on your toes for these people die like flies. I'm learning a lot on the Tb. wards too. I've had 3 deaths in the last week. Two of them had in addition to their fatal tuberculosis acute appendicitis found on autopsy. The other death I hold myself partly responsible for bringing it about earlier than need be. I started her on a pneumothorax and collapsed what good lung tissue she did have. I think I at least learned more about selection of cases for the pneumos. There is surely lots of Tb. here. I picked up two cases one day at Charan Kanoa. Charan Kanoa is the village where all the natives other than Japs and Koreans stay.

We are now getting a few natives from Yap, Ponape, and Truck in the Carolines. They are all called Kanakas. They can't understand Japanese, English, or the Chamourro language. In addition to these we also have a few natives from the Marshalls—Eniwetok& Kwajelein who understand nobody else.

I got the pictures of you all and surely liked them—Ole Tom in his Civies. Also received the book "Green Years". Thanks a million.

Rankin, my roommate—Baker, and myself have found a football and have been throwing it around for a little exercise.

I believe that is all the news for the present—Till Later.

All my Love, Bill

*   *   *

Thursday Nov.8,1945

Dear Bill:

Before I go to get ready for the bridge club I will pen a few words to you,off in Saipan. I had my hair set in the new all up in the back way this morning and from your Dad all I got was "There is a place in the back that is sort of bare.". Tom did somewhat better for he ahaed a little after I had called his attention to the fact that is had been done differently. I wonder if you would have noticed it either. Well the ladies at the club will pay attention to it even if the men dont. the cold wave that was predicted for last night did not arrive then but guess it will reach here tonight for it is already much colder than it was this morning. I can wear my fur coat tonight for about the first time this year. think of that. Being so warm that I could not show it off.

The Toms got home some time late in the night, I was too sleepy to be sure just when it was. Tommy had had "a fair time" so guess he is not very crazy about that little girl. He seems to think he best efforts will have to be spent not in catching her but in getting rid of her. He seems to think that she is desperate for a man.

The little maid did not show up today so the ironing that I thought I would get time to do this morning I had to do this afternoon. If she had some it would have relieved me of the dishwashing and bed making so I could have done the other. Mrs. Stone was here however and got aunt Fans room all cleaned up ready for the curtains which I will get at tomorrow.

The hens did not do so well today as yesterday. I got only three eggs today where the day before I had seven. Maybe if it gets real cold they will not do that well

Mr. and Mrs. Woodruff went to Denver last Friday thinking that Tommy would reach there about Saturday and he is not there yet. I think he did not get away from California till about sunday eve or later perhaps.

Think that I had better start getting ready so Mr. Sisson will not be put out at me by having to wait for me so so long honey. Think from the conversation that I just heard Tommy and MacClusky having over the phone that for once the little Sisson boy is tired and intends to go to bed early.

*   *   *

11/11/45

Dear Mother, Dad, & Tom,

This has been quite a long day. Yesterday I was OD and didn't get to sleep until about 12:00 then up at 4:00 A.M. to pronounce a woman dead. I then went to 5:00AM Mass with Miss Orlando at Charan Kanoa. Their chapel was crowded and we were a little late so we had to stand outside. Of course we had our usual Early morning shower, but we found cover. It was surely dark, but quite pretty. However I don't think I'll go to 5:00 AM Mass very often even to have such a pleasant companion.

Listened to the Army Notre Dame Game today and was surely sympathetic for ole Notre Dame. That Army really has a team.

You wanted to know something about the natives. As I've told you most of them are Japs—about 13,000. 2-3,000 Kalans. And about 4,000 Chaumorros the true natives of the Mariannas.

Most of the Japs are Okinawans. The Chaumorros will probably be the only ones left here. By now the Chamauros are Pretty well mixed—Mostly Spanish from early Explorations. There Is a noticeable German strain in them from German control of Saipan till the end of the last war. They are very much like our Mexicans, and nearly all Catholic. They have two priests and 3 nuns from Spain.

They as well as the Japs are an unhealthy lot. Life expectancy is short and the death rate in children is very high. Many diseases such as diabetes, appendicitis, hypertension, arteriosclerosis, and cancer are rare. The largest cause of adult death is Tuberculosis. They have an abundance of worms of all kinds. The most common are hook worm, strongyloides (much like hookworm), and ascaris. Ascaris is a long round worm very much like the common earth worm. We can always treat them for worms. The record for Ascaris something over 100 worms following deworming. These worms often are vomited by children and sometimes even crawl out of their noses. At autopsies if this patient has this kind of worms the intestines look alive as the worms try to get out. They have dewormed all the natives mass production, but even so only very few don't have some sort of Infestation as it is impossible to remove the source of infection. Worms are so common among them that we hardly think it too abnormal. Perhaps you'll find this interesting Mother, but I doubt that the Toms do. They have 9 lepers in the Leprosarium. They are the first ones I've ever seen. Another very common disease is Yaws, which is much like syphilis in that it is caused by the same sort of organism and produces a positive Wassermann Blood Test. However it is non venereal. It can produce large skin ulcers, but responds miraculously to treatment. Syphilis and Gonorrhea are surprisingly rare, as are Difficult labors and pregnancies. There are lots of diseases as well as many common Medical problems.

The boy who developed the tetanus from the burns much to my relief has pretty well gotten over it. But of the 3 cases only one died.

They still don't what is to be done with our G-10's. And so we shall just wait and see. I rather imagine they'll just leave us hear now. I surely hope we don't have to go out again to a place like Yap where some Fellows who were here went. Dr. Wyatt just came back from a two weeks in Yap and the other Island and says they are really living the primitive life. The boys who have control are back at Hawaii.

Had a surprise the other day when the Capt. who I was under at Okinawa and his assistant who was my pal came through. They are now on the staff of Cincpac and are stationed in Hawaii. They were making a routine inspection of the hospital. I was surely surprised to see them and vice versa as they thought we'd be anywhere except Saipan.

I guess that is all the news I can think of.

All my Love, Bill

*   *   *

Monday,Nov.12,1945

Dear Bill:

This is a big evening for your brother for he has gotten a date with a little girl he has seen and thinks is pretty cute. Her name is Ona DeBona,sounds like a movie queen and they are going to the dance,American Legion,about eight so I must have my letter ready so as not to keep him waiting one single moment.

Being Armistice day the big game between La J and Rocky Ford was played but I did not see how I could spare the time to go so stayed home and replanted the tulips, an all afternoon job. There were so many little bulbs that I put them all around the shrubbery in the front of the house. Hope they will grow for I have always thought they would be pretty there.

Dad and Tom and a bunch of the boys,Roy Black,Ham, Bob Mann and Tom Woodruff went to the game and though La Junta beat 31 to 13 they say it was a good game. Ofcourse La J was able to play the second team after the first little while and even some of the Gas House Gang got to play. The Lamar game comes off Friday so I will go see that.

Every one is talking about Frank Bradford again marrying Charline. Funny isnt it to have such a big wedding just to remarry ones own wife. Guess she did not like her wedding gown the first time.

Justine says she would like to marry Johnny again so she could have a different gown for she did not like the one she had. She ate dinner with us yesterday for her mother went out to cook dinner at the farm and she does not think that is much fun. She stayed all the afternoon and the four of us played bridge till Marg and Bobby came along then Mary took my place and I played with Bob.

After supper last night Dad and I went down and worked on the change he is making is some of his books. After about an hour Mac came along to get the key to the drug store to get May a coke. Well that was the end of our working for he stood there and talked to us for about an hour. Bet May wondered why it took him so long to get a coke.

Mr. Inman was telling Dad that some friend of Bob's wants him to go in with him on the manufacture of some invention the Boy has perfected. Tom says this fellow waited tables with Bob at the dorm,has very bad eyes but is evidently very brilliant. Had Bob ever told you about it? Mr. I seems to think that it is a very good deal for Bob. I must try to go see Betty before she leaves. They say her baby is really a cute kid but I have not seen him.

The Hollis family have heard from their boy, Don. He is in Oregon going to school just as they supposed so ofcourse she had nothing to worry about but she is just a mama like the rest of us.

Hear T. out of the bath tub now so guess I had better stop and get this in the envelope and addressed so ta-ta.

*   *   *

11/15/45

Dear Mother, Dad, & Tom,

Yesterday was again my turn at OD and I didn't get a letter off to you. Every Wednesday we have a meeting of the Staff Officers at which time we present interesting cases and deaths during the past week. As usual I have several deaths to report. We have Autopsies on every case so can establish most of our diagnoses—right or wrong. I had 3 yesterday two—Tb and one a heart disease. One of the tb cases was a boy about 12. He had involvement of his heart.

I received Tom's letter today of the evening that you were all going to hear Rubinoff. How I'd like to have accompanied you.

In a few days I'll have passed my 26th birthday—The first that Auntie Hi won't be able to celebrate. This time last year I was at Oakknoll.

Haven't really much news tonight. Till later,

All my Love, Bill

*   *   *

Thursday Nov.15,1945

Dear Bill:

While the two Toms get a little muchly needed sleep I will write a little to you. I dont know what the plans for the young Tom are but the big one has the bridge club before him yet tonight so that is the reason that he has to get a little rest. I took a nap this afternoon for I cant let him get the best of me at bridge again.

I just ran(in the car) out to the Sabins with a handout, a very nice handout,12 fresh eggs, about two lbs of butter and a half pint of good cream and found Aunt betty, Mrs. Johnston,Mrs. Mays and Mrs. Woodbridge still playing bridge at five thirty. the rest of the family were all arriving for their supper so bet AuntB. was wishing the ladies would pick up and leave. John,I learned is going to Denver tomorrow to try to get some of the things that he needs for his store. Counters are the hardest of all for him to get and he says they will have to be just make shift at best for the present.

Guess Tom and Ida had a good time last night at least they had a long time for they danced till two. But he got an invitation to dinner tomorrow night with Ida's boss at their home in Rocky Ford. They had invited Ida so suggested that she bring him along. The boss is a Major but cant remember his name but guess it is not important as you would not know him anyway,I dont.

Think that Dad has it arranged so that both he and Tom can get off to go to the game tomorrow afternoon. I will accompany them since my work is rather light for a little while.

Think that I had better wake Dad up so that he can get his bath. Oh,yes. This afternoon I thought that the softener had better be regenerated before we would all be taking baths tonight and tho I had never successfully done it Dad thought that I could with a few instructions he gave me and with those hanging in the basement so I started. Well the thing acted up some way and I got all balled up so had to send an SOS for Dad and he came up and finished the job. I am sure this time that I will know how the next time.

*   *   *

Friday Nov.16,1945

Dear Bill:

This has been rather a blustery day but not cold tho the weather man had said that it would be cooler last night. It did not get down as low as predicted,30 or lower and I think that it could not have been much less than 40.

We went to the Lamar La J. game this afternoon and it was a good game ending up with a score of 14 to 6 in our favor, ofcourse. The best part of it was for me at least that I had the lucky number in a pool which Mac and some of those close to us got up at the start so I came home ahead by $2.50. Dad was the money holder and in some way he had $3.25 in his possession after the game instead of the $2.50 so we are both ahead.

There was not a very big crowd because of its being on Friday afternoon instead of at night. Ofcourse when they planned the schedule they did not know that the weather would be as nice as it is but even at that I guess one would get somewhat chilly at night out there but the crowd would be much better at night,we know.

Right now Tommy is sleeping in preparation for another date (the one to the boss' house in R.F.)with Ida. I hardly see how he could sleep any this evening for last night he went to bed before nine and slept till eight this morning. Mr. Sisson is a little tired I guess tonight for he has had two nights out in succession. He did not do so well at the club last night as he did the week before but his proud wife took home the money with what I call a very mediocre score,4580. I had no idea that such a one would get the prize.

Later—It is now 8:30 and I have just come in from a little practice on our tenor part and so will finish your letter before I put Aunt Fans car up.

Aunt Nell appeared about five thirty so that was the cause of the interruption. She and Aunt F. are out to the Sabin household. She and Fan will go out to the ranch tomorrow if the day is good to see the calves that are being weaned. Ginnie seems to be on the up and up out in San F. at least according to Aunt N and evidently Margaret May gives the same report of her success. At present she does not seem to be particularly interested in the marrying game but is directing all her interest to the advertizing.

Even my hens went to town today and layed me eight eggs. A pretty good record for ten hens, I think. they are getting good care for I feed them and them all day and Dad closes them up at night.

I will now cut out some clippings that I think will interest you and then go mail this.

*   *   *

11/18/45

Dear Mother, Dad, & Tom,

I'm tired this evening since we had a game of touch football this afternoon in the Saipan Sand and Sun. I'm surely out of any kind of shape.

Last night we had our usual every two weeks party, and luckily I had a date,though a short one as Miss Orlando had to go to work at 10:00 p.m. This morning Dr. Wyatt, Miss Orlando, and

Myself went to Mass and this time went to the seaplane base. Father Gallager was long winded—45 min sitting with the sun in our eyes, while he talked about Birth Control. This evening had a dinner, a ride over a little of the island and a show with Orlando so have really been sociable this weekend.

Our skipper Dr Goss is leaving and we are getting a new one this week. Our status here hasn't changed a bit.

Gosh I'm tired so had best hit the sack. Till Later,

All my love, Bill

*   *   *

Monday Nov.19,1945

Dear Bill:

Since Tom has gone down to play cards with Shirley and the Mesch couple(Nancy Gardner and husband) I wont have to hurry with your letter for Dad will mail it when he puts up the car.

We had a letter from you on each of todays mails the first on this mornings mail which you wrote on the 7th and the other this afternoon which you had written on the 11th, Armistice Day. Both were good letters greatly enjoyed by the entire family.

Well, Bill I guess you are learning the hardest lesson in the practice of Medicine, that is seeing some of your patients die and not letting it get you. When you have done the best you know how you have nothing to grieve about and must learn not to dwell on it. The woman whose lung collapsed would have died anyway from some other cause for the Lord had decided it was her time to go and you just happened to be His instrument in that case and no doubt He was letting you learn something thru the experience.

A little interruption—Aunt Betty came and had quite a visit. She read your letters and like us says you must not let the cases that do not do so well bother you.

Yes, you have been in the Navy a year on the 6th of Nov and it wont be very long till it is a year since we have seen you. Tomorrow it will be 26 years since you arrived on this mundane sphere. I still wish I could send that cable tomorrow but you will be in our minds even more than usual tomorrow.

I am so glad that you got the book and evidently that sort of package goes thru quicker than most of them for there are others on the way that I had sent long before I did that one. As soon as I get the others they will be on the way to you.

The party honoring Mrs. Stark has caused a lot of feeling among the ladies of the city, especially those that have worked hard at Red Cross and things like that. I went to the party however yesterday and it was very nice. On the way down Goerings big armored car was out in the street so Dad and I went over to try to get a look at it but there were so many people around it that there was not much chance but this morning I saw it right near as I was at the mail box at the post office they drove into Needhams station for gas. It is really a big car and I bet those boys whose duty it is to drive it all over the country are really having a big time doing it.

Sure glad you got the family group picture, and liked it. You must have a very hard time trying to find out what is the matter with those people over there when they do not speak the language. And so many different languages it is quite a muddle.

You and Miss Orlando had quite a time going to Mass at 5:30 AM and in the rain. Your letter was very interesting especially about the worms. I dont think that eve would like to be nursing one of those in the process of being dewormed.

How do they get all those worms? Is it thru the skin or through the stomach?

Dad may go up to the Springs tomorrow to see the game, the winner of which we play on Thanksgiving. Then next week he and Aunt Fan are going to Denver to see if they can buy some more bulls. I wont go but stay and take care of my "little" boy, who in turn will stay and take care of the office and me.

Must stop now and let Dad get this mailed and then to bed for us.

*   *   *

Tuesday Nov.20,1945

Dear Bill:

This is a perfect day for letter writing, dark and snowy and not the least bit inviting out of doors. It all started up quite quickly too for when Aunt Fan and I went to Mass at seven this morning I remarked what a perfect morning it was, about nine thirty it began to be quite cloudy and started to snow thick and fast about noon or a little before.

Dad went to Colorado Springs with Mr. McCauley, the two coaches and Mac and they do not have a very good day for the trip so for the game which they went to see. There is no wind so the snow is not drifting and it is not very cold so it is not freezing which helps a lot.

I looked back in my files and find that I sent you "Green Years" on Aug. 24. Over two, nearly three months reaching you but since it was sent to your Okinawa address that is not so bad at that.

Woke up with a headache this morning,sinus I think for it was right between my eyes, so I have not been worth shooting today and invigled little Justine to go to bridge club this afternoon in my place. It is about gone now but I fell like a rag, just good and lazy from lying around all day when I should have been ironing or doing something useful.

Guess the girls in the court house are getting a big kick out of your brother like they do your dad, with all his kidding of them etc. A day or two ago when he and Leila were over there reading Mr. Moorhead came over to see them and when he got to the door he asked the girls "Where are my two girls" so since then they have really been razing Tom, calling him Mr. M's girl etc.

I think when you were here last year you got your eye on a cute little teacher,Miss Rasmussen(dont think that is spelled right but it sounds like that) and now you brother has his eye on her too but he goes one farther than you do and is going to try to get a date with her. Mac, (Bob Mc.) is trying to fix it up for him and he has been very anxious lest it would fix it for tonight and he has his high powered?

date with Martha for tonight. "He says it would be just my luck for this to be the night" but so far Mac has not called so guess he is safe.

Aunt Mayme went up to Idaho springs yesterday to spend Thanksgiving with the Farthings. The Sisks wont come down, Tommy will go to the game so there wont be many of us at the Sabins for dinner, four of them and three of us. Marg will be with her mother that day but maybe when Christmas comes both she and Bud will be with us. Next year I hope we can all be together again in one great big family like we used to be. Maybe even the Rourke clan would join us then. It wont be really Christmas till we have you and Gene both home at least in the states. Fred is wishing he could be out by Christmas so they could have one more Christmas together before the Sisk give up their house in Trinidad. Those two kids are a bit unreasonable about the sale of the house I think for neither of them will ever live in Trinidad again so why should Aunt Nell and Charles want to live there just to keep the house when they come home,maybe once a year, for a few years longer and after that maybe once in ten years.

Johnny is still having a hard time to get the things he needs to start up his business. He has quite a stock but no counters etc over which to make his sales and it is so hard to get anyone to do anything. It is good that Bert Jones is home and working again but he too is already busy as a bee but is trying to help John get going. They are going to make some changes at the drug store after Christmas. Take out that dirty hole of a refreshment room and put the soda fountain clear back against that north wall, throwing the whole thing into one room, and get the place cleaned up and with Fred Jones now on the job maybe it can be kept that way. It is surely dirty now.

Seems good to see so many of our own now getting into things here at home. Stu is working away in the bookstore and H.F. at the hardware store, Tom is in the Abstract office Roy Roath with his father, Marsh Seirks with Larsens. Marsh and Ella Jane are not planning on remaining here tho but expect to locate somewhere else for themselves. Bob Barnes it out of the army too and will go back railroading.

It is getting quite dark tho it is yet early but I had better go out and close the hens up for the night. They did not falter today but gave me six eggs so had better try to keep them warm tonight so they wont let up the good work. Eggs at the stores are about 60 cents so you see they are really profitable old girls.

*   *   *

Wednesday Nov.21,1945

Dear Bill:

While I was at Pomps this afternoon Marjorie Perry came in and so ofcourse the topic of conversation became "Bill" She asked if your birthday was not right here somewhere and when I told her yesterday she said for me to send you belated greetings from her. She told me that Betty is living in a trailor following Jim around just now they are somewhere in Missouri,I cant remember the little town by name. She says Betty gets quite a kick out of the baby's talking to all the darkies down there.

Speaking of tactless people I think that Mrs. Marshall, Archie's grandmother is the world's worst. She came in the bank this morning where I was selling bonds and seemed sort of befuddled which to me did not seem at all unusual but she explained it in this way. She said "I have seen so many sad people this morning that I am all upset. First I went into the beauty shop where Mrs. Strain was and when I asked her what they would do on Thanksgiving she began to cry. Then I went up to the flower shop and Mrs. Kendall was in there and I asked her if they would be with their little daughter on Thanksgiving and she began to cry." Can you beat some people? Then when I was telling H.F. and Tom about it H.F. said "that is like the break Mr. Woodruff made in the store yesterday. He was telling me how glad he was to see me home etc. and then he turned to Mr. Kendall and said 'Dean isnt it great to see all these boys back again'." Well that was even worse than poor Mrs. M.'s but ofcourse neither of them thought of what they were saying.

Pop is having poker club tonight and everything is in complete readiness,the new table all set up and the cigars etc gathered in. Aunt Fan and I will go to church and as usual I will stay for choir practice. Dont know what T. will be doing but he has a big day tomorrow for he and a load of kids are going to the game in Pueblo. At noon he had eight and more accepting his kind invitation to go to the game so think that the decision finally was that there should really be another car to take all the crowd who wanted to accompany him. Aunt Betty has the turkey all ready for the oven,a job which I had said I would do for her but I had forgotten that I had to go to the bank this morning and so she did it herself. There is simply no sense in anyone being in the bank to sell bonds these days for no body is buying them this time. Maybe they just have us do it for the advertizement it is. Sort of keep the public conscious that the drive is still on.

Wonder if you are or have eaten turkey today. It did all most come on your birthday this year. I bought you a new hair brush this morning when I was at Pomps. One of those good ones, not quite as good as the Fullers used to be but they are not obtainable now. I will send it in a package and end of this week.

The Wests were telling me that Junior had received some of his Christmas packages so your should be getting some too. By the way have you had a letter from Aunt Gertrude lately. She says that she has written you several but that she has had no reply. Too Aunt Fan wrote you about the time you left Okinawa. Did you ever get that letter.

We had a letter from Uncle John this afternoon in which he said that Gene was coming to the U.S. He was to be in San Diego yesterday and from what he said guess he is on his way to New York. Gene says it will be some time yet till he is out of the Navy. I suppose their route would be via the Panama canal and John did not know how long they would be in San Diego so unless they had other news their plan was to be in San Diego when he got in.

Tommy got thru the date with Martha but did not have a real hot time for "that girl gets in my hair".

Aunt Betty called up the Sisks this afternoon and Nellie thought that they would drive down for dinner tomorrow. We just cant understand what has come over "Charlie" but just hope it lasts whatever it is.

Dad and the men who went to Colorado Springs to the game got home about 8:30 but were sort of cold as it was awfull cold at the game. The storm did not amount to much here and the sun came out nice and bright this morning but it has stayed pretty chilly today. The weather man says it will warm up tomorrow. Even with the cold the hens laid seven eggs again today.

Now I will go put the supper on the table and then wake your brother up to come get it. He has acquired the habit of taking a little nap every evening just before supper time.

*   *   *

11/22/45

Dear Mother, Dad & Tom,

Today is Thanksgiving and we have a holiday though I unfortunately have the duty as O.D. We are to have our big Dinner this evening and have seen the menu with turkey with all the trimmings.

I passed my birthday quite quietly. I have received several of your boxes including two X-mas and the book. I opened one with the cake in it and it was o.k. Thanks a million.

Had a big time last night Nichols another of the jg's, and myself had dates. We went down to the Fleet Officers Club to the dance. My date was Orlando. It was a good orchestra and good date, but the place though very large was hot and crowded. Since we had dates they let us sit in the Senior Officers bar. It was a good time.

This morning they had Four Marriages at the Charan Kanoa. One of the Girls works on the Male Tb ward and invited me down. Orlando also was invited to another one so we took it in at

4:00 AM. (when we had to get up.). After the wedding we then had breakfast at both houses,which was really not bad food, but hope I don't get any worms.

This afternoon the Milt. Gov't is having Boat races and a swimming meet. Tonight there are several dances, but I'm OD.

You asked about Dr. Wyatt. He practiced in Canon City until the war and knows Best, Donahue, and Fred Jones. He has enough points and is now waiting to get his orders to go home. If he gets to L.J. he said he'd give you a ring. He is a swell egg.

I just got a V-mail letter mailed in May now think that airmail is the best bet.

I used up another roll of film this morning and am about out, so if Dad could get a few rolls of 616, for me I will probably be here to use them.

Our set-up is still unchanged. I surely hope that this G-10 never functions. We have already sent two of our men back to the states and several more in the near future.

I was interested to learn of Geraldine Serafini's Marriage. John and she were never headed for the altar, mainly because she is a Catholic I think.

Bob has had this Business venture of his in mind for some time and they are a good bunch of boys. I tried to talk him into letting me invest a little in it. So maybe if I can borrow a little money from the folks one of these days I'll do it.

Ole Tom and his women. He always has about six he is interested in. I'd surely like to get the low down on them.

One of the big Carriers—Bon Homme Richard left here the other day with about 4,000 men. There are now very few waiting for transportation.

I guess that is all the news for now.

All my Love, Bill

*   *   *

Thanksgiving Day in the evening.

Dear Bill:

It is now about five thirty and we are home after a very pleasant day at the Sabins. The Sisks did come down and have just left waiting for the sun to set so it would not be in their eyes all the way home. The turkey was good and in the serving Aunt Betty saved all the dishes she could so that it was no burden to wash them. I walked home with Justine to get in her daily exercise and then took her down to the shop where poor Johnnie has been painting all afternoon. He was thru and now that the glass for the window has come and he can get that fixed dont think it will be very long till he can open up.

Tom and his gang,which finally settled itself at six got off to the game and have had a wonderful day, cool but nice and clear all the time. The game did not come out so well for La Junta,32 to 7 but suppose they have had a good time any way and may spend the evening up there if they can find anything to do. Am anxious to hear what he thought of the game. If the boys could have made that one touchdown at the beginning instead of in the third quarter I think it might have made some difference.

I think that I had better finish up my Thanksgiving by ironing a shirt for Tommy to wear in the morning to work for I had to iron one for him to wear to Pueblo this morning. I had been so lazy I had not done one bit of the ironing yet this week and since I did not wash last week his shirt supply was very low. There was still one white one in the drawer this morning but when he went to put it on the sleeves came most to his elbow. He keeps saying that he will buy some more, the colored ones are obtainable, but he just does not get the job done.

The Dr. Cashes are expecting another baby the first of Dec. cesarian of course and a few weeks or maybe it was just days ago she had a bad fall and hurt her back. They took her right to Denver and she is now all right but the Dr. wont let her leave there. Her mother was buried yesterday but they would not let her even come to the funeral. Dr. Cash is trying and hoping to be here and out by the first.

Aunt Nell talked to Virginia today. She was having dinner with her artist (the girl who works at Magnins too) and all was fine with her. She has a reservation for the 23 of Dec on the air line but is a bit worried for now they say they are going to cancel 75% of the reservations for the boys who want to get home for Christmas. She and Margaret Mae could not get them the same day so M.M.'s is the day before.

Since all did this afternoon was listen to the game over KOKA,did not even get any gossip I am all out of news so will stop for this time.

*   *   *

11/28/45

Dear Dad, Mother & Tom

It has been quite awhile since I wrote a letter to the office. I've been neglectful w/ my letter writting these last couple of months.

Thanks a lot for taking care of the Ins. Policy for me. That makes about $180 I've put in that thing. Now that I've got it I don't know what to do with it.

It really sounds like quite a football season L.J. has had. Have been following it right along. Poor ole Boulder lost to Denver. We hear a game every Sunday. This Sunday it will be Army and Navy.

Glad to hear ole T. has put on a little wt. I weigh about the same I imagine as I did when I was home. Put on a little in Hawaii lost on Okinawa, and back to normal on Saipan. Okinawa now seems like it never happened. I couldn't ever have been that far from Colorado.

Inclosed is the little checque with which I'd like for you to get something for Mother for Christmas. Till Later,

All my love, Bill

*   *   *

11/28/45

Dear Mother, Dad, and Tom,

Missed writting to you Sunday, and shall try to make it up today. Sunday Rankin had a couple of Army doctors down for the day. They have been helping him with his pathology and we've learned the real diagnosis of a good many of our cases. We played Bridge on the beach, went for a sailboat race, had a good dinner and a show. We may go up to their hospital this Saturday for a dance.

There are lots of rumors around here about sending the Japs back to Okinawa and Japan. If they would It would almost close this place down. However it is all rumors without basis. They still have a few Japs on this island that haven't surrendered, but plans have been made to do so this Saturday.

My female Med. Ward has been busy this past week. Two cases of meningitis—two peritonitis one a ruptured appendix which died last night. I'd surely be in the dog house in the states, but—I wonder if I should even turn myself loose on the public. Also have a case of cancer and a Gall bladder.

This afternoon Rankin and I went sailing. Dr. Wyatt left today for Colorado. He left his old sailboat to Rankin and I and can have a lot of fun with it.

The staff of the hospital has surely gone down. Four doctors have left and we have one more on temporary duty. It doesn't make much difference in our work because we were doing most of it anyway.

Have received several more Christmas packages from the Rourkes, Aunt Gertrude, and two more from you. Also the Money order from Aunt Fan. Hope that next year that I'll be enjoying Christmas with you.

Had announcement of Bill Davidson's Marriage. He married a girl from N.Y. he's known for some time.

You asked how these people get worms—Eat the eggs for one way. Hookworm from the mud through the skin of the feet.

I have a favor to ask of you Mother. Being unable to find appropriate gifts for X-Mas here I wonder if you might find a little something for Dad Tom and Aunt Fan w/ the inclosed checque. Till later,

All my Love, Bill

*   *   *

November 29,1945

Dear Bill:

It is now about 9:30 and since Tom is at the show this letter will not be mailed tonight but perhaps is will go out sometime tomorrow morning so I will write it. I have a lot of clippings,four days papers to cut from, so will have to put them in two envelopes so that they will not weigh over the six oz (the limit in weight), some of them will not interest you perhaps but I have made a guess them might. Do you remember Vera Mae who got married? The little fat girl who used to work for me and lived over the North La Junta store and how thrilled she would be when I would send you to take her home.

The best of all news that I have tonight is that Bud will report at Ft. Logan the 4th for his discharge. Marg and Bobby are going up to meet him and then Bobby can have a look at the sights especially the May Co windows decorated with animated figures, Santa etc. for Christmas.

John Geiger is home and already out and Tom Stjernholm (guess that is not spelled right) is on a ship on the high seas for his Navy assignment.

Tom is going to start this trip to Boulder tomorrow with Tom Woodruff accompanying. They spend tomorrow night in Colorado Springs where Tom has a date with Julia. She called this eve in response to a letter he had written her asking for a date. She can not spend the Christmas vacation with us but did not explain over the phone or else Tom did not get it, something about her father coming out this way about that time. She will get a date for Tom W. too.

Dad and Aunt Fan have deserted me for the "hay" so guess I had better follow. I have to get up in the morning and go sing at 7 for a High Mass so had really better get some sleep. Tom and Roy Black went to the show saying they would be in really but dont know just what that may mean, midnight perhaps.

*   *   *

12/2/45

Dear Mother, Dad, & Tom,

I've been in the Pacific for 11 mo. now, hope I don't have too many more to go.

We have a new Captain or Skipper of the hospital by the name of Frezmann. He seems to be a good egg.

Last night they had a big party with free drinks and everything. Rankin & I thought we had dates with some army nurses, but they were on a hospital ship and the darn thing left yesterday. I spent the evening at the show and then went up to see Walsh on the hill and played bridge. Rankin did an autopsy. I returned just in time to be the escort (all dates have to have an accompanying armed male) for the Captain who lives on the beach here. He'd had plenty to drink & It surely did not take long to find out what kind of a fellow he is. I wouldn't stay in the Navy even if I had starved outside.

Went to Mass with Miss Orlando this morning. She sewed the sail on the boat for us yesterday so we are now all set to sail around.

Today I'm O.D. so shall close as haven't much other News. Received three packages the other day from you with canned food. Haven't Inspected your special job, but will let you know how they are. Till Later,

All my Love

*   *   *

Monday Dec.3,1945

Dear Bill:

Your very good letter of the 22nd,Thanksgiving day came Saturday and we did enjoy it a lot. Too bad you had to be OD that day but it looks as if you sort of made up for it the week end before with all the activities you attended. Glad to know that you had turkey and all the trimmings just like we did here in the states. Glad to know that the cake went thru all right and if you like fruit cake I could send you another one like that if you want so let me know.

I see that there are advantages besides just being entertained to taking a girl to the dances. You got to sit in the senior officers bar. by now you should know whether you got any worms from eating the Native food in their home at the weddings. I wish you had told us what sort of food it was and how it was served. Do they have dishes like we do, tables, chairs etc.? And how about making yourself understood. Did the girl who worked on the ward speak English? Now there is material for another letter if you run out of news for us. Oh,yes. And why the early hour for the event.

Dad talked to Fred Jones this morning about Dr. Wyatt and he says he is the best internal medical man that he knows but that Dr. W. does not like surgery. Dad also got you a couple of rolls of film this morning and so I will send you a box this week with them in it and hope it goes thru to you as quickly as possible.

Mrs. Inman says that Bob will not get here for christmas as he had thought he might. Things just have not moved along as quickly as he had planned they might.

Tom has not yet arrived from Denver and may not come today. It just depended on how they got along and ofcourse I think that they would want to stop again on the way home in Colorado Springs.

Martha Klob Hummel died Saturday from a Caesarian in Denver so you see other doctors lose their patients too when it seems like it should not be but just as I told you the Lord takes them when he wants them regardless of the care etc they have. I dont know what happened that they had to take the baby (it is living) for it was about 7 1/2 months.

I did a lot of work today, washed this AM and then went down town to try to get a few things this afternoon. It is a very slow process for there are not enough clerks who know anything in any of the stores. Ofcourse the morning is the best time for such business but I could not make it just now.

Better run and get Dad and will finish this later.

Dad was talking to Dr. Rowden this afternoon and he said that he got the letter telling him that you were on the island the very day he was leaving. He knows right where you are though and the hospital you are in.

We had a letter from Aunt Hattie this morning telling us about their visit with Eugene. She did not tell us what he is to be doing or any thing like that but did say that this will be the third Christmas that he has been away from so guess at least he does not expect to get home for that event. Said that some of the officers on the ship had a two week leave but that she thought Gene wanted to save his till later. Dont know what she meant by that. They evidently met Gene at San Diego and then went home with him for a day and took him back again when they went on the ship and all. Said she would not have missed that for anything.

Will stop now and go get in the rest of the laundry.

*   *   *

12/5/45

Dear Mother, Dad, & Tom,

Here it is December—Only one year ago in December I was with you all in Calif. That was a lucky break for me.

Yesterday Rankin and I went up to the Army Hospital where he was to present a case to a Pathological conference. He & I sat in the front row, afterwards during the discussion one of the voices sounded like one of the fellows in class. After the meeting I found that it was he. A boy from Utah by the name of Karschner. He has been on Saipan for quite a while & is now a Captain. Though we weren't ever very close friends it was surely good to see him & hear of some of the other boys.

I am enclosing a picture another doctor took at the club one afternoon, and from it you  can see what a rough life we are having. The other fellow is Dr. McClintock who had temporary duty here for awhile.

This afternoon Walsh and I went sailing and took his dog along. It was quite windy and we shipped a little water occasionally but our expert seamanship kept us on an even keel.

Haven't much other news for the present—until Later,

All my Love, Bill

*   *   *

Friday Dec,7,1945

Dear Bill:

This should be a newsy letter for I did not write yesterday so I have news of two days to make up the contents of this epistle. However there are just the usual happenings of the day to report. We had the club last night and I really had a rather hectic time getting ready for it for I had electricians here all morning putting some floor plugs and doing a lot of just little things that have been needing attention for a long time but since the war began could not get anyone to do them so these fellows said they could come as they had a day or two between big jobs so did not dare put them off. Then just after lunch was over and I was about to make a good start at getting the house in order Mrs. Lane came over and sat for about an hour. Just the same everything was in apple-pie order and I had my hair all pretty and everything when it was time to go down and eat.

Do you remember meeting the Boyds when you went to the dinner with us last year at Major Moberlys up the street in the next block? they belong to the Thursday night club now and last night met Tom for the first time. Mrs. B. told Dad that we surely do have the finest boys. ofcourse we know that but were glad to know that she knew it too. Really they have never forgotten about meeting you and always refer to it when they ask about you.

Today was a big day in two ways. Johnny opened up his shop and it seemed to over in a big way. He had almost more business than he could take care of by himself and was as happy as a kid with a little red wagon. By noon he had ten watches in for repair and I went in just after,when I took the men back to the office and there were two more in there then. He had five or six big boquets of flowers, gifts of different stores and individuals. The Needhams had sent a basket, the Sheridans, The Roaths, The Democrat, Mrs. Mayer, and the Sissons, are the ones I recall.

The big thing was that we got your two letters with pictures in them. The first we have had since you left Hawaii, so we surely did fill our eyes. None of us could see that the two very professional fellows looked like you but guess it is the moustache which conceals your identity. Ofcourse your dad had to show the one with the open air latrine to the girls at the office and make a few remarks. You can guess the sort,I think.

I got the check for $15 and will try my best to do as you wish but it wont take the place of having you here to do it yourself.

Am so glad that you got the Christmas boxes and only wish that we could have sent you something worthwhile but when you open them there will be a lot of love spilling out to you with each little trifle so maybe that will help.

Speaking about the rumors that are about over there(I sure hope they are true if it would mean that they would send you this way) Dr. Rowden told Dad that they are going to close all the hospitals on the island but one and that that one would not be the one that you are in. dad said that you thought that you would be home by June and he said he will beat that by considerable. More rumor? Perhaps.

I heard this eve, but not from the Herrons that Rosy is going to be married soon to a boy by the name of Karney. His uncle is Joe Karney, a sort of cripple who used to work around out Higbee way and now lives out in the Fairmont way. The Herrons like him because he neither smokes or drinks but she has been going with him only a short time and is only 18. Gosh!

Aunt Fan went to Pueblo today and had a car full. Hay, Mrs. Herron, Mrs. Morris and Mrs. Lane. They were back by four oclock so guess they all got done in a hurry.

Julia is coming tonight so we will wait and have a little supper after she gets here, about eight. Dont know what she and Tom are going to do for entertainment this eve and may have to resort to a game of bridge with the old folks.

The gang with Tom as the spark are planning a dance at the Country club the Sunday eve before Christmas for about twenty five couples. They will have exclusive use of it that night and with dinner and the orchestra will cost each one about $4.25. for the couple.

Sounds like you and Rankin had quite a time with the army medicos and hope the return party was as much fun and they got you a date or were you to take Orlando to the dance. Surely was good of Dr. Wyatt to leave you and Rankin his boat, but dont go out too far in the thing.

Think that perhaps I had better get the table set etc for the supper so will close for this time.

*   *   *

12/9/45

Dear Mother, Dad, & Tom,

Another weekend has passed which has been a very enjoyable one. Yesterday was rather an outdoor one with sailing and tennis and ping pong on the porch. The sailing was really good as we had a fine wind. In fact too much at times as Walsh with whom I was racing tipped his boat over and sunk. He and Nichols raised it ok. I fell out of the one I was in but fortunately It didn't tip over. I bailed it out and made it back to shore. They have just completed a grand tennis court next to our quarters and we tried it out.

After Mass this morning with the Captain and Miss Orlando, Mary (Miss Orlando), another nurse, and myself went to the Japanese games which were held yesterday and today. They were much like a track meet with about three thousand children participating. Went to Mass yesterday, too. This afternoon Nichols, my roommate (Baker), Mary, and the other nurse went riding and saw most of Saipan. This evening the show with Mary—So had a quite a day with her.

Am Enclosing an Invitation to the Japanese Games held a week ago—that I didn't get to see—thought you might like to see their style of writing. Also Enclosed is a menu for a Japanese dinner we had last week. It was really Japanese—Though very interesting not a very good everyday diet.

All my love, Bill

*   *   *

Dec.10,1945

Dear Bill:

Whew! the weatherman came all in a hurry night before last and in the morning all was white with snow about two inches. It looked as if it was really going to keep it up so we persuaded Julia to wait till this morning to go back to Colorado Springs, chiefly because she would have had to go on the bus yesterday and you know how I like the idea of buses on slippery roads. However it cleared in the afternoon but got very cold, in fact the temperature went to 10 below in the night. I went to Mass this morning not knowing it had been that cold. Guess if I had I would have about frozen,as it was I got along very nicely,a little trouble getting Aunt Fans car started but saw many people being pushed and others just standing along the streets and when I got to Hartmans after church for the milk found that they could not start either their car or pick-up so I did a little good deed and brought Roberta in to high school.

The Toms got Julia down to the train for 8:30 but T.waited there with her till 9:30 and then they put him off the train so he left and isnot sure just when she got started on her homeward journey. We enjoyed her visit a lot but are all a little puzzled about a ring that she is wearing on the third finger of her left hand. It is not the conventional diamond but a pearl and none of us had the gumption to ask about it so do not know whether it has any significance or not.

We just had a telegram that Marian and Marsden will get here Wednesday afternoon on their way home for good. He is discharged and so they will be home for Christmas. they are in Springfield and staying there just one day so I imagine they will leave here Friday. Ofcourse I dont blame them for wanting to get home as quickly as possible.

I have to go to USO tonight and I dont want to get out in the cold. Christmas eve will be my turn again but I am going to tell them "so soap" for if I get the turkey stuffed etc,I think I may be somewhat busy about that time. I had hoped that it would be closed before that time but it looks now as if it may go on for a while longer.

Tom and Julia did not do anything exciting but I dont think she was bored. After she came Friday eve we had dinner and then just sat and talked for quite a while and about time for the old folks to go to bed the kids went off. Think they went out to the Country club and sat about etc and danced a time or two. Sat eve we played bridge(Julia is really pretty good at it) till again it was bedtime for Dad and me and then they went out to the inn. Last night we again had a little round of cards and later about seven (I made a mistake, it was afternoon we played cards) they went to the show. Saturday afternoon Julia and I made her duty calls, the Sevitz especially, the Larsens and the Garlingtons, she wanted to go there.

See I am about out of paper so will stop.

*   *   *

12/16/45

Dear Mother, Dad, & Tom,

Here it is Sunday night—a week has gone by and I haven't written to you.—It seems difficult to get down to write letters. I have not written anyone this Christmas. We could send Christmas greetings by cablegram if we got them in by yesterday noon— Before doing so a fellow in the Male Tb. ward Developed a perforated appendix, which consumed my attention for the rest of the day and I forgot all about the cable till today. The guy is still alive, but he has so much Tb. I don't see how he can live anyway. Appendicitis is more common than we previously thought and very difficult to diagnose.

Today I had a very enjoyable time. I went to Communion this morning (confession last night). Had lunch on the beach at the nurses area with Mary, a couple other nurses and Walsh. We swam and had a fine time. Had dinner and were to see a show, but could not find one that sounded appealing so just sat around the Club.

It surely doesn't seem like Christmas time. They are having dances at the Club Christmas and New Years and fortunately asked Mary before the others so have had dates for both. It will make it a lot nicer now.

Can't think of much more news for the present; so until later,

All my love,

Dr. Rowden was right about closing all the hospitals except three—one army—one navy and this one at least for a while. Even if they close this one there is only one way I'll get back to the states and that is when my 18 mo. are up. So doubt that I can be home before August or September—unless something happens.

*   *   *

12/17/45

Dear Mother, Dad, & Tom,

Another month we've been on Saipan which makes three all together. Today we got our orders for Permanent Duty at this hospital; so it is no longer G-10 Comp24. I'm surely glad of that. I rather imagine that we'll stay right here now until our 18 mo. are up or they close the hospital down which is not likely. I don't think you could ask for better duty as far as work goes. The living quarters can't be Beat, a wonderful Club, lots of transportation, and for the present at least a good date once in awhile.

You asked about the meal for the wedding Breakfast in Charan Kanoa. These people have rather inadequate housing and about 4-5 families live in one house. They had a table set in the backyard setting the bride, groom, and Americans, and a few big shots. The rest of the neighborhood stood around and watched us eat. They served the food on plates, which consisted mostly of starchy things like rice, several different kinds of bread and cake. The protein was mostly G-I forms even Spam fixed up in their own style which I'm afraid I can't describe. They had coffee which was very good. It tasted much more like our food than the Japanese dishes do. I took some pictures but something has happened to the camera, and they did not come out very well. Till Later,

All my Love, Bill

*   *   *

Monday Dec.17,1945

Dear Bill:

Just a week from tomorrow will be Christmas and we will be thinking more of you than anything else. I guess it is a good thing that I have to get the dinner for I cant sit around and gloom about your not being here or else the turkey might burn. You have not said if you were keeping your packages to open on Christmas or whether you are opening them as they come. I imagine it wont seem much like Christmas so guess it is just as well if you opened them as they arrived. I will be glad when 1945 is gone for then it will be getting pretty close for the time to come when you will be heading this way.

We got your letter this morning with the picture of "Sisson, the surgeon" in it. We all like it better than that one taken on Okinawa entitled "Really Professional". No one can see any resemblance in it to you,except your posture. In the one that came today we think you are working a poor colored boys hand.

Cant quite see why it is necessary that one on a date must be accompanied by "an armed male escort". Has it been that way ever since you have been on Saipan? One cant do much love making that way, can he?

Tommy and I are finally going to go out to Cransons this eve and take a wool blanket as a gift for Walt and his bride. last eve about six he and Margaret Driscoll (she seems to be the lucky one just now) came in and announced that they had come for something to eat. I made some sandwiches and cocoa and with some store cookies,that was it. Afterward we played bridge till about ten. Margaret has not played a great deal of contract but will make a very good player when she has had more practice. You know your brother tho, he likes to play with some one who can really make tricks out of nothing, like his brother but since it was Margaret guess he was not bored.

I trimmed a little tree yesterday which I set on the table. It looks quite pretty for I have a good many lights and ornaments on it. I put the table right in front of the middle west window and behind the tree on the window sill I have that seven candle electric lights so when it is all lit it serves as our Christmas decoration, and not too bad.

Dad had to make a trip out to Cheraw just after noon today to inspect a house for a loan. He gets five dollars every time he makes an inspection like that but he did not relish this one much but after the day warmed up a little he did not mind so much. We have wondered all weekend about Marian and Marsden and how they got along. Bet from now on all the vile language they can use will not be strong enough for them in describing Colorado as compared to lovely California?. I began to fear that Dad was going to put Marsden out in the cold for he did not hesitate to tell us continually the wonders of his native state.

Mrs. Stone told me last night that tomorrow would be the last day she would help me for a while at least as Lewis is on his way home to stay and they will be busy hunting a house. guess I will send the shirts to the laundry for a while at least till the holidays are over. And the warm weather comes again. I have a little bit of ironing to do in the basement now so must run along and get it out of the way before we wash again tomorrow.

*   *   *

Christmas eve, Monday Dec,24,1945

Dear Bill:

Your Christmas is about over and ours is yet to be. We are so glad that we had your letters today and yesterday for we have been thinking of you and Mary having a nice time at the dance. The one that you wrote on Monday came yesterday,Sunday (we had mail delivery since it is so near Christmas)—telling us that you had been made permanent party at that base and the one you wrote on sunday did not get here till today. We did enjoy reading about what you ate at the wedding and how it was served etc.

It was good news to us that the chances of your being moved to some of the little out of the way islands are now out of the picture and coming just at Christmas gave us quite a lift to fill up the vacancy your absence causes.

Surely hope you can get your camera fixed up so that you can again take pictures for we do like to see them.

In about half an hour we are going to open our presents and then all the family but me will retire to their snuggly beds. The Toms are going to go to church at 9:30 in the morning and if I get things ready to night so I can get away will go with them again for the choir is supposed to be there to sing carols. when we were practicing yesterday Fathers, both of them and some of the ladies were fixing the crib and they all complimented us on the music, said it sounded grand. We sing the "Silent,Night" achapello, (That is queer spelling but guess you get what I mean.) in the dark.

Aunt Nell and Ginny are coming down in the morning as Chas. goes out tomorrow morning for four days. They will stay over one night at least and since Jimmy Taylor is here I am wondering if perhaps he will persuade Ginny to wait for the Koshare formal on Thursday eve.

Jimmy has asked some of the boys for "Tom and Jerrys" in the morning. Bud and Bill Guthrie are also among those asked.

After all his bother and fuss,Tom did not get to enjoy the party last night very much for he was not feeling well and came home about ten-thirty. He had the trots yesterday and got to chilling out there. I thought that he might be getting the flu. I covered him up good and put hot water bottle to him. He felt sort of sick to his tummy so finally got him to take soda water and after a while he got to sleep. This morning I gave him a dose of castor oil and after it did its work he began to feel a lot better and seems very normal tonight. He did not have any fever any time so I abandoned the idea of flu when I found that out. Was I right,Doctor.

Guess Dad has told you that he had your license renewed for you. So you are in good standing in the state of Colorado again.

Aunt Mayme is with us tonight and that helps to swell our little Christmas tree party a little. She has just talked to dud. I said "hello" too. They are fine and Judy had been in a little program at the church.

Well Tom has come and now if Aunt Fan has her prayers said we will open the gifts, the five of us.

*   *   *

12/26/45

Dear Mother, Dad, & Tom,

I'm surely letting myself slip at this letter writing. I have hardly wished you all a Merry Christmas. I have lots of unanswered letters waiting for me.

It has been really quite Christmasy around here though it just doesn't quite seem that it is really that time of year. Christmas Eve we had a half day holiday—After a short while on the beach Rankin Orlando and I went to Charan Kanoa for the school party. It was an interesting event with all the children doing little songs and dances. You could see the influence of Uncle Sam for they waved the flag and sang some of our hymns. They had a Santa Claus who brought them each a present. He rode up in a cart drawn by an old black cow dressed up like the real thing.

In the evening Mary, Rankin and I had dinner together—then a short while in the club. Then with another nurse we went to the 5th Marine M.P. Battalion to meet her date and pick up Walsh. We then went to Mid night Mass at Charan Kanoa, where they had hard seats reserved for us. Most of the people had to stand up outside as the Church is really small.

I really enjoyed opening your Christmas packages, I couldn't have wanted anything other than what you sent. Aunt Gertrude sent a big can of fudge w/ nuts, Marion & Marsdon some nuts & candy and the Rourkes a nice stationary outfit. Unless things are sealed in cans they don't keep too well. Aunt Betty sent a neat box of anchovies, olives, and other things. Two of the Chamorros from the dispensary—Delores Panglenian and Jose Torres, each gave me a present—a small necklace and Bracelet from Delores and a woven bag from Jose. I don't know what I'll do with them, but I think they may have thought they would be nice for Miss Orlando. I asked them if they could get me some flowers for Mary and I went down yesterday to pick them up—You should have seen all of the flowers. Two card board boxes. Enough for all the nurses and more. One of the Tb. patients gave me a nice Cane someone made at Charan Kanoa.

Christmas I fortunately had an all day date with Mary. In the afternoon they had a dance at the headquarters for the Military Gov't Farm. It was cool and beautiful there. They have a place where we dance then sit on the lawn—really like a vacation. Last night had a dinner on the beach—and another dance at the Club with the best band on the Island—16 pieces all professionals I think.

I can surely use all of the gifts you sent. I don't know how I managed to do it, but I really didn't open them till Christmas day. I was surely lucky for all my packages came. Some—as Rankin and Mary didn't get their packages. The chess game, cards, cans of food, hankies, stationery and everything was surely appropriate. But next Christmas I only want one present and that is to be with you.

Next week is New Years and I have a date. All these dates aren't going to last as Mary has her points and will soon be going home.

Haven't much other news. Hope you have a happy New Year & that before it ends I'll be home.

All my love, Bill

*   *   *

Wednesday Dec.26,1945

Dear Bill:

Christmas is over and now we can begin to look forward to 4th of July and the day when you will come sailing home.

Everything went off in splendid order starting with Mid-night Mass. I had a beau to accompany me and as I had to go alone as far as Family was, I was glad to have him. He was Dick,who came up early and left his coat he would wear here and then went down town for the evening. About eleven he came back and we started about 11:30. My goodness!when we got there all the parking places for blocks around had been filled do Dick said "If you want to get out here I will park the car." I was a little flabbergasted for I did not know he knew the first thing about driving but I accepted his offer and guess he got along fine for after Mass (the choir was late getting out as we received Communion after the Mass) there he was waiting for me at the front door with the car just in front. I could not sleep very well for the music kept going through my head. Guess I was a little tired and nervous, so got up with a little headache. I had set the tables while waiting for 11:30 to come the night before so was pretty well along and went to the 9 o'clock Mass with Dad and Tom. The Sisks phoned they would be a little late so dinner was set up for 1:30 at the earliest which gave me still more time to do the few things that were left to do. aunt Fan and to our great surprise, Aunt Mayme went to the eleven mass so I had the house all to myself and no one to interfere with my work by too much conversation. About 20 minutes to two we decided that I would put the rolls in and eat with out the Sisks so just when we had the plates ready and were setting them on the table in they came so all went off just fine. Bobby was so cute but he did want Aunt Justine to go to the little room in the basement and play. His Dad was getting more fun out of the toys he got then he was I think. He had a silly cat thing which when the string underneath are pulled did all sorts of silly things like sitting down etc and Dad kept telling Bud "Let the poor kid have his toys for a little while at least" You know the kind of "ribbing" Dad would give him. About four Marg, Bud and Bobby went home and soon after that Virginia, Aunts Betty and Nell went to the show, Justine and Johnny went over to see the Hahs and what the twins got for Christmas so while they were all gone aunt Mayme and I had naps and Dad and Aunt Fan listened to "Fibber and Mollie". Ofcourse Tom was already off with Margaret. About eight John and Justine came back and we played bridge till the rest of the folks came back and then we all had a bite to eat. So it was about ten when the day was finally over and all went home.

Mayme went back to her ranch and Nell and Ginny went to Trinidad today. Ginny is coming back for the Koshare formal tomorrow night so spect Nellie will bring her. They had a call from Fred last eve telling them he will be here next Monday for a ten day furlough before getting his discharge. He wants to look up a location while out here.

My! My! I did not report on the gifts opening or tell you what you gave all the family. Well you gave Dad a down comfort. Can you beat that? But I bet he appreciates it more when he has slept under it. I put it on his bed this morning and bet he is surprised for I think that he thought I persuaded Tom that he and you should give it to him so I could use it and my motives was not like that at all. You gave Tom a tie clasp set with chain for keys etc. and you gave me a lovely lapel pin, the first sale that Johnny made,after he opened up. the Sabins gave the Sisson family some nice drinking glasses Aunt Fan gave me some pretty bedroom slippers, Hay, a nightie, Eleanor a cute apron, the Sisks some bath powder and lotion, the Rourkes, Ballards Lees, Mrs. Reed and Virginia all gave us fruits and nuts. Wish you had some of them for they are really nice. Perhaps I had better candy some of the nuts and try sending them to you. What do you think about that?

This afternoon I have taken the trimmings all off of the bassinet and washed it with the little wardrobe for the baby clothes and now when I have the trimming washed and a little color added to them I will iron them and put them on again and it will be all ready for little Lloyd to sleep in. We took some pictures yesterday afternoon and Dad got one of Justine, side view to send to you. She said that might be a good idea for with your knowledge of those things you might be able to tell her when the arrival would be. You see there was a lot of that sort of kidding going on around here yesterday. Anyway we will send them on to you if any of them are good. There is no finder on the kodak so one just has to guess if he is making a picture or not.

One of my hens died a few days ago but even tho that leaves just nine I got eight eggs today. When Nellie was leaving today we loaded her up with cream,eggs and meat. Jack had also brought her some cream when he come in to get Mayme so she will be living high while her children are home.

We did miss our Billy Boy but just the same it was good to think that he was not on Okinawa or some other little out of the way island and that there was some sort of companionship which he could enjoy on that day. I am so glad that you did not do like you always did at home and decide you would go to those dances on Christmas and New Years the day they were due to take place and then it would have been even worse then here to try to get a date. I bet there are a lot of boys envying you when you and Mary step out. So really I guess we had a lot to be thankful for at this Christmas time.

Dad it going to the poker club tonight and dont know what T's plans are but fanny and I will be turning in a little early I think.

Now I will go make a few sandwiches for the folks to eat.

*   *   *

12/28/45

Dear Aunt Fan,

I'm a little slow at answering your good letters and thanking you for remembering me on Christmas. I really appreciated the money order and have already made good use of it.

Our situation here has not changed much from what you've learned from the folks. The four of us who came here from Okinawa are to be permanently assigned here. The only thing now is to get our orders written which seems to be a slow process. Our only hopes for getting back are to complete 18 mo. which will be up the 1st of July. I surely hope I get out of the Navy then.

The other afternoon we watched the natives butcher some hogs. It was quite an interesting process for I don't recall witnessing such a thing before. I believe it was no different from a stateside Job. The natives here produce quite a few vegetables which we get being the Military gov't. Mostly it consists of Squash, carrots, radishes, corn, potatoes, egg plant, and cucumbers. There are no horses, but do have a few old cows which pull their carts.

Hope you had a Merry Christmas and best wishes for the New Year.

Love, Bill

*   *   *

12/29/45

Dear Dad,

I haven't been very good about answering your good letters. I enjoy them very much. I'd surely like to have been with you this Christmas, but perhaps this next year will make things different. I surely hope so. There are rumors about sending the Japs back to Japan. That would surely reduce the number of patients we have, but if it does occur it will be some time before it happens.

Am now looking forward to New Years and know I have the duty New Years Eve I expect to have a very enjoyable time, as there isn't much to do and they can always call me if necessary.

Sound as if you do quite well with your poker game. I played one night here at the club with the boys and did all right for a while, but soon lost all my money that I'd allotted myself—$8. Haven't played since. Did I thank you for sending in the check for the life Ins.—

Enjoy hearing about the Drug store. It was quite a worthwhile Investment. Now that you have a good manager things out to run more smoothly.

Am enclosing the last of Okinawa pictures. One is on the ship to Saipan with Walsh's dog. On Christmas eve the Dog was killed by a car. Poor ole Walsh was really broken up about it.

*   *   *

12/29/45

Dear Mother, Dad, & Tom,

Am waiting this warm Saturday afternoon for an army doctor by the name of Brown who is to come down and look at some of the X-rays and Tb—patients. He is a chest surgeon and had quite a little experience with chests. He is from Colorado Springs. His sister married a classmate of mine.

Yesterday afternoon a boy by the name of Lloyd Wright who was two years ahead of me in med school dropped by the hospital.

He is in the army and has been on Saipan for three mo. He knows Capt. Brown who told him I was here. He and I exchanged all of the latest news on everybody. It was surely good to see an ole Phi Rho.

It really sounds as though you have been having your share of the cold spell. Would surely like to be home to see Julia & the Burns's. I didn't see the eclipse that you sent the clipping about though we do have a nice moon and stars.

You do not need to worry about us in the sail boat. There is a reef about 1-2 miles from shore that stops all the surf. It is only about 5 ft deep all the way out to the reef and we never go out to it. The only thing we have to worry about is that in the late afternoon the wind usually stops and if you get left out you have to pull the boat back. Would really like to have some of those Fresh eggs. Until later,

All my love, Bill

*   *   *

Monday Dec.31,1945

Dear Bill:

This is the last time that I will be writing 1945 and so am hoping that 1946 will be very good to you and us and see you home ere the season advanced very far. We, the whole family,Toms Aunt Fan and I are going to the Garlingtons for supper and to ring out the old year and in the new. I really tried hard to persuade Hay that it is too much trouble for her tho I did not tell her that the real reason of my great consideration for her was that I just dont quite like to try to sit and play bridge for about four hours while one waits for 12 oclock to arrive. Well we will get there a little late I am sure for both of the Toms are now trying to take a few quick winks of sleep. We were to be there about six thirty but think that it will no doubt be nearer seven when we get there.

Of course Tommy has a later date with Margaret so he will have to be stealing away later in the evening and I spect that Aunt Fan will want him to bring her home about that time too. Aunt Betty called me this afternoon to tell me about a colored woman who has been helping some with her work particularly ironing so I called the gal and she will come to me Thursday. I am so glad for since Mrs. Stone left me I have sent the clothes to the laundry and my! they look as if they had been put in dirty water and then just taken out and run thru the mangle, dirtier than when they went. When I straightened this paper I seem to have moved it and so there is that jog in the margin. You wont hold that agin me will you?

Dad hear something very nice about you today which I think you will really like to hear coming from the source which it did. Mrs. Girsh was in Canon City over the week end and saw Dr. Wyatt. He told her that "That boy will go far in his profession." when he spoke of you. So just think of that when things dont go quite to suit you. Then Sunday morning when Aunt Fan was coming out of church she had a little visit with Mrs. Carey,Winifred's mother. She asked about you and said "We think he is a wonderful boy."

Pop and I went to the McCune's tea yesterday and it was very pretty but like most men dont think that Dad got very much of a kick out of it and doubt that he would go if he did not like the McCunes so much. Marg told me today that they had been over to see us during that time but ofcourse did not find us here nor Aunt Fan either for she had gone to see the Thomasons.

Aunt Mayme was in just a minute at noon today on her way to Rocky Ford for some business deal. She had had a letter from Dud telling her about their Christmas and how much Judy liked everything. Tho she had lots of them Dud had to give her a doll for he said he thought a little girl just should have a doll under her Christmas tree.

We suppose that Fred arrived in Trinidad today and tomorrow Ginny will go back to California by plane. She leaves Pueblo about one and arrives out there about seven in the evening. Jimmy took her to Trinidad Saturday and I think that he stayed at the Sisk house Sat night and maybe Sunday too. He said that he was going up to Monument to see Smitty but that could have been just an excuse.

Think I shall close now and get this ready to mail so we can take it with us when we go down.

*   *   *

1/1/46

Dear Mother, Dad, & Tom,

One year ago today I boarded the USS Telfair which departed on Jan 2, for Pearl Harbor. That seems like a long time ago. I hope by the time 1946 is half way over I'll be back to the States.

The Commander of the Military Gov't Unit says they are going to be sending the Japs back by the 15th of this month. If they do there soon won't be much left here. They are going back on old LST's which have been stripped of their equipment. It sounded like a good way to get to Japan; so I asked the Captain if they needed a Medical officer if I could go. I've been here longer than any other place and a move would surely help make the time pass faster. It probably won't happen.

I got two packages from you this morning. Gosh you've really sent me a lot of them. I really enjoy the stories, magazines, and newspapers, and cans. I have still quite a few cans now since all of your packages have arrived and the Christmas packages. And since I may change address one of these days you don't need to send any more.

Last night we saw the New Year in from the Club. They had no special party, but about everyone was there. I was OD, but had a date anyway. Was only called once for only a sort time. This morning went to Mass. This isn't a Holy Day of Obligation because we really came under the Jurisdiction of Tokyo, where it is really not a Holy Day of Obligation.

Today is quite a rainy Cloudy day which is really nice for a change, for it is really warm in the sun.

Am enclosing some pictures that were taken at Pearl Harbor.

All my love, Bill

*   *   *

Wednesday Jan.1,1946

Dear Bill:

This is the first time that I have written 1946 so you see you are the first guy to get a letter from me in the new year. I got very much mixed up yesterday and thought it was Sunday so thought that Dad was writing to you and I didnt. When I got my bearings today I thought that I had let a whole day slip by without sending any sort of epistle to you.

This morning your letter written the day after Christmas came and we found it very interesting. The description of the school party with the children saying their pieces and waving the US flags and singing our hymns was quite enlightening and the black boy all dressed up for a reindeer must have been a bit on the humorous side.

You were very special, I take it when you had reserved seats for the Midnight Mass,with most of the other people standing.

I am glad that you waited for Christmas to open your things. You did not say just which things did not keep so well in the shipping but dont think that I sent anything that was not in cans except that first fruit cake and even it I think was packed in a can by the baker. I was thoughtful of those native people to give you gifts even if they are not things that you can use the thought was very kind and showed that they like you. Why dont you try to send some of those things that are hanging around in your way home. Some of the boys seem to send things.

The flower business was interesting too. And it must have been nice at the Milit.Govt.Farm. We cant seem to realize that you are warm over there. I has warmed up some here in fact the weather now is just perfect.

Aunt Fan and I have to go to church in a little while and must wash the dishes first so think that I had better stop for this time. Oh, yes I must tell you that I was talking to Justine this morning and she is all excited about building a double garage on a lot if they can get one and fix it up to live in. Bath,Kitchen, and living room. It would be made out of cinder blocks and stuccoed and then later

WILLIAM ROURKE SISSON, M.D

when they can build they will have their garage all ready. I think it is a good idea if they can get things to do it with.

*   *   *

1/4/46

Dear Mother, Dad, & Tom,

Today Dr. Brown came down and we Bronchoscoped a few Tb. pts. On one we found what may be a lung cancer which I've suspected for some time. It is surely good to do something for these people for a change though most of them, at least the Japs surely don't realize or appreciate what is being done for them. I really don't care, for about all I get out of it is a little information anyway.

I am O.D. this evening. I had one Jap come in Comatose and die in less than 2 hr. and I surely don't know what was wrong with him. Had been sick only 1 day. Am now waiting to decide whether another pt. has appendicitis and whether to operate tonight. Hope don't operate or it'll be past midnight when I get to sleep.

The rumors about taking the Japs are stronger than ever. The latest scuttlebutt is that they'll start Sunday. They evidently won't take any of our personnel; so it looks like my trip to Japan has again hit a snag. It'll take them quite awhile to evacuate all the Japs & Koreans. What they will do with this hospital after they've all gone, I don't know. They will have less than 50 pt. by then I imagine. Everybody hopes they will close it up and send us home, but that's wishful thinking I'm afraid.

Sunday—

Didn't finish the letter. They operated the guy Sat morn and found acute appendix. Yesterday I saw a fellow at the clinic in Charan Kanoa who I think has leprosy. This medical game is no fun. When you do a good job medically like finding a cancer of the lung or diagnosis leprosy the patient surely does not Benefit.

The guy with cancer will die a lot sooner than if he had Tb. The leper will have to be segregated the rest of his life.

Still lots of talk about moving the Japs perhaps they'll start this week.

The armed male escort deal has been in effect ever since I've been here. The MP's have lately been arresting those who don't comply. It all started I understand when a colored boy shot an officer and his date.

Sounds like a wonderful Christmas you had—hope I can celebrate the next one with you. I wouldn't give ole T. castor oil for the trots. The idea is good, but there are better things than castor oil such as Cascara or good ole Epson salts. I never use castor oil except on confirmed goldbricks, which is very rare.

Am enclosing some snaps taken at Iroquois Point Pearl Harbor of Max Carter and I and the fish he speared. One of them is really a whopper.

Until late—All my love, Bill

*   *   *

Tuesday Jan.8,1945

Dear Bill:

One week of the new year has passed and we are still waiting for the Lloyd baby to arrive but they think now that it will probably be about ten days or two weeks.

Your letter, telling us about your asking that you be allowed to go to Japan if a medical officer is to accompany the Japs came this morning and since all the family think that be an interesting experience for you I guess I do too but right at first I thought, "Gosh you are getting farther away all the time" but when one is so far away a little more does not make much difference. I dont wonder that you want to see a little more than the islands afford and that is one way of doing it.

We liked the pictures too and especially to see what Rankin of whom we hear such a lot,looks like. He looks like a great guy to us. The picture with the little dog is good of you. Just such a shame that he had to get killed. Wish I could send Walsh another one.

So I wont send you another package this week but hope that you get this letter before the LST takes off to Japan if you get to go on it. I think that you must have thought that there was a good chance of your going when you said to stop the sending of packages.

Wednesday—

Joan came in at that point to bring back some cream of tarter which they had borrowed and so stayed for a little visit and I did not get the rest of the letter written before supper and rushed off right after for a library board meeting and when I got back T. was in a hurry to keep a date he had with Margaret so the letter just had to wait for another day.

Tonight there is Rosary for Francis Mallouf but I will not get there as it is church night too and as Irene has to be at the funeral home and Tom's Margaret will play the organ for the first time, I am to be there to help her on when to play such and such and so on. I accepted an invitation from the Rockwells to attend an open house for Bob and his bride tonight too but think that I will have to call and tell them it will be impossible for me to make that.

Hope that Dr. Brown was a help to you with you T-B patients and also the Exrays. Strange how small the world is after all and how good it must have been to have a good talk with Lloyd Wright and hope you can see more of him or rather did if you are leaving the island.

Was glad too to hear the situation about the sail boat and the reef which lends itself as a protecting wall when you are out in it.

We hear that "Marsh" Archie Sierks is going to locate in Trinidad.

We had a snow storm this morning, and if it had kept up like it started out we would have really had some on the ground by night but now the sun is shining and the snow is all gone. It is like a spring day out now. Guess it did not scare Mary and her men out from taking their horses up to Denver today to the stock show.

Once I told you that Rosy Herron was to be married soon. Well that is all off now. I sort of thought that it would not last. Those violent affairs are often fleeting.

We have not heard a word from Jimmy since he was in Trinidad nor have we heard from Aunt Nell. Guess the relatives are off with us for we have not heard from the Rourkes since Christmas either except when Aunt Fan called them and had a little visit over the phone.

Think this is all the news for now.

*   *   *

1/9/46

Dear Mother & Dad,

Tis only another day on Saipan and I have the duty. Such evenings are pretty much a bore for there isn't much to do. Other evenings I usually go to the movies and as frequently as possible with Mary. After the movies have a coke or beer at the Club or at the Nurses area. It is really very nice, but she is now just waiting for orders which should be here by now.

Today they loaded their first batch of Japs. I understand it is really a mess getting them to piers and then on the LST's. I don't imagine it will be a pleasure cruise. I hope they have more ships soon; for at this rate they are going today it will only take about 6 more such loads.

Dr Brown came down today and we have lined up some operations for him on some of our Tb patients. I surely get a lot out of his trips down here.

Enclosed are a couple of cards in which you might be interested. We didn't get initiated when we crossed the 180° degree parallel for there were over 1,200 of us on that little boat, which was once a freighter.

Until later,

All my Love, Bill

We are finally really attached to this place.

*   *   *

Friday Jan.11,1946

Dear,dear Bill:

I was too near the edge so had to put in an extra dear, but then maybe I meant it. What do you think? Too I nearly called you a very uncomplimentary name at the salutation but that I did not mean.

It is snowy tonight so think that it is a good night for all the family to stay at home. However T. is going down to the office to do some typing for a little while but suppose that he will find some body to stay out with after his work is done. He is right now talking to Margaret so perhaps that will be the reason he will be out late.

I did a little typing for Aunt Fan this afternoon (it was a mess) in making some copies of her income from investments etc. and it took me about all the afternoon,so much for my speed.

Our evenings are getting quite a bit longer and now the chickens do not go to bed till about five when a few weeks ago it was bout four thirty when they retired. I got eight eggs today, quite a record for there are no only nine hens since one died and then one other one is sick so cant count on her eggs. That really makes an egg for every laying hen.

Had a letter from Aunt Hattie yesterday and in it she said that they had had a good letter from you and that she was going to write to you to see if she could not persuade you to make them a visit on your return home. She told about all her church parties etc and their Christmas dinner with the Goldsmiths. She admitted it was pretty cold the night that she was writing and said that John predicted frost that night.

I am still knitting on the little jacket for young Lloyd but if the event keeps in the future perhaps I will have it ready at least by the time he or she is ready to wear it.

The Manuals out at the ranch have a little baby about a month old. She went out with it when it was about two weeks old but they have gotten along fine till this even when she told Fan that they all even Manual have colds. So many people in town hare have had them and they seem to be the kind that stick on for a long time. Mrs. Herron is not really entirely over the one she got just before Christmas. She has been out a few times and thinks that she has taken a little more each time.

Poor little Jo Ann was running for girl leader in junior high and got beat today by about 200 to 80 votes. I just cant understand it and dont like it a bit for I think a thing like that is apt to give a kid sort of an inferiority complex.

Fannie is ready to wash the dishes or rather to dry them so I had best get busy and do the washing and then too Tom just came in so guess the boys are about ready to go down town.

*   *   *

1/1346

Dear Mother, Dad, & Tom,

Mary left this afternoon and so I shall again be without a date. She got her orders Thursday and had arranged transportation on the Hornet Tuesday, but the big guns decided that there should be no nurses on an aircraft carrier. They then put her and another Navy nurse on the hospital Ship Relief. A friend of the other nurse and I got them aboard then after they chased us away, we sat on the beach drowning our sorrow with a bottle of beer and watching the ship sail out of the harbor. We had a look at the ship and it was very nice. The only difficulty and it isn't much is that they'll have to work and they only have five nurses on the ship.

I received the books the other day and they are just the right thing. You surely know what kind of books I like Mother.

Yesterday Capt Brown came down for a look at a few X-rays then a sail in the lagoon. The boat needs a new Sail So will try to get one made. The boat also needs several other minor repairs including a paint job. We beached it yesterday and scraped all of the barnacles off of it. It is really a good little boat and goes right along, but you need two people when it is very windy or it will tip over.

I am OD today, but got Nichols to cover for me when I went to see the girls off. While I was gone an officer from a ship was drowned at the officers' beach which isn't far from here. They just were reckless and didn't use their heads.

Guess I have related the startling news. Thanks again for the books.

All my Love, Bill

Enclosed are some pictures of the Mormon Temple on Oahu.

*   *   *

1/14/46

Dear Tom,

It is about time I have penned you a note after the many letters of yours that I've not answered.

It is surely good to think of you at home, and know that you are out of the army. I like to hear of your escapades around the ole Town. As I'm writting, the latest flame was Margaret Driscoll and I am wondering if she is still # 1. I remember her and as most Driscolls is very attractive. What's the latest?

You are going to Boulder in March—and then will finish around September—Is that about right? I hope I'll be home by then and will call on you in that little town of learning.

Dad was telling me of your trips to see Dr. Cooper. As usual I can offer very little advice as his information was a little scanty.

My guess is that you have a little Chronic Prostatis which responds very well to finger waves—You will know what I mean if Dr. Cooper has been Massaging your prostate. Such things are often rather persistent and ole Dr. Cooper knows what he is doing. Can't give you much other advice without some more history, a urinalysis, and a physical Examination.

Haven't many other little pearls of wisdom so will close.

Love, Bill

*   *   *

Wednesday Jan.16,1946

Dear Bill:

Have spent most of this day, it is now about 4 P.M. getting, wrapping and sending a gift to the bride-to-be of Ed Leonard. We, Fannie, Bessie and me, on a blanket, a very nice one, yes for it cost the neat sum of $20.00 with the tax but by the time that I had bought an inclosure card and wrappings it was another dollar. There is so little one can buy in the way of gifts. No silver,no linen, no electric things like toasters or percerlators that one pretty nearly has to resort to bedding. Oh,well, we know that sooner or later they are bound to need a blanket, so.

There was little in the way of mail today but you did have a little letter or card from Denver which I am sending on by air mail so that you will get it some time in the near future. I almost opened it since I am possessed of that womanly quality,curiosity, but was afraid that the men of the family would not approve so held myself in restraint.

When I was in the F&A this morning Helen Cash approached me to tell me that Mrs. Aeneas Cash wants me to be the Godmother for their new little son. They want to wait till Father Prinster comes down here so he can be the officiating Clergyman. I think that he married them or else started on her instructions.

They are gradually clearing away all the stone etc. from the old Columbian school and Dad says that the school board is asking

$1000.00 for a 25 ft. lot of that ground which would bring 12,000 dollars if they get it,a nice start on a new building.

Your brother, Hughie, Ham, Bob Kann and Roy Black are quite the bowlers. Of course it makes it more interesting since some of the girls like the sport too, Margaret for one. She does pretty well for she does around 130 quite regularly.

If I did not write by the type method you would be forever getting the same thing over and over for I cant remember whether I have really told you things or just thought that I would so when I refer to the carbon copy I can be sure. I am wondering if I did tell you that I saw Paul Needham the other day and that both he and his wife plan to go to school.

O yes too while in the FandA this morning Mrs. Mishou came out from the back when she heard and recognized my voice and we had quite a chat or rather she did for I just could not break in as much as I would have liked to tell her how wonderful my sons are for she was full of Shirley and all about her going to Manilla,her wonderful trip over there by plane and so on and on and on. Major Mishou is ordered out to Camp Beale and does not know for what as his orders did not state. Gossip here tho says that he is to get out.

We had a good turkey dinner last night for the choir members and just a few remarks so were home about eight thirty and I got a start on the little cap to match the jacket I did for Justine. I hope that I get it done in less time than I did the jacket or else the baby will be too big for it before I get it done.

Think that I have covered this session almost entirely so will close now and see if there is not more of interest to write by tomorrow.

* * *

1/18/46

Dear Dad & Mother,

Surely have had lots of free time since Mary left. Took the sailboat out of the water, scraped the barnacles off, painted it, and Repaired the Jib sail. Still have a little more to do to it.

Dr. Brown Came down Wednesday afternoon and did a couple of operations on some Tb patients. I believed we really got results with the Operation. It was the first time I'd seen this type of operation. Dr. Brown is a very good surgeon and knows a lot about it.

Last night I went out to where Lloyd Wright is stationed— Isley Field. Had dinner with him, a show, and a few drinks. I got a terrible headache and couldn't understand it until this morning when I awoke with a full blown cold. Feel better tonight, but my nose is still a little runny.

Last Tuesday we went to the 148th hospital to a meeting in which they discussed a case I had on my ward and then sent the specimens from the Post Mortem up to them.

I surely enjoyed the pictures. Bobby has really grown in 1 yr. I'm anxious to see him. It also looks like Justine will also have a child by the time I get home. It ought to be quite a few months old by then.

Boy have the Deposits in the bank increased. Almost 6 million now. I have quite a while to go until before I'm Lt. Maybe around May or June I'll make it.—Till later,

All my Love, Bill

The pictures aren't good, but you might like them.

*   *   *

Friday Jan.18,1946

Dear Bill:

This letter wont get mailed till in the morning for all the men have gone off for the evening and as it is now about eight oclock Fannie and I wont be getting out any more. Dad has gone to a board meeting of Rotary. Tom and Fred to the basketball game, each in his own special company. You can guess by this time who T. is with and ofcourse Fred is with Bud and Marg. He,(Fred) came down by way of Colorado Springs yesterday. He is looking all around for a possible location. He did not think that the prospects in the Springs were at all promising so today went to Lamar. There did not seem to be much inducement there but on his way back he stopped in Las Animas and seems to think that there is a good out look there,at least he had a lot of encouragement from the editor of the paper there who is also the sort of strong voice in the county and local government. This man seemed to think that Fred could be appointed the deputy district att'y and possibly county and city atty also. That would be e very good start for in those cases one has something to live on while he gets his name before the public.

I guess I told you in a recent letter that I was a bit concerned about the progress of little "Chuckie". Well tonight Fred voluntarily cleared up most of that for me by saying that he thought by this time the baby was probably starting to walk for he was trying to stand alone when he left which was very good news to me.

The Belt (Hazel Bickett) baby arrived yesterday according to tonights paper. Bet old Charlie is excited.

Lea Garlington is going up to Denver the last of next week to go to Post Engineers school. He thinks then he could be assigned out here for quite duration for he thinks they will leave an engineer here as a sort of maintenance man for a long time, even tho they close it up as a field.

I have been sitting here thinking that I was hearing something like rain but did not realize that could be possible till I got up just now and went to the window and sure enough the streets are quite wet.

A letter from Uncle Murray today tells us that he thinks that they will be starting on their trek westward about the middle of April, that will be almost Easter for according to my prayer book Easter is on the 27th of April.

Bud Lane is doing quite a job on his house across the street and doing most of the work himself. He is changing the rooms all around so that he can have the bathroom between the two bed rooms instead of off the kitchen as it was before. Then he is lowering the ceilings too so it will be a nice little house when he gets through. I am wondering if he is not about to take a wife so he is going at this with such a vengeance. He must have some real incentive.

Thought I had a cavity in a tooth but this morning went to Dr. Klob who exrayed it and found it all right. Said my gums were in pretty good shape but to get some Lavoris mouth wash and he thought the use of that would clear up some of the sensitiveness which I attributed to a hole in the teeth.

Justine and John have taken an apartment 821 San Juan, the old Sexton house across from the junior high. She wants to get in before the baby comes but her mother thinks that she should wait till three or four weeks afterward so dont know who will win out. It is a rather big apartment for it has two bed rooms which will be nice for the baby and is nicely furnished but cots $75. a month. However they can rent another bed room upstairs and that will reduce it about $20.

I dont want to use any more paper for I want to put in some clippings and dont want it to over weigh so will just write on the back. John has more repair work than he really likes to do for it is very nerve racking work when one tries to stick at it too long at a time.

Just called Mrs. Inman. She was up at the hospital last week for a few days taking shots of penicillin for sore muscles but got home wednesday. She says that Bob expected to leave Honolulu last Tuesday so guess he did not catch a plane or would have arrived in the states ere now so is evidently on a ship. Virginia is out at Dorothy's waiting for him to arrive. She has her car there and they will drive home by way of Albuquerque where they will see his sister,Virginia and family. He has eighty days terminal leave but wants to go to Boulder the first of March. He had been in exactly four years the day he got out.

Think this is all the news for tonight so will close.

*   *   *

1/20/46

Dear Mother, Dad, & Tom,

Church this morning wasn't quite the same without Mary. One of the new nurses is Catholic; so the Captain and I took her and the other Catholic nurse Miss Schulte.

Yesterday afternoon Lloyd Wright came over and I showed him the Leprosarium and the nine lepers. Also, took on a tour of Charan Kanoa. Then for dinner and a show, it was an enjoyable afternoon.

I got two more boxes with the films and more books all of which really look like good ones. I now have a good supply of good reading material. Aunt Hazel also sent a book which I got at the same time and it also looks like a good one. Received a Christmas card from Mrs. Eddy tell her thanks a million.

As you've learned now my propose trip to Japan is out. When they close this place—maybe in 3 months, we will go up to the Navy hospital dispensary, unless I can work up a better deal. Am glad you like Rankin. He has a girl who is going to school at Boulder.

When I came out here, I too didn't quite realize how long it would be before I would get home, but now it seems like a measurable period.

Believe I've reached the end of my new so 'til later,

All my Love, Bill

Some more pictures

*   *   *

Tuesday Jan.22,1946

Dear Bill:

Things happened a little too fast yesterday for me to get a letter ready for you before Tom went to his date last night. It was a little different kind of date to the usual one for it was a poker party but began at 7:30 so took him off early. About the time I was ready in the afternoon to get to writing Aunt Mayme came in and had not much more than sat down when Aunt Nell and Fred arrived so there was no letter writing then for a while. Nell went to the ranch with Mary but I did get a bit extra supper for Fred as they do not have much of a dinner at noon. Well Fred went to Las Animas today and from his report tonight is definitely locating there. Everyone seems to think that it is a good location for the one good lawyer is now a state senator and does not seem to be going to practice there very much again and the others are quite old and will soon be out of the picture even tho they are not much competition even now. He was sort of promised the other day when he was down there that he could get the district (deputy) attorney job but today could not get any thing definite on that but the state senator lawyer promised to keep him busy with business coming into his office which he can not take care of, having to be in Denver most of the time so Fred made arrangements for an office and when he gets a place to live will go back and get his family. He has Father Lacquer and several others hunting for him so is hopeful tho the house question there is about as bad as it is here.

Your letter written Jan.9 came yesterday and the one on the 13th, the day Mary left came today. Gosh I bet it was hard to take seeing some one who had been at least a good pal going off home when I know you want about as much as anything to come yourself. I am so glad that the books arrived just at that auspicious moment. Maybe they will help to dispel some of the gloom.

Am glad that they really got started to taking the Japs back to Japan and I have been wondering if they have to use compulsion or if they go quite willingly. Are most of the natives of Saipan or of Japan?

Am glad that you are having the opportunity of working with Dr. Brown for I know you must be learning a lot from him about TB and the treatment thereof. Maybe you will specialize in it when you get back.

I went to bridge club today but was not much force and had a poor score. I met with Jane Kendall and I had the nerve to tell them that I will have it in two weeks. Now I will have to look the house over and see what has to be done in the way of cleaning before that time.

I have a big day tomorrow beginning with a Requiem Mass at seven. Then there is a funeral at the Spanish church at 10 at which they want another high Mass so Mrs. Herron and I (the official choir) have to do that. At two I have to go to PEO for a change since I have to take a part in the programme, not must just read some article and dress up in one of my mothers old fashioned dresses, it is founders day. Then at seven thirty there is the usual Holy Hour so again I spect I will not get a letter off to you.

The George Halsey baby is still just hanging to life by a thread. I dont understand just what was the matter with it but some way the esophagus (I cant spell that but you are a good guesser) got mixed up with its breathing apparatus and before it could eat they had to operate.

I made Mrs. Clyde Davis a card table cover for her dining table since she had often mentioned to me that she wanted one and could not get it and was she surprised, and I think pleased today when I gave it to her. I had her guessing tho for at club I told her that I had something for her and it was hers if she could use it and if not it was mine and she got the idea that it was some garment which I could not wear which I was offering her. I had told Jane about it and she went right along with me in making her guess and get excited about it.

Aunt Fan is going to have all the dishes done if I just keep on writing a little longer and tho I would like to do just that I spect since she is just recovering from a cold I had better give her a lift.

Before I do that tho I think of another interesting bit which Aunt Nell brought down when she came yesterday about the Edward Leonard wedding last night in Pueblo. All the invitations, 300 of them read that it would be the Catholic Cathedral in Pueblo but for some reason which the Francis Leonards could not then explain when she talked with them on their way thru Trinidad to the wedding it was to be at the Episcopal church. It must have been very embarrassing and we wonder if they had a notice posted on the Cathedral door directing the guests to the other church or just how they took care of things. We will hear one of these days what happened to change things for them. I bet poor Grandmother Leonard about had a fit at its being in the Episcopal church for that automatically ex-communicates him.

*   *   *

1/23/46

Dear Mother, Dad, & Tom,

It has been rather rainy around here, and not quite as hot. I guess it is the winter season—at least I'm surely having a time with a cold. I've had it for about 2 wks and though it doesn't bother me to the extent of incapacitation it is surely a nuisance.

Today we put the sail boat back in the water and it really seems to go right along without all the barnacles it had on it.

Since I've been here I figured out today that I've had 20 patients die on my wards. Of these 15 had tuberculosis in advanced stages. I'm beginning to tell when these people are sick—at least more than I could at first. Tomorrow we are going to test about 400 school children for Tb. Don't know how we'll get along.

Your letters have surely been coming along. The last three have arrived in 6 days after they were mailed. Would surely like to sit by the fireplace with the fire on at home and read some of these good books I have. Both Walsh and Baker, my roommate enjoy them, too. Have enjoyed the serials cut out from the Post. You can't ever count on seeing consecutive magazines out here.

Left you in Mid air about the Jap who died 2 hours after admission.—Well according to the autopsy he had no reason to die. The only Rankin could see was that perhaps he might have been poisoned, but I guess we will never know.

The little letter you just about opened was from a T. Rabe Taylor of whom I've never heard. Evidently he expects me to get into trouble as he is a lawyer who just got out of the navy and was announcing the opening of his law office in Denver.

Not much more news for the present.

All my love, Bill

*   *   *

Wednesday Jan.23,1946

Dear Bill:

Well I have been to the PEO meeting and had Ahs and Ohs over my mothers lovely taffeta dress and her gold watch and pin which I wore to compliment it. And now having a little time before the "boys" come home from the office I will write a little to you. I want to go to the post office to send back to the Denver Dry Goods some articles which I sent for by mail and find they(brassiers) are too large.

A nasty hard wind blew up about five this morning and has been disagreeable all the day tho not really cold. The weather man does not predict any storm so maybe tomorrow will be nice again. I am glad that my laundry was done yesterday but think that aunt Betty had planned on today for hers. The twins came in about noon today and Nellie and Fred went off to Trinidad. Aunt Nell really seems quite thrilled over the prospect of moving in to the apartment for she will not be tied down with furnace etc. and can run away and come down here whenever she has the urge.

Gosh I almost wish you were a father for just now I heard over the radio that some congressman wants all fathers to be home by July. O well maybe you will be here by then anyway and we hope even before.

We got thru all our singing this morning all right, I guess but at the Spanish church we got a bit worried for Irene could not start the organ and I had to make a scurry,for the funeral was almost at the door,into the sacristy to tell Father Pecorrela our perdiciment.

He sent one of the altar boys who understood the intricies of the motor to help us out and we got going. The motor sounds like a washing machine and the organ itself sort of squeeky. The stairway up to the choir loft is really quite treacherous,I would say and dark as a well.

Aunt Mayme sold her fine stallion,Fred Bailey while in Denver. I seems that he was getting pretty stiff and was 14 years old. She got as much as she had paid for him in the beginning and a young horse to boot so she thought she had done quite well.

Dad is going to the poker club tonight and I to church but dont know what Tommy (dont tell him I called him that) is to do.

Do you remember Guy Hewitt? His mothers name was Cap Foxworthy, and he was here one summer when you all were little boys but we could not make you boys very much interested in him. He was then a big soft kid. He went Boulder under the army and studied Japanese, and since V-J day has been in Japan but is now home or on the way but wants to return to Japan and wants his mother to go along. He says that they could live elegantly over there. Guess she is not so much interested.

Well the "boys" are here so I will go to the post office and mail my package and this letter so ta-ta.

*   *   *

Thursday Jan.24,1946

Dear Bill:

Wish you were here to have some of the rolls which I made this afternoon but just wait I will be bussing around one of these days making a lot of things that I know you like, and how—

There was not much of interest happening today but just the usual days routine,breakfast,dishes, dusting, dinner etc for me and the office for the men. I did go out to east this noon after I had the dinner ready for the family. The Operating Committee of the USO met at noon at the Kit Carson. From the meeting the understanding developed that the club will be closed the 28th of Feb. so I still have a couple of nights to go down there, it would seem. I also got another little job out of the meeting when I was put on a committee to arrange for a sort of party of recognition to those who have given of their time and effort down there. It will be on Feb.3, so have some time to get ready for it. Guess there will not be much work to it as the plans are about made. When I am asked to do something like that is when I realize that I am not as young as I used to be for I just dont want to do it and it sort of makes me mad inside to even be asked. I once thrilled to put on affairs like that.

Mac had an attack like the one you had on Okinawa a week ago last Sunday. He was down at the bank doing some work when this terrific pain struck him. He finally got the phone and called Dr. Stickles who gave him a shot of morphine. He said he must have been a big one for he hardly got home and into bed when he was out and slept till the next afternoon. May is away so he was alone in the house and it seems to me that it was a bit dangerous for him to be there alone. The doctor does not seem to have done anything about making the stone pass so has given him some morphine tablets to take in case he has another attack which he says he probably will. Nice to think about. No?

Guess George Wright and Rita are to be married as soon as he gets settled in a job. At first he thought that he would go back to school for a masters degree but seems that he cant get anything at Boulder which he would need so has given up that idea. I have not seen him since he got home.

Your dad is slipping for he did not bring home the bacon from the poker club last night. I think for about the first time in my married life did any of the family slip in without my hearing them but I sure did not know when he came and evidently slept right thru for did not even know I had not heard him till this morning.

Think That your brother has a date tonight so will mail this letter (if he does not forget) when he goes for her.

I took a pan of rolls out to the Sabins for their supper about six and Justine was there still feeling fine. Each morning I think there will be a call to tell us about the arrival and every time the phone rings I just dash to it.

Its time for the supper dishes now so will close till tomorrow.

*   *   *

Friday Jan.25,1946

Dear Bill:

Big news! The baby arrived this morning about 6:40 and weighed 6 1/2 lbs,a nice little girl with lots of black hair. Now for all the details which I know you will want to hear. The water broke yesterday before noon but little nagging pains did not begin till late in the afternoon. After the Sabins had had supper Justine being pretty restless thought if she could play some bridge it would help to pass the time and divert her attention to the pains but she did not want to let anyone know that it was about her time. Finally she decided that they would ask Bud and Marg to come over and she would just tell them all about it but when they called the young Sabins were going to the wrestling match so then the Lloyds and Aunt Betty played three handed for a while but about 11 she decided they would go to bed and maybe in between time she could sleep a little. Well at least Aunt Betty and John did drop off to sleep and about one Teeny called them and thought they should call the doctor and for half an hour tried without any luck to get central then John went over to Dr. Coopers house and could not rouse anyone so he went down and called from his store and got central and the doctor so they went off to the hospital. After a while Uncle Earl woke and finding them all gone he too tried to call the hospital to find out about it and he too had to try for about 20 min. before he finally got a girl to take his call. He was plenty mad about it and I bet someone hears about it. You know Uncle Earl. Well the pains did not get really bad enough to call the doctor back to the hospital till a little after six so it was not long then till the baby was here. I think Justine had to have a few stitches but is fine and dandy and the baby when Aunt

Betty looked in at her this afternoon was screaming her head off and pounding her fists so guess she is really a husky little girl. John called his Dad this morning and it was hard for him to believe that the baby was really a girl. He was so determined it was to be a boy.

We have all been so excited over the arrival today they none of us have accomplished much. Aunt Mayme just happened to come in today so she too got to hear the news. Aunt Betty called the Sisks this morning to tell them and Mayme was going to talk to Dud anyway so about all the relatives know the news this eve.

I am going to have a turkey Sunday so asked the Sabins to eat with us and I can send Teeny some too.

Your two letters addressed to the men of the family came today the one to Tom was written the 14th and the one to Dad the 18th. We like the pictures of you and Mary and the others even tho the one of Mary with you was a bit blurred. It is so nice to see what the surroundings are like as well as what sort of people you are associating with. It looks quite nice and comfortable at the MG farm. I think that the picture of you with Mary is very good of you. While getting accustomed to doing without Mary's company was a very good time to do the repair and cleaning job on the boat. What color did you paint it?

Hope the operations which Dr. Brown did on you patients were of some good to them and they are recovering well. Isnt it good that you have a contact with such a good surgeon? Hope the cold did not affect you very much. I would like to have known more about the discussion of your case,I mean the case which they discussed from your ward but perhaps that is not for the laymen to hear about.

Tommy is going to the Junior college formal tonight.Roy Black asked him so guess it is a bonified invitation. Ofcourse he is taking Margaret,she is still ace-high. That is rather steady for Tom,dont you think so?

The weather man says we are to have a little snow tonight and much colder weather for just a day so guess we can stand that. It had been unusually warm for this time of year. It was about this time of year about nine years ago when Tom came down with scarlet fever. I remember the sudden change of weather we had that day that we went to the ranch and how cold it got for the trip to the dinasour tracks. Poor Tom. I still kick myself when I think of making that kid go or rather of not making him stay at home that morning.

Guess I had better now make the waffles which I promised for the supper so will stop here.

*   *   *

1/27/46

Dear Mother, Dad, & Tom,

Have just completed the duty, and am now looking forward to a quite day on the beach, sailing, and a show in the evening.

There are surely lots of rumors running around about this place now. The Captain last night said they had set a dead line to have all these people out of here by February 15. What will happen after that I don't know. Since we will probably have to go to the Naval Hospital when it closes up, I'm not quite so anxious to see it close quite so quick. The census of the hospital has gone down a lot. When we first arrived it averaged about 190 and now it is about 140 and now it is about 140. I guess they will open a couple of Wards at the Navy base for the Chamaurros. They ought to make this a Tb. sanitarium for I know they could just about fill it up with Tbs. We tested about 400 children between 7&11 with tuberculin and half of them had positive tests.

The mail has really been making speedy time I've received two letters in only 5 days. Was glad to hear that ole Bob Inman is now on his way to being a Civilian. You'll probably see him soon.

Believe I have covered all the latest news, so till Later,

All my Love, Bill

Enclose is a Picture with long hair.

*   *   *

1/28/46

Dear Dad, Mother, & Tom,

What a student at C.U. Med school in the Medical Clerkship of his Senior year would have given to have seen the cases I saw this morning. Two fresh Yaws, 1 leper, a Liver Abscess and two new Tbs. I wonder If I'm learning anything by it however.

Saipan Surely looks like a different place now than when we arrived. There were over 400 ships in the harbor and now about 25. Many activities have close and there are lots of empty quonsets everywhere. However there are still lots of people here. It is kind of hard to watch everybody leave, but one day I'll leave too.

They are really getting anxious to close this place and I think I've learned why. The Captains at the Navy base want our quarters to house their families.

Went surf board riding yesterday and was really quite a lot of fun. It pulls pretty hard on your arms and shoulders and I'm a little sore today.

Your last letter written on Sunday arrived on Friday. That was really a quick trip.

Believe I've run out of news.

All my Love, Bill

I've surely had good use of my Wrist Watch. Not one bit of trouble with it though I've worn out four bands.

*　　*　　*

Monday Jan.28,1946

Dear Bill:

It is now 6:30 and T. is taking a few quick winks while Dad and Aunt Fan listen to the news. I have just been down to get some meat from the locker and take my secretary's report to Mr. Harms so now before I get a little bit of supper will type a little letter to you.

The baby and mama are coming along fine but guess the poor little child will have to go thru life just as "She" for the parents cannot decide on a name for her. I saw her that is her forehead and black hair Friday afternoon. From outside that was all we could see. She was in the back row and the covers were pulled well up around her but ofcourse she was by far the best looking baby in there and there are twelve of them now. Three have come to life since Friday.

Yesterday I had a turkey for dinner so had asked The elder Sabins and John but John had a previous invitation and Uncle Earl wanted to work at the farm so did not want to come in at noon. Being my table would only take care of about eight I had not asked the young Sabins but when the crowd dwindled like that I asked them. Bobby staid all afternoon with me while Marg went out and helped Aunt Betty get the announcements as ready as they could without a name for the baby and Bud went to the office to work. When they came back Bobby thought it would be nice if they had a sandwitch here and as Tommy was bringing Margaret home for one they did stay and we about finished the turkey. There was just about enough scraps for our dinner today and the rest will be creamed for supper.

Bobby thinks the baby is wonderful and is so excited about her that he has to tell everyone he meets about her even tho he does not know them. Dad thinks it would be nice if they named her Eva so that when she says "Uncle Tom" he can answer "Yes, Little Eva".

Olive and Judy were just a little while Saturday morning and maybe they will see us again for they have gone out to the ranch for a little visit before they go back to Idaho Springs. At least I think they have for I heard that Mayme and Jack were in today but I have not seem them. Duds grandmother, about 95 years old died Saturday morning. She has been a wonderful old lady but guess one could not expect her to live much longer than that. Judy is sure cute and talks so plainly. She has had cold almost constantly, Olive says since October so that is one reason they came down to Pueblo so that Dr. Schwer could see her. He has perscribed vitimin C for her. She does not look as if it does her much harm for she is as plump as ever. Still has as Bobby says "Cute legs"

Wonder if I should begin to send you some more books or any thing or do you still think that you might have a change of address?

In another month Tom will be going off to school and we will be alone again. Then if the weather is good and if Nellie,now free from caring for furnace etc goes along Aunt Fan may be streaking off to the ranch and they we will be alone. Guess the Murrays will be coming along in April.

It is now six so had best be getting busy so will close now.

*   *   *

Tuesday Jan.29,1946

Dear Bill:

What a wind has come up this afternoon and the weather man says more snow which we dont like to hear just now for Fred left this morning for Ann Arbor to get his family and we had hoped that the weather would be nice for him. Maybe by the time they start back it will have all this out of its system. He has his office all right but as yet did not have an apartment or place to live unless something had turned up that he did not know about. The Sisks got moved yesterday so he came on down this far last night as he wanted to stop in Las Animas for a little while today and of course is anxious now to get Jean and Chuckie. I guess the Sisks found moving a six room house stuff into an apartment was a bit hard but it will adjust in a little while. Things just seems to fit into corners etc after a while.

Well the baby is finally named. Linda Justine so the announcements will be mailed now. Aunt Fan was up to see them this afternoon but of course did not get a very good look at the baby.

It seems that Justine is going to have to feed her on the bottle as she does not seem to have sufficient milk. Perhaps it is just as well for then if the milk is not right for it they can change the formula which cannot be done so easily with mamma feedings.

I did a very foolish thing last night or at least I thought so then. I tried to bite a thread off and broke out an inlay in one of my front teeth. The dentist found however when he looked at it today that there was some decay under the inlay so maybe it is best to be out. He put in a very temporary porcalin filling for I have two parties to go to tomorrow and next day. Then next week he will make a jacket crown for it. It feels tonight as if there is a wad as big as my hand in my mouth up there and it interferes with my bite so guess I will be forced to diet for the next week or else eat soups.

Your letters with the two pictures taken on Oahu, a large one of you and one of a pineapple field came today. Am glad that you found another nurse to take to church and then perhaps you can get some other dates with her. Am so glad that now you have some good reading material. It was good of Hay to send you a book I must ask her what it was. Lea went to Denver last Friday to take the Post Engineers training for eight weeks so guess the Garlington Girls are a bit lonely these days but I am sorry to confess that I have not been down to see them since he left but then I have only once been to see the new baby so I must have been busy.

Leila Hayden(one of the girls in Dads office)'s sister is in the same room with Justine. If she is as good a talker as Leila Justine wont have much peace and quiet but then it is only for about five days now for she thinks that Dr. Cooper will let her go home next Sunday.

Think I had better get this letter ready for mailing for T. might take off at any minute as Ham called a little while ago and from the sound of the conversation I think something was hatched up for this evening.

*   *   *

Wednesday Jan.30,1946

Dear Bill:

While the rest of the family finish their supper I will write to you.

There is no poker for Dad tonight for most of the members are going to Blair's dinner. Last year we were invited and for some reason I did not tell Dad about it, just left the invitation which I thought was not important laying around for him to read and he never read it so the party came and went and he did not know he had been honored so this year he did not give me a chance to say I did not want to go, he just did not tell me anything about it. It is one of those hot parties with much to eat and drink so you know that I dont fit too well.

T. is going to bowl in the American Legion league and I am to church and choir practice so everyone is accounted for but Aunt Fan and guess she will read a book.

I went to a luncheon at Mrs. Lagerquists today and was so sleepy all afternoon that I could not do a very good job of playing contract and ended up with a very mediocre score.

We got your letter written on the 20th today and were glad to hear that you are getting our letters in good time. Also the report on the jap who died so suddenly on you. Guess no one else could have diagnosed his case since the autopsy showed nothing.

Will they give all those children who show they have T.B. treatment? How many natives will be left on the island when the Japs are all taken back to Japan?

Mayme and Olive and Judy were here just as I was starting to Mrs. Lagerquists so I did not get to have a visit with them. Olive and Judy were leaving on the 2 O'clock bus anyway and wanted to go out to see Aunt Betty before they left so there was not much time to spare for them either.

Hope tomorrow is nice(is sort of cold tonight) for I want to wash a few things before I have the club next week. Bed spreads pillows and bathroom rugs.

Think I had better get busy now at the evening dishes so will close.

*   *   *

Friday Jan. no Feb.1,1946

Dear Bill:

There is about a half hour before T. goes a-dating so will get a little letter ready for him to mail when he goes. Margaret has been home sick with cold all this week so he has not had any dates but tonight she seems to be on deck again and they are going to a Junior College game(basket-ball).

T. went to a party at the Mesh's (Nancy Gardner) last night with all the married folks. The Bob Barnes,who by the way are expecting, Dot Vandetti and hubby, the Jay Millers and I cant remember who else except Tom and Shirley. We went to the club and neither did any good so did not get any money but had a good time.

I went to a luncheon today which Mrs. Bickett across the street, Mrs.Pomp West and Mrs. Robert Strain gave. I did not want to go for I just have to get this house a little cleaned up for the bridge club but did not like to refuse for they had never invited me before and I was afraid Mrs. B. would think that I just did not want to go and I am glad that I did accept for as I was leaving Mrs. B. said to me "I was afraid that you would not come and so I did not know whether to invite you or not".

I went up to see the little baby and mamma yesterday afternoon and got a good look at the baby for she was on her back and not too much covered up. I think that she looks a little like Justine except she has a big mouth like Johns and Justine is thrilled about that. It seems that now big mouths are popular. Justine is going to stay at the hospital the full two weeks since they are not too much crowded just now. While I was looking at the baby the George Halseys came along to see their baby so I got to see the poor little thing too. It is now gaining a little and they have a ray of hope that it will get along. Last week they thought that at any moment it was going to die for it seemed to be choking and then with a terrible effort something seemed to happen inside its throat or somewhere and since then it has been better. It weighs five pounds now and seven at birth.

Nellie came down last night and went right off to Marys ranch but stopped here just long enough for a message that we were to call Fred in Ann Arbor and give him a message about the office he was renting in Las Animas for she had had a letter from some real estate man down there about it and did not know what Fred wanted to do. Keep the one he had or take this other one. As we were going out it was Aunt Fans job to put thru the call so she did and got Fred about an hour after he had arrived there. He had had no trouble with weather on his trip back. Will be there a week or two before they start back here to live in Las Animas. He is a bit squimish about how Jean is going to like it for she had told him no to locate in a town smaller than Colorado Springs. Guess these girls just dont know where the best opportunities are. There is a new red neck doctor locating in Las Animas too so maybe they will strike up a friendship.

Guess I have related the gossip for today so will stop right here.

*   *   *

2/3/46

Dear Mother, Dad, & Tom,

Received the letter this morning informing me of the new little Lloyd and was surely glad to hear that there was such little difficulty with the recurrence of the accident. Hope It won't be long till I can see it. What name have they selected for the girl. Am glad it was a girl for there are not enough girls in our generation. Perhaps the next will be more girls.

Last night Rankin and I went out to the USS Boxer one of the Big aircraft carriers for dinner and a show. Our host was a fellow I met here on the beach. We couldn't get a boat back and had to stay all night. That is the second big ship I've been on—the other was the USS Shangri La an aircraft carrier at Ulithi. I've seen enough of all the types of naval ships to realize how lucky I am to have had all shore duty. Even Okinawa was better than any ship I've seen.

This morning was very rainy, but this afternoon cleared off wonderfully and we really had a grand time swimming, sailing, and speed boating.

Had a letter from Cowgill the other day and he is back in the states as they took all the doctors off of destroyers. He is now in Seattle, Washington, on another ship that is being Decommissioned. He has seen Woody Brown who is also back in the states as they decommission his CB. Battalion. Woody has duty at Glenwood Springs Naval Hospital. Nice Break, eh? Wallie Gist is in China. Believe that is about all of the news for the Present. Don't see how they can close this hospital before March 1.

Till later,

All my Love, Bill

*   *   *

Tuesday Feb.5,1946

Dear Bill:

The ladies have just left and I have the tables and all put away so now can relax and write to you. I did not let the Toms come home this noon so maybe they will be starving tonight. It seems so often that Dad is hungrier the day he goes to Rotary than any other time and I have to get him a little more supper so perhaps we will have a little extra tonight. Even I could be a little bit on the hungry side since I did not stop for much to eat at noon. I had thought that the house was practically ready yesterday but last night the wind blew a furious gale with plenty of dust so I had about all of it to do over again this morning. I was so sort of provoked at the man for not coming yesterday to wash the windows on the out side but this morning was glad he had not for they too would have been a sight. There was just enough rain with the wind that the dust stuck to everything. Well enough of my difficulties.

Bob,so Mrs. Inman told me sunday is now in the state and in civvies. He and Virginia are having a visit with the Inman girls out there and sort of honeymoon before they get here. Ofcourse Mrs. I is getting pretty anxious for their arrival and surely they will be getting here ere long.

Those poor little children who had positive tests to TB wont have much chance if all the hospitals close and they have to remain with their families, will they? Here I think that a positive case is usually have some sort of treatment probably hospitalization if at all possible, and surely isolation from the rest of the family if there is TB among them.

Dad and I wondered if the long haired picture was taken recently or in Hawaii. If recently, then you have let it grow out. We like the picture very much whenever it was taken and think it is very good of you except of course that it does not show your pretty brown eyes.

My I should think that you would be learning a lot seeing in just one morning all those different cases and I take it it was your job to diagnose them too, and that is something.

I sent a letter this morning with just clippings in it and wonder if it will arrive any sooner than this one does or not. I put it out for the mail man to take and this will go down to the office pretty soon.

Aunt Fan would not stay to see the ladies today but went off to the ranch. Of course she had a good excuse for Tommy Richards went out to look the light plant over and put in an extension or two for her. She wanted one over the stove in her summer kitchen especially and I dont know where else.

Just ten days more till all the Japs will be going if they stick to the dead line the captain said they had set and sure hope they do and that your stay at the Naval Hospital will not be long. I have a feeling that your are going to get to come home before too long now. Perhaps I am all wrong but you know how psychic I am.

Will close now and finish a letter I started at the USO last night to the Rourkes. I got one off to Gene so think that I did pretty well and did not neglect my duties there at all either.

*   *   *

2/6/46

Dear Mother, Dad, & Tom,

Had the Duty yesterday and believe it or not I needed a blanket. The room where the OD sleeps is open at the end towards the breeze. There was a nice breeze and occasional rain and the blanket felt good. The breeze has been nice for about the last month and it hasn't been too warm at all. There has been plenty of wind and the sailing has been good till the other day when Rankin and a new Dr (Craddock) were out almost to the reef. As they turned around the boat shipped too much water and sank. It was over their heads and they couldn't get it floating again. It's still out there.

They seem to be gradually getting the Japs out and suppose they will get this placed close in about a month. Will surely hate to move from the beach.

You asked if the Japs want to Return. They surely do except for a few. There are lots of them who think that Japan has won the war and that's why they are being sent back. If they have been here on Saipan more than 10 yrs they can stay, but this is a very small portion.

I guess it would be better not to send any more books as can't tell what they might do with me when they close this place.

Am glad they named the baby. It has quite a name to live up to—Justine.

Enclosed is something we are dishing out to the Chaumarros to try to teach them a little about tuberculosis. Till later.

All my love,

Bill

*   *   *

Friday Feb.8,1946

Dear Bill,

While the men finish their supper I will dash off a few quick lines to you. They are going to the basketball game in Rocky Ford so must leave pronto.

We have had another little flare of weather today,a little snow and quite a bit of cold but the weather man says warmer tomorrow.

Last night after supper we went out to see Linda for that is the only time that she seems to stay awake for more than a few minutes. I got to hold her for a bit and look at her feet and the back of her head. Her hair hangs down on her neck in the back. Fortunately she has been a good baby so far but ofcourse feeding her at 10,2, 4,and 6 A.M. sort of got Aunt Betty night before last for she could not get back to sleep quickly after each feeding so was awake most of the night. Last night Justine took all the responsibility of her bottle during the night so all went fine.

Aunt Fan brought in an egg from the ranch the last time that she was out and it was a whopper. I measured it tonight before I broke it and the long way around it was eight inches and the short was six and a half. That is nearly big enough I think to put in believe it or not.

Aunt Fan may have to change the color of her chickens at the ranch for the women she gets the baby chicks from in the spring each year told her today that she is not able to get the white rock eggs. It seems that the hatcheries have to get eggs from flocks that have been tested for disease and the white rock owners flocks do not meet the requirements. So thus far she has not found any place to buy the white rock eggs. Aunt Fan thinks that because we have the hens here she will see if Manual will take care of the baby chicks out there for her and then she will buy his chicks for him/ She says that he had such good luck with the little chickens last year. He has a little stove, oil, which he keeps the house warm with and that is much better than my set up here for the globe does not make enough heat if the spring is sort of cold.

Dad will be telling you when he writes Sunday about the change to the basement for his office. He thought that Mr.Morrison would not like the idea but says Mr. Woodbridge told him today that Mr. M. is very enthusiastic about it. I guess he thinks it will be a time for him to see that raise Dads rent,a subject that has bothered him (Morrison) for a long time.

I got my feet all fixed up in Pueblo yesterday,bought a couple of dresses, some sheets for the baby bed, some material for a skirt for Justine and some panties for myself so thought it was quite a profitable trip. Crews Beggs announced that they would have a nylon stocking sale at three but none of us wanted them badly enough to get in that line which extended out the door and about half a block down the street. A couple of policeman were kept busy seeing that the ladies stayed in line and did not break in ahead of where they belonged.

Time to quite now so ta-ta.

*   *   *

2/10/46

Dear Mother, Dad, & Tom,

Never can tell what's going to happen in the Navy. It looks like the big wigs on this Island have been thwarted in their attempt to close this hospital as the higher-ups at Pearl Harbor said no soap. The latest now is that they will keep about a 75 bed hospital here with 3 medical officers. Don't know who the 3 medical officers will be, but the Captain Recommended that Rankin and I stay and they will probably ship in a Lieut. Comdr. to be the Skipper. There was a chance of getting home Early if we went to the Naval Base Dispensary as they are overstaffed and we have more time than any of them. If we stay here we'll probably have to wait to July 1 anyway. Doubt that I could swing a deal to get home anyway and this is a good place.

Had a letter from Geo. Motter the other day, and like the rest of us he doesn't think he'll make the army a career. He is still at Whipple Treating Tb's which is a discouraging thing to treat.

Had five letters yesterday, two from you, two from Mary (Guess she must have reached the states) and a valentine from Dorothy Duffy.

The days have been sort of like Colo in the Winter with Clouds all over but not dense. The water is much cooler for swimming now. Went out twice to try to find the Sailboat, but were unsuccessful.

Rankin and I are going to try to get to Guam this weekend for a little vacation trip.

There will be about 4500 natives left on this Island when all the Japs have gone. If we find any Tb. in the school children we will treat them, but treatment means only limiting their activity by putting them in the hospital and watch to see whether they get better or worse.

Am Enclosing some pictures of our Quarters. Till Later

All my love, Bill

All the pictures were taken standing in one place and Just turning around.

*   *   *

Monday Feb. 11,1946

Dear Bill:

Dad went to Pueblo this morning and I would have gone along if I could have scared up any reason for doing so and neglecting my household duties but just could not find a single thing to do up there while a thousand things here at home were calling for attention so I let him go alone and evidently he did all right without any back seat driving for he was back in town about two oclock. The table that holds Hazels typewriter fell the other day and damaged the typewriter and as there is no one here just now to fix them he made a hasty trip to "Pu" town to get attention for it.

Aunt Fan just talked to Aunt Betty and found that all is going fine out there except that Linda wakes about half an hour before her feeding time and is fussy till she gets her bottle and then she is O.K. so I guess they will be having to enlarge on the supply of food she gets. She is in her third week now and the food seems to be all right for her for her bowls are in fine shape.

Yesterday afternoon Dad and I went to the office and finished the work we have been on for some time. Transferring some records from an old style book to a new one. I just did the writing for you know he could hardly do both the reading and writing both.

Marylin Hostetter called this afternoon for Tom. Ofcourse he was at the office so I directed her there but dont know if he saw her or not. She just landed from India last week at Portland. She does not think that she will be discharged for she does not have points enough. Dont know how Tom will be able to handle two girls but guess he can work that out all by himself, so I wont have to bother.

The weatherman keeps trying to scare us with a threat of storm. Last night he said it would snow but none appeared so then this morning he said that it would come late this afternoon but so far there is none. I rather hope that it does not snow for I would like to hang out the laundry which I expect to do tomorrow. bob is now in Boulder so guess it wont be long till he is home. Mrs. I. is getting pretty anxious but I think that it is fine that he and Virginia have had this really first time since their marriage by themselves. Has really given them a chance to get acquainted, with out mama dictating their actions.

Dad and I have to go vote as soon as he gets home at five on the bond issue for the school district. There does not seem to have been much talk about it so doubt that there will be much objection and think it will surely pass.

Thought that surely we would have a letter from you today but none came. We have been getting them on Monday but suppose that this time the mail did not go thru as quickly as ordinarily and we will probably get it tomorrow. The last of this week should see the last of the Japs on Saipan if the Captain knew what he was talking about and hope that he did.

T. said that Mr. Morehead was like a chicken without a head this morning. When things are busy he gets all flurried and bothers the girls to death. Wants them to stop what they are doing and do this and as soon as that is started he wants them to do something different and so they dont accomplish any thing. When Dad is there he sort of keeps him quiet at least jumps on him if he gets to doing that.

Dick Willett is home and will go to Logan soon for his discharge. He says that he will just loaf for about a month before he goes to work. Guess because of his seniority he will have a job with the Santa Fe and I surely hope so for dont know where else he would get a job now.

It is about five now so will close and be ready to go vote with Dad when he comes.

*   *   *

Tuesday Feb.12,1946

Dear Bill:

A holiday for bankers and all such including Abstractors so the young Tom slept till about noon and dont know that he would have wakened then if Bobby had not come over and his little shrill voice filtered thru the doors etc to arouse the sleeping beauty. Bob and Marg came to borrow the clothes pins, a weekly process since they are among those things which just cant be bought or at least any that will keep the clothes on the line if the chances to blow a little hard. The colored woman who helps Aunt Betty mornings now that she has the baby and Justine there, said that they had some at the Western Auto Supply Co. and she would get me some so I told her to do so at the ten cents a doz. which she said was the price. But low! the ones that I wanted, and a very flimsy variety compared with the pre-war one that I have cost me 24 cents a doz. $1.44 cents for six doz. which is not many. I used to get a gross at a time and then often did not have enough to hang all my wash and used to borrow from Aunty Hi.

After writing your letter yesterday I found that the day offered a lot of news but just saved it for todays letter.

First; I knew I should have gone along with your Dad to Pueblo to keep him out of trouble and sure enough he got arrested. As he was coming thru Avondale he thought he slowed up but evidently not to the satisfaction of the courtesy patrolman for the fellow caught up with him a little way out and told him he had gone through at 45 and the speed limit is 30. Dad is sure that our speedometer does not register right for he had kept it at 50, he says, on most of the road and the patrolman said he was going 60. Anyway Dad took the ticket for $8:00 and sent it in last night with an Abstract Co. check for that amount without arguing with the fellow about it. Dad says the fellow thanks him for being so nice about it.

Then while he was in Pueblo he had lunch with Frank Leonard and three of his sons, Charles,Edward and George. Poor Ed had taken his Dads car on his honeymoon trip to Santa Fe and on the way it got a leak in the crank case,I believe that was the spot, anyway in something which caused a lot of trouble and the call all but went to pieces evidently for they had to leave it down there and it will cost the dad about $200.00 to get it fixed.

While in Crews-Beggs Dad talked to Bill Grants dad who said that Bill is always writing wanting your address so Dad gave it to his dad to send to him. He is still on Guam but expects to me moved and says it will be farther—away instead of nearer. I was sure that he went in to the regular Navy but his dad says not that he is in the reserves.

Then here yesterday Dad saw Mr. Geiger and had a talk about John. He and Jewel are running a camp(cottage) at Glenwood Springs. An uncle of Johns helped him buy it. Seems that John had saved $6500.00 during his service which he used. Then the uncle loaned him another $_6000.00 and put in $12,000.00 himself. Seems that John is to get about two-thirds of the income for his share and for running it but during the dull months he is to get the whole profit, which so far has been about $12.00 a day.

Aunt Fan has her eyes on a brooder for our hen house so guess we will have to go out there after a while and look at it. Some man out at the old Walker Chicken Farm has several of them for sale. So will close now and go with her if she wants me to. I have to get part of the laundry done tonight for I have to sing a Requiem at nine in the morning and just get it done tomorrow.

*   *   *

2/13/46

Dear Mother, Dad, & Tom,

Well I guess I'll be on Saipan for awhile yet. The latest plans which have been approved by the big shots are that this is to be a 75 bed hospital. They have sent in the list of officers who will be available for return to the states and it doesn't include me. There will be only three jg's left. Oh! Well perhaps in June.

Tomorrow, if we get a plane and get aboard we will be in Guam. I am all set to go, but Rankin isn't feeling too good. If he decides not to go I think I'll go anyway for there won't be much opportunity with only 3 of us left here.

Monday evening Nichols the other fellow selected to stay and I went to a USO show and for a change it was really good. They had about 14 in the Cast with good music, singing, pretty girls and costumes. It was more or less a selection of Jerome Kerns songs. Most of the USO shows are not too good as they seem to be mostly amateur and not well put together. The service shows are usually better.

This afternoon I painted Dr. Brand's sailboat, but got most of the paint on myself. His boat is a little larger than the one that sank and has a flat bottom. It is really a nice sail boat.

Will let you know about the Trip later.

Enclosed are some pictures.

All my Love, Bill

*   *   *

Wednesday Feb.13,1946

Dear Bill:

Well your letter of Feb.3 came today,about ten days this time. But we were sure glad to get it and what a lift it gives us at least me and so I guess I speak for the others to get it.

Am glad that you had received the news of Lindas arrival and by this time you already know that her name is "Linda Justine". Aunt Fan and I went out to see her this afternoon and tho it has been only a few days since we had seen her before she showed that she had put on a little weight probably only an ounce or two but that shows on one so little. She is a good baby but guess she would like more milk than she is allowed to take for she seems very hungry.

I surely hope that it wont be long till you can see her for yourself. I think that everyone is well satisfied that she is a girl and Justine can hardly wait for her to be big enough for dressing up and fixing hair etc.

Sounds as if you and Rankin had a nice evening on the SS Boxer and spending the night too. I think that Gene too thinks it very monotonous on a ship all the time. We had a letter from him today and he is supposed to be thru with the Benson on the 6th of Mar. and then will come thru here for a "very,very short visit'" but later when he is out says he wants to take the folks on a nice trip and that they will see us then for a longer time.

You must have really enjoyed Cowgills letter with all the news of the fellows. Gee it would be really a break to be at Glenwood like Woody is especially for you if and since John is over there. We hear tho that they are closing that Naval hospital over there right away so he will perhaps get another change.

Night before last about ten the Sisks(Fred,Jean and Chuckie) came thru town on their way to Trinidad. They were pretty tired and had had a blowout at Dodge so had no spare but it was a pretty moonlight night so they went on as they were very anxious to be at their journeys end. Suppose Fred will be down to get started at Las Animas tomorrow or the next day as I think he announced he would open his office the 15th.

Guess I told you that Faunie Decker had had some sort of attack and was pretty sick. Well some people from out there who know John well and had been to see Faunie at the hospital brought the news that she had had a coronary thrombosis and that the doctor says that she has to take off 100 lbs of the 275 with which she went into the hospital. Can anyone imagine her weighing only 175?

Aunt Fan is ready for the dishes now and as we are going to church I had best hurry along so ta-ta.

*   *   *

2/17/46

Dear Mother, Dad, & Tom,

Back from Guam and it was a pleasant interlude. It wasn't quite like Hawaii last year, but was a change from Saipan. The best part was that I ran into 3 CU M.D.'s. The first morning there while trying to see a friend of the Captain's we met Dyce Thurston, who was in the class behind me. He knew where Bill Grant was so we soon found him. We then went out to see Tom Boyd also was in my class at school. We hashed over all our news of the Boys.

Saturday Grant, Rankin, & I took a trip to the Southern end of the Island. Guam is over twice as large as Saipan but not quite as large as Otero County. The Northern part of Guam is almost entirely airfields and Supply Depots. The Southern Part has not been very much disturbed and is about like it was before the war. It was really beautiful with all the palm trees, hills, and lovely coast-line. There aren't many palm trees on Saipan. The little villages look like typical South Sea Island towns of the Movies. We went to the military Gov't hosp there and they have about the same medical problems as here—Tb. is very prevalent.

The airplane was quite punctual this afternoon and we arrived in time for a swim. This evening are going to a friend of Rankins for dinner and the Stage Show that was so good.

On Guam we stayed at the quarters where they keep all the USO Show People. Some of them seem all right, but many are surely crummy appearing.

Haven't much other news for the present so shall close. Till later,

Love, Bill

*   *   *

Monday Feb.18,1946

Dear Bill:

Tonight I go to the USO and am saying for the last time but I have said that so many times that now no one believes me, hardly do I believe myself when I say it. However Mr. Harms is making all preparations to close on the 28th so guess it is real this time. We,the volunteer group are planning a party for him and his wife on next Tuesday evening so after we do that they had better leave or will their faces be red as will give them a parting gift.

This morning when we awoke the ground was covered with about four inches of very wet heavy snow. Dad says he thinks he never did see such slippery snow. When he stopped at the curb out here to bring in the milk he would not have gotten away if T. had not been on deck to give a little push. I got out as did all the women in the neighbor hood and cleaned all the walks. By noon the sun was out and it was like a spring do so in a little while all the snow was about gone and the walks that had not been cleaned were just as dry as those we had worked so hard on so my stiff shoulders tomorrow will be just a reminder of how foolish I was to work so hard.

Bob and Ginny Inman were up again Friday afternoon and it was good to see old Bob. He is not one bit different than the last time that I saw him which must have been more than two years. They were going down to Albuquerque to see His sister over the week end and will be back today or tomorrow and be here a few days then they will go up to Helena to pack up some things that they will want in their apartment and be back at Boulder in time to register on the first.

Tom and Margaret were up to Rocky Ford last eve to Marty Covers wedding. Tom saw a lot of people he knew among them the Merrifields and Mr. Wilson (supt). Mrs. M. very much wants him to go up to see her so I told him that some day he and I would run up if we find the time etc.

Bud,Marg and Bobby were over in the afternoon and then we went to their house and had some sandwitches after Dad and listened to Charlie Mc Carthy and Fred Allen.

Eleanor Willett called me this afternoon. She has a phone now after waiting for months for it. She had put in for one when she first went out to her present house but ofcourse they were just not putting in any then. Dick is out now and will go back to work at the freight depot the first of the month. I am so glad that he had seniority so that he has a job to go to. With them both working now they should get along pretty well. I still miss the neighbor on either side of me. Poor Aunty High and Aunt

Mayme. I dont run in to any of the houses around here now like I did than but maybe some of these days I will feel more at home will all these people.

Aunt Fan had thought that she would go out to the ranch or at least try again yesterday but it got stormy looking so she did not venture. Now since this wet she will probably not go for a little while. Of course the ground is very dry or was so this wet will sink in pretty fast. She may go to see Dr. Lassen tomorrow for the highways are all dry this eve.

Justine took Linda to the doctor Saturday afternoon and found that she has gained 13 oz. since birth which is very good so the little mama was very pleased.

I am wondering now if the Japs are all gone and you know what the next move for you is to be. Hope it is no worse that Saipan. Guess you have really been somewhat lucky in being able to practice a little medicine all along for Bob was telling us that Bob Maul is in Hawaii and is just a sanitation officer. Bob said to him one day when he had some little thing bothering him, a pimple or some of the sort, "What should I do for this" and Bob answered that how should he know for he did nothing but look after sanitation. Paper has run out and so have.

*   *   *

Tuesday Feb.19,1946

Dear Bill:

Dad is out to a drug store meeting and T. has just gone over to Lamberts to play bridge(Margaret went to Rocky Ford to see Marty Covers gifts and he refused to go along) so I did not get my letter done in time for it to get mailed tonight but since tomorrow is wash day I shall put two days letter in this one and send it on in the morning.

I went to bridge club this afternoon and while I played very poor bridge still I got the prize due to the fact that I had good partners.

I heard that the Kendalls had a telegram Saturday telling them that Dean had been killed and that a letter would follow immediately so evidently some real evidence had come to light about what happened to them. Saturday was Janes birthday so Dean did not show her the message till Sunday. Barbara and her husband came last night on their way to Florida where his home is and where they will locate now that he is out of the army. The Kendalls are going to go as far as St Louis with them and Dean will do some buying for the store there. They have to leave tomorrow as he has to report for his discharge in Florida in a few days.

Your letter of the 10th came this morning and gosh it seems as if that Captain should have let well enough alone and maybe you would have gotten to come home and then again maybe you would not. We will try to think that again this is a good break for you for maybe if you had gone to the Naval Base Dispensary you would have been shipped off to some more foreign place that Saipan and since the set up at that good old 202 is not bad and you are getting some experience,perhaps you are in luck. July 1, is not very far off.

So you had two letters from Mary and a valentine from Dotty. That was a pretty good days catch along with two from us.

Wonder what happened to you little boat. Maybe some one else got to it first and raised it, or do they do such things on Saipan?

Maybe if you went to Guam you got to see some of the other fellows or do you still know any who are stationed there. Guess there are still a few from here over there,I think that Bill Driscoll is, but of course you would not see them not knowing their addressed or anything.

We liked the pictures very much and gives us a good idea of your location and living quarters. The sand must be very white and clean.

Did I tell you that Bobby is wearing glasses for stigmatism. Lately his eyes would not snap back when he would look sideways as they should and sometimes he would be very crosseyed. Marg took him to Dr. Hopkins but wondered if she should take him to some one else too for she hates to have him wear glasses so much.

Dr Hopkins did not say how long he would have to wear them but she is hoping that by the time he goes to school the correction will have been made. Today Bud went up to have his eyes checked and they took Bobby so that Dr.H. could check the glasses for Bobby. He has worn them about a week now.

The USO last night showed that it is soon to close as things are being cleared out and so very few boys around. I did not check a single thing in or out and answered two questions about the time the bus would leave for the base. The janitor came in about nine so I left shortly as there was no need for anyone except just to keep the doors open till closing time.

*   *   *

2/20/46

Dear Mother, Dad, & Tom,

Another beautiful day on Saipan and we swam and sailed this afternoon though the wind was not very good. As for the rest of the news in Saipan there isn't very much. Am slated for this place I guess after they get the Japs out. Have only about 5000 left which means they have sent about 10000 back already which is really not bad, although I don't think they've lived up to any of the dead lines I've heard.

Ole Bob will soon be in La Junta. Give him my best. Would surely like to see the ole boy and will one of these days.

Tom is having his usual woman complications I see.

Dad said Al Shand is now at the Santa Fe Hospital. I remember him, He was a senior when I was a studious ? freshman. He was from Pueblo as I recall and a friend of Fisher's.

Haven't much news. Till Later,

Love, Bill

*   *   *

2/22/46

Dear Dad, Mother, Tom,

Today is a holiday—which means that we work only half as hard as usual—which isn't very much. I usually finish up all my duties by noon so that in the afternoon I can take it easy. The mornings are not quite so hot and you can do a little work. Man should only do very light things or nothing in the afternoons except go for a sail or a boat ride which is not so hot. We practically always take a nap after lunch for 1 1/2 to 2 hrs. Really is a rugged life.

Really sounds like you are having quite a lot of business these days. Moving to your new location sounds like a good deal for it will not be as noisy there and cooler in the summers I should think. The Drug store has just about been remodeled by now. There have been quite a few changes since a year ago in October when I was in L.J. Including the little Lloyd. Tom will soon be returning to Boulder. Am glad he has a room in the Dorm.

I mentioned in My last letter that I remembered Dr. Shand. He is a fine fellow, and very intelligent.

They are taking the Japs back mostly in LST's. However some of the ships are Japanese ships. I went down and looked at one of the Japs ships. It was a DE which is somewhat smaller than a destroyer. It was surely a dirty ship. They put about 350 civilians on it. Where they put them I don't know. They had built several wooden shacks on the deck and on the Fantail. They had erected a wooden out house which hadn't been emptied for some time— May have been saving it to use a fertilizer back in Japan.

Believe I have given you the news to date.

Lots of Love, Bill

* * *

Thursday Feb.21,1946

Dear Bill:

As I said probably would happen I did not write to you yesterday. I washed in the forenoon and ofcourse there are always the clothes to bring in and fold etc in the afternoon and then to church in the evening. We have begun to practice a new Mass for Easter using just the soprano and alto,just womens voices. There were about 18 present last night and if they will just keep coming we should be able to make it sound pretty good. But like always, I suppose they will come to a few practices and then drop out. Did I tell you that I am now singing alto. There are only about four altos and all those sopranos so while I am not much more help there then in the other place I feel a little more important. At Christmas time I say tenor so I guess it does not make much difference where I am they dont hear me anyway.

A week from today T. should be going to Boulder but sometimes he talks as if he would weaken and not go to September but that is probably a bad idea, better go and get it over with, and like your stay in the Pacific it will pass before we know it. I keep trying to remind myself that life is short and that I should be using my time to good advantage not just diddle the days waiting for you to get home. My mother used to say that it is wrong to wish our lives away, that is where I get the idea. But still I keep counting them anyway but try to do something useful so I wont feel so guilty.

Had a card from Aunt Mayme,she is in Idaho Springs, saying that she would be home Saturday and also that Dud had been very busy, was down to Pueblo for a body on Monday.

Justine and John expect to move to an apartment in the old Sexton house across from Junior High next week. Aunt Betty thinks they should stay at their house a little while longer but they are so anxious to go to themselves so guess that is the best way to cure the desire. Think she will sometimes wish she were back where mama could help take care of Linda. However if she were away off in another town like so many girls are she would get along so guess she will when only a few blocks apart from the home nest.

Had a letter from aunt Gertrude yesterday in which she said they had had letters from you. From the sound of her letter I guess Uncle Murray and Kitty are to have Aunt Gertrudes house while they are out in California for she said she had served eviction notice on the occupants and when she had written Kitty about it she was delighted and wrote right back to thank her. I rather think Aunt G. is glad of an excuse to get these people out as I recall she was not very well satisfied with them when we were out there last year.

Mrs. Duncan, the colored woman, is ironing for me this afternoon and that is the reason that I sit here so leisurely writing to you. She has been helping Aunt Betty in the mornings ever since Justine and the baby came home from the hospital. She is a good old soul and very faithful. But charges 60cents an hour and is very slow so it runs into money like a house a fire.

My! I most forgot to tell you that I am getting two pair of nylon hose this afternoon. Hose for ladies has been the biggest source of worry to the women and to the shop owners as well. when a shop has a few pair the women just fight over them so last week Ruben Inge put a notice in the paper that he would distribute what he gets by turn of cards which the ladies could get at his store,fill out and mail in. they would be filed according to the time of the postmark and then in turn each woman would be notified he had two pair waiting for her and she could come and by presenting the card and paying the price get them. So my card came this morning and Dad took it down this afternoon to do the purchase.

I think Reubens idea is a good one and the Denver Dry Goods send out cards to their charge customers about like Reubens so I sent that in and in due time expect I will get some from them so then I will be fixed for a while if I dont fall down and tear them to pieces.

Tom's girl Marilyn seems to still be trying to intice him for she comes up here with this Jack Davis and then they hunt up T. and take him to eat with them. Last time she told T. that she wanted to talk to him so think that he has evaded her since. Arent you glad that you are away off in Saipan where the women cant chase you around.

I believe that I am getting to be a "gabber" for I thought when I started to write this letter that there was nothing to say but I seem to have strung along here for quite some time. Well I will stop now and give you a little rest.

*   *   *

2/24/46

Dear Mother, Dad, & Tom,

Tis Sunday, but have the duty so have to sit around the room. Nothing ever happens, but we are not supposed to go on the beach or lagoon. It is a nice breezy day and it would be good sailing.

The last two days we have towed the sailboat behind Doctor Brands big power boat out beyond the reef. Then put up the sails and sailed it in the Ocean. It really goes out there, but is pretty rough. Dr. Brand leaves this week. There will only be one officer left who was here when we arrived. We now stand for duty every third day. Ours census yesterday was 92.

Our Tb tests were positive in 70% of all the children. We are now X-Raying all of them which is really a job.

I saw Bill Grant about the time Dad saw his father. Bill is in the reserves as I am. What probably confused you, Mother, is that Bill took a navy internship. At that time all Naval interns were in the Regular Navy, but when they finished their internship they went into the Reserves again unless they took special Exams for the Regular navy. He wants to get out of the navy as quickly as I do. Tom Boyd and I have only 26 points (47 required to date).

He is the only fellow I've seen with as few points as myself. It would have paid to be married and interned in the navy—oh, well.

Interesting note of Ginny Woodbridge's coming marriage.

Lots of Love, Bill

*   *   *

Monday Feb.25,1946

Dear Bill:

Saturday brought quite a thrill for us in that we had two letters from you. There was no delivery on Friday or perhaps one of them might have come then. One you wrote just before you went to Guam and the other after had returned. Am so glad that you got to take that trip before you get so tied down as surely you will be with only three doctors at 202 and especially glad that you got to see Bill Grant. Bet he was a little surprised. And Tom Boyd and Dyce Thurston, I dont remember him but do the others.

Maybe from now on there will be better shows for you as they do not have so many places to put shows so perhaps will just use the better ones.

From the sound of your letter there will be just three (jg's) at the hospital. Which one will be the big guy? Bet you try to get out of it because of the reports etc.

Your painting of the sail boat (Dr.Brand's) sounds a little like when you and Tom painted the house over in east part of town for Dad one summer. Most of the paint then was on you boys.

Is the hospital close to the officers club? The pictures dont show it, nor the mess hall where you eat.

We had a little dinner party Saturday eve at the Kit Carson. The inspiration being Hays birthday and the fact that Lea was down from Denver. Margaret also was present and after dinner we came up here and played fan-tan with matches till nine oclock when T. and Margaret had to leave. After that Shirley settled herself with a book so the old folks played a little bridge and about eleven we had the birthday cake that Shirley had bought for her "Mom", and some more ice cream. I had been to a luncheon that day so I had two big meals and ice cream twice. That was a little hard on my figure.

We went out to see Linda yesterday afternoon. My! how the little thing is filling out. Now she looks around when she hears a noise and notices things. John went to Denver Saturday eve to see his folks and do a little buying too but was to be home today or tomorrow. Uncle Earl has had arthritis in his foot. It is quite a little swollen and pains him quite a bit. Guess if he would stay off it for a while it would help but the farm needs attention just now. Aunt Betty has wanted him to go to the hot springs but he says he cant leave. Dr. Cooper gave him some vitimin D and it seemed to help some.

Went down town with a woman this afternoon to buy the gift for the Harms to be presented at the dinner which we have tomorrow eve and spent the whole afternoon. I could have done it in a half hour if I had been alone but this other woman wanted to go into every store in town and look and then too she had some other shopping which she wanted to do so used me and my car to tote her around. It is very tiresome to shop that way I think. Especially when the wind is blowing as it was this afternoon.

Had better close for Aunt Fan has the dishes all picked up and ready to wash. Guess i can start sending some packages now that you are to be in the same place for a while yet.

We heard over the radio a few evenings ago that a girl who went to CU Med school now a research worker somewhere, I dont remember, had discovered some property in the white blood cells which has something to do with cancer, they think. Perhaps we will be reading something about it ere long. Was she in school while you were?

*   *   *

2/27/46

Dear Mother, Dad, & Tom

Another day with the duty. Nichols and Walsh may go to Guam this weekend and then I'll have the duty every other day for a few days. Walsh is Still with the Marine MP's, but takes care of two wards here. He doesn't have the duty. Walsh will leave in about a month on points.

I had a real nice surprise the other day. I was reading the Alnav for figuring out points and found out that my internship in the USPHS counts towards points which gives me 5 1/2 more. If the points for medical officers continue to go down 2 points a month I should get out by Christmas.

Was sorry to learn about the two Dean's. Has anything been heard about Ben Bloom.

So young Bobby is wearing glasses. He will get used to them. It is important that he wear them now to prevent from becoming cross-eyed. His eyes will probably change as he gets older, but he may always have astigmatism, as does his father as I recall.

After tomorrow I understand there will only be about 500 Japs left. We have about 35 patients left to go. Six from my Tb wards. They are all pretty sick and would hate to be on the receiving end for them.

Believe have run out of news.

Lots of Love, Bill

* * *

Wednesday Feb.27,1946

Dear Bill:

Yesterday was a pretty busy day for me so did not get a letter off to you. It was the party for the Harms at the USO and I had to fix five lbs of potatoes,scholloped, and that took most of the afternoon and when I was about ready to take my bath and get ready to go down, they wanted me there at 5:30. Hay came so I was pretty delayed and then rushed and that always makes one a bit tired so by the time I had done all the money end of the party,collecting from the 75 present for the dinner and the gift we gave them, a lovely wool blanket and getting all those who had paid out money for this and that etc I was very tired by 10:30 when I got home.

Today I have not done enough to earn my salt for none of the family was here for dinner and I went to a luncheon at Mrs. Woodbridges. T. went to Rotary with Dad and Aunt Fan went out to the ranch. It was a nice day but the air just a little too cool for comfort without a wrap on. There were only eight at the party and Aunt Betty and I won high and second. Does not that speak well for your relatives at the great game of contract?

T. is going up to boulder with Al Jackson from rocky Ford tomorrow and since Al is to keep his car up there for a couple of weeks T. sees a chance that he will be getting home for a week end in that time. That is good news for him as well as for us.

Shirley G. came up this morning and helped me to get my unruly locks combed into the semblance of a hair do. Aunt Fan told me that it did not look as good as when I do it myself. Tomorrow I will go to Pomps for a set as we go to bridge club tomorrow night. We are rather doing society this week as with the Merrifield Club on Sat. eve.

Bobby is getting used to his glasses very well and we hope that wearing them may make a difference in his high strung nerves. Little Linda is growing right along. Bobby likes her and seems to think that she is his property.

People have been irrigating their lawns these last few days but so far I have not started. Suppose I will get in line soon however as the ground is really quite dry.

This is church night and so I had better quit now and get the dishes washed before we go. We are trying to practice a new mass for Easter but it is slow going and seems hard at first.

*   *   *

Friday Feb. no March 1 1946

Dear Bill:

You will have to have the carbon copy of this letter tonight for this old typewriter has a poor ribbon and the original is so dim that you could not read it. T. took his machine to Boulder yesterday and Dad took yours to the office. Now if Fred just takes this one, he asked if he could have it for his office, then I will have to do all the letters long hand. That might be better for think poor as my scribe is sometimes it is more legible that my typing.

Aunt fan, Betty and I went off to Pueblo today to shop and did not have much luck for there are just not any clothes to be had. Fan and I did buy hats but that was all. had a pretty good lunch and then came home. when we got here your letter was waiting and that was a thrill to come home to. Mary looks pretty cute in the pictures where you do not show and the other one looks as if you were really having fun, which we like to see.

Justine and John got moved over to their apartment yesterday and last night had a cousin of Johns, returning from service as their first house guest. We did not hear how they got along by themselves but hope that it was fine.

Heard yesterday that Blanch Todd(John's wife) has a spot on her lung and has to be in Glockner Hospital for some time. She has had other such sieges and because her sister and brother died of TB she worries about it. It is so hard for the mother to be away from home when there are two young boys like they have.

Dad is going to have the poker club next Wednesday so will have to get this room all cleaned and straightened up unless they will play upstairs. Think that they like it down here for it fools them into thinking they are so very private and secluded.

Last night at the club your Dad and I were having terrible luck and score till the last game when we met up and then he bid and made a little slam and that sort of helped not enough but that I had to give up my place as high lady to Naomi Davis and he did not pass Jim Driscoll as he would have liked to do.

One of the men last night told me that Dr. Davis says he thinks young Dr. Shand is going to do all right over at the Santa Fe. Wish young Dr. Sisson was over at the Santa Fe.

Dad is home now so will close.

Oh I forgot to tell you that Barbara Kendall and her husband are going to locate here and he is to go in with Dean in the hardware business.

*   *   *

3/3/46

Dear Mother, Dad & Tom,

Yesterday was quite a day as Jap ship came and took our patients. It was supposed to be a hospital ship, but the only thing that made it so was a couple of Jap Doctors on it. It was a Destroyer Escort and about as dirty a ship as I've ever seen. We put 37 patients on it—I know a lot of them won't survive the trip. They, also put the five lepers on it much to the Consternation of the Jap skipper. Everyone is so afraid of the lepers and they were isolated from the other people by putting them up on top of one of the little shacks. No one could get leprosy no matter where they put the lepers, but the six Tb. cases we sent were put down into the crowded hold with everyone else. I wonder how many will get Tb. out of the journey.

We put several Jap children who are orphans and have serious physical ailments. Everyone had come to like these kids and really felt sorry for them on that old tub.

We now only have 50 patients left of which 24 are Tb's. Three Medical Officers will not be kept very busy with that many. I'll still go to the Charan Kanoa and still take care of the Tb's I guess so will have something to do. There are now only about 200 Japs left and these will stay to clean up the Camp, and then be sent to Tinian. No Japs will be left on Saipan. Those who had been here a long time had a choice of going to Tinian or Return to Japan.

Tinian is not quite as large as Saipan and is only about 10 miles from the Southwestern end of Saipan.

Tom is Probably at Boulder today. As you say it won't be long till he's finished there. I remember my mother telling me life is short and we ought not wish it away, but nevertheless I wish I could hurry up and get home.

Walsh and Nichols are in Guam, but will be back tomorrow. In the meantime I have most of their patients, which isn't very many.

I got myself a new pair of big shoes yesterday. It will be my third pair. They are just the ticket for all this coral.

Believe I've run out of news. Am Enclosing a little note from the Skipper at the Military Gov't.

Till later,

All my love, Bill

*   *   *

3/6/46

Dear Mother, Dad & Tom,

Tonight for some reason I'm all excited about what to do when I get out of the navy. It's always a good Idea to think about the future. I have seriously considered being a rancher. Perhaps I shall.

Medicine however is my present job and I enjoy it very much. I would like more training in it If I'm to amount to anything. The chances are not very good until next year to get a residency. The notice about the residencies at the State Hospital might be good.

If I can get such a chance for more training there will no doubt be a lapse of at least 6 mo. between the end of my Naval career and the beginning of such a residency. I've been thinking a long time about a trip for all of us for such an interim period. Why not all of us taking off for England or probably even better South

America. Rio de Janerio or Brazil. Wouldn't that be fun. I'd really try to be a better traveling companion than I have been in the past.

Everything here is just the same. Rankin is now the Officer in Command of USNMGH#202. However, not for long as they are going to send in a Lt. Comdr. to be skipper. I'll stay for I have less points and unfortunately a little less time overseas than Nichols. The quarters are about 75 yards from the hospital.* I hardly leave the grounds except Charan Kanoa and the show every night.

Am Enclosing todays newspaper because of my name in it. Everyone is accusing me of unethical advertising.

Have not much other news. Till later,

Lots of love, Bill

*In the letter there is a little diagram of the buildings in this area.

*   *   *

3/10/46

Dear Mother and Dad,

When you receive this Tom will probably be at Boulder, but as I write it he may be spending the weekend in L.J. He has another interest in L.J. now so he'll have to keep tab on her.

The Ships have been coming here awfully slow lately and Dr. Brand has waited two weeks already for one. There is surely a difference in this place than when I arrived six months ago. There were about 400 ships in the harbor, and now only about 10 that I can see and these are a minor task force. There is supposed to be a ship this week that will take Dr. Brand, the Captain, and two military government officers. There is supposed to be a ship this week that will take Dr. Brand, the Captain, and about 7 Milt. Gov't. Officers. Our club will surely be exclusive then.

Officers who will be here for some time are looking to having their families come out. One family has already arrived—the wife of a Captain at the Navy Base. The Skipper of Milt. Gov't. and Capt. Reed, the Senior Med. Officer of the Island are expecting their families this week. There isn't much here for a woman, but I think they should enjoy it as they won't have to cook or anything. I don't know what they'll do to spend their time. No place to Shop.

There surely isn't much happening here. There is rumor that all reserves will be out by Sept. I surely hope so, but am not counting on it.

Are you thinking about a trip to somewhere when I am available. It surely sounds good to me.

Yesterday went boating, Passed the football, went to the show and played poker till 3 AM. That's the second time I have played and am now on top $ 48. Till Later,

Lots of Love, Bill

*   *   *

3/13/46

Dear Mother & Dad,

Just another pleasant warm afternoon on the tropical beach of Saipan. One of the big differences in the appearance of Saipan and Guam is the Scarcity of Cocoa nut trees here. The Japs for some reason did not like them and there now only a few left and most of them were damaged badly during the invasion. In Guam they have lots of Palm trees and it really looks like a Hollywood version of a South Sea Island.

The beach where we are was one of the big beaches, for the first landings on this Island. Not far off shore there are a couple of Stranded Tanks and a half-track. There was a sugar mill at Charan Kanoa, but there is only the wreckage of it left.

Tom is now well settle in Boulder. I'll bet he hates being away from L.J. When you're a long ways away you just resign yourself to the fact that you can't get Home, But when it's not too far away you want to go all the time. This affair seems to be pretty serious—Eh? Maybe ole T will be the first Sisson Hitched, but I hope not the only one. My heart is still open for some little girl however.

Surely enjoyed Tom's Letter. I'll bet he quickly gets into the swing of things and will be through with School before you know it. Boulder will soon be getting pretty. He picked the best time to be there. Winter quarter surely used to be a dreary one.

Really not much other news. Till Later,

Lots of love, Bill

*   *   *

3/17/46

Dear Mother & Dad,

Very little has happened on Saipan since I last wrote. I have been on Saipan now 6 months. That is the longest I've been anywhere since leaving the States. It has been a good 6 months as far as good quarters and duty. The duty really rounded out the 9 mo. internship I had. And would now like to concentrate a little more on something else. Surgery is probably the best thing to look for because (1) I've not done much surgery and (2) I think it is more of a financial factor. Not that I'm entirely mercenary but if a man expects to practice in a small place he cannot send all of his surgical cases to someone else. If he does he will loose those cases and others who might draw the conclusion he doesn't know enough to operate. I also need a little more Ob. I had good medicine in my internship. My last six months has been pretty good medical experience. Pediatrics doesn't scare me as much any more for I treat 15-20 children everyday. These of course have not received the refined treatment expected in the States. I'm now not quite as alarmed by complex cases as I once was. I think I've gained a little self confidence. At least I have had lots of patients die and it doesn't bother me as much as it did.

Now at the clinic I just about decide the diagnosis, and treatment as they walk from the door to my desk.*

Enough of my medical problems. Your Yellow stationary is perhaps not so beautiful, but even if it were old newspapers used for stationary I would still enjoy your letters. The biggest event of my day is mail delivery. I surely enjoy your letters.

Till later,

Lots of Love, Bill

* The clinic at Chanan Kanoa is held daily. The patients do not speak English. I had an interpreter, however. there were so many patients which I had to see in the allotted time that there was no time for history and physical.

*   *   *

3/20/46

Dear Mother & Dad,

In 6 more days Tom will be 25 years old. I forgot about it until today when it dawned on me.

This afternoon I played 3 sets of tennis in the hot mid day sun. I didn't win any of them, but got plenty of vit. D and Exercise. We surely have a good tennis court right in back of our quarters. The difficulty is finding a cool time of day to play.

Today the wifes of Comdr. Findly and Capt. Reed arrived. Comdr. Findly has 2 small sons and I believe Capt. Reed has a boy also. It surely seemed strange to see the two white boys out here.

The navy announced their points for June 15 as 39, which is 3 points lower than on May 15. At this rate they be down to 35 Aug 15, and I should have 35 points by then; so maybe I'll be home and out of the service by Sept 1. I guess I'll just have to wait and see.

The mail has surely been slow this last week. Only one letter during the whole week, but one day I'll get several and that will make me very happy. Until Later,

Lots of love, Bill

*   *   *

3/24/46

Dear Mother & Dad.

I started to write Tom a little birthday greeting and found that I'd thrown away his address after I had written him a short note.

Yesterday I saw Walsh off. He caught an LST to Guam, where he'll catch a big ship to the States for discharge. If I were married, I could start home next month. Since my points will make me available to return to the States about the 1st of August. I am afraid that they will hold me here until then. I'll be home though before too long anyway; so I won't worry about it. Will just wait and see what happens.

There are two cases of measles in the children that have come from the States, and they are all excited about it spreading to the natives. However, I understand that the natives here have had it before so don't imagine it will be very severe even if they do get it. Our new skipper just arrived the other day. He is a fairly young fellow in the regular Navy. He is a Commander and seems to be a pretty good egg.

Received quite a little mail the last few days so am pretty well up to date at home. Sounds like you have a full schedule for the spring. Don't miss the chance to go to Atlantic City. I probably won't get home till you get back to L.J. Would surely like to be there for the Sisson and Winchell visit.

I saw the clipping about the La Junta girl coming to Saipan. It's not bad here now, but they don't have 5 Room furnished quonsets. They'll be two Roomed. My Roommate Baker is getting ready for his wife who will come in 1 1/2-2 mo. He is trying to find furniture.

The Murray Sisson's surely seem to have more than their share of Difficulties with their health. Hope it doesn't hold up their trip. Glad you like the suggestion of a trip. I don't know who I could get for a partner to take. Since you like the Target will Enclose a Sunday Supplement Edition we got today—too much cut—next Letter.

Not much other news.

Lots & lots of love, Bill

*   *   *

3/30/46

Dear Dad & Mother,

Didn't get a letter written this last Wednesday, but don't believe it would have reached you any sooner than this one will.

We have been having quite a bit of excitement for the past three days. They reported a hurricane heading in our direction. It was a pesky unintelligent storm for it would just not arrive when and where it was supposed too. Everyone got all jittery about it. They tied down all of the quonsets and made all sorts of preparations.

Yesterday afternoon at 4:00 p.m. we evacuated all the patients left in the hospital to a cave that the Japs had conveniently built. In the morning we had discharged all those who could walk. I was OD and was afraid I'd have to stay in that disagreeable cave. Rankin relieved me for supper and at 6:00—Just 2 hr later they decided the storm wouldn't arrive till today sometime. Fortunately for me everyone wanted to stay all night with the patients except myself and I was excused from an uncomfortable night.

This morning they decided the storm had passed us and we are no longer in any danger; so we brought the patients back from the hills. I guess the storm is about at its height right now, for we are having a lot of wind and this morning had a heavy rain. I imagine the Chaumorros enjoyed humoring the American for they got out of a couple days work. They all said it wouldn't do much except blow a little, and I'm surely glad that's all it did do. A few old trees were blown over and there was some damage to the awnings etc from all the precautionary measures.

You surely had the Abstracty Business this Month. Am enclosing the Sunday Target.

Lots & lots of love, Bill

*   *   *

3/31/46

Dear Mother & Dad,

Today is the last day of March and Tomorrow I'll be starting on my sixteenth month away from the states. One of these days I'll not be counting the days weeks and months till I get home. It can't come too soon for me.

Our storm is over and last night had a movie again although it was a Roy Rogers western I went and enjoyed it. The storm interrupted a little party we had planned for the new skipper. However, we'll have it this week sometime. We had prepared the invitations and everything. I'll enclose one. Rankin was the composer of it and it is pretty clever I think.

We have surely been lucky with transportation all of the time since being overseas. Many medical officers have not been as fortunate. After leaving the G10 COMP 62 jeep in Okinawa we brought a couple here with us and they have worked very well, although they aren't any beauties.

Over a year ago tomorrow was Easter Sunday and the day they started the invasion of Okinawa.

After Mass this morning am listening to the Sunday morning music on the radio and writing you this note. There is still a little breeze, but may be able to play a little tennis this afternoon. We really have a good tennis court.

Believe I have exhausted my information. Till later,

Lots &Lots of Love, Bill

Dr. Brow has his orders and will be going to the States soon. He has surely given me lots of Help.

*   *   *

4/3/46

Dear Mother & Dad,

Thought all our moving to the safety of the caves was over after our experience last week, but last week we again moved to the hills. Yesterday afternoon they got the news of the tidal wave in Hawaii. Somebody also added Guam to the list and within 30 min. we found ourselves in the cave. I was pretty disgusted for as soon as the patients were moved we learned that the announcement of it's having reached Guam was purely fiction. We stayed in the hills and I had to stay too as I didn't stay the last time. I had the watch from 4:00-8:00 A.M. and really looked ferocious with a Pistol at my hip. I didn't relish sleeping in that completely dark, and windy cave. Surely felt sorry for the patients. I guess the wave really hit Hilo.

We are just getting settled from last week's experience, and getting all the patients back in and now have to do it all over again. We just got our X-ray machine fixed, and I am now looking at the results of some of my treatment of the Tb's and it is surely discouraging. I also now have the prisoners of war and the pediatric wards.

Have received several letters and learned of Gene's stop in L.J. The mail is sort of sporadic and inconsistent as I received the letter after he left before I knew of his expected arrival.

Congratulations Dad on your election to the Rotary presidency. Now the trip to Atlantic City is for sure.

Believe I've exhausted my news for this evening. Until later,

Lots & lots of Love, Bill

*   *   *

4/7/46

Dear Mother & Dad,

Here it is evening & I've not written my Sunday letter home. This morning & afternoon we played tennis, and stopped. despite the fact that everyone has a pretty good tan it is easy to get sunburned here. We played tennis yesterday afternoon too and my shoulders were a little sore today.

This afternoon the fellow I met from the USS Boxer was here. He is a slap happy fellow by the name of Jolly. He tells me the aircraft carriers based here are to go on a trip to China, Hong Kong & Shanghai. Boy that would be a good trip. I don't see how I can ever manage such a deal.

Had a couple of letters today, and as always surely enjoyed them. It is surely good to get the latest news of the family. I can just see most of the events happening, and even little Sisk & little Lloyd.

We picked up another leper at Charan Kanoa this last week. That's the second I've found. Who in the States would pick up two lepers in 6 months.

Have the duty today, but it is not very rushing. The only thing is we can't go sailing when we are OD. We even go to the show which is about a mile from here.

No other news at present.

Lots of love, Bill

*   *   *

4/10/46

Dear Mother & Dad,

This evening the husbands are having a dance at the club for their wifes. Lots of the husbands and wifes of the island are there and it looks like a real stateside affair. I dropped in for a minute.

They have a Japanese telescope at the club now and it is really a good one. We looked at the moon saw the craters. We were also able to locate two of the planets and think they were Jupiter and Saturn. We could even see the moons around them.

The band for the dance is now playing "Winter Wonderland" all about snow and ice and it surely makes me homesick. However everything can be interpreted or transposed to home. Haven't seen snow since the winter of 1942-43, except for the tops of Mona Loa and Monakea on Hawaii from and airplane.

I've included everything I can think in the way of figuring up points including V-12 and now have 32 3/4. I saw in the paper— the Navy News from Guam, that they have now arrived at a procedure of getting all reserves out by Sept 1. So am pretty sure I'll be home for Watermelon Day. Hope you can manage to get that car for T, for it will be better than a motorcycle. Sounds like T. is doing ok in school work even after having been away so long.

Glad that Ed G. is home. What are his plans—Believe I've covered the news—

Till Later,

Lots and Lots of love, Bill

*   *   *

4/14/46

Dear Mother & Dad,

Today is Palm Sunday and in one week it will be Easter Sunday. Hope my wishes for a happy Easter Season will not be late. I have already done my Easter duty by going to confession and communion, but will repeat on Easter Sunday.

Yesterday much to our surprise we received a replacement for Walsh. He is a low point boy so will be stuck out here till reserves are turned out. Nichols should leave next month. An Alnav came out the other day giving the procedure for getting all the reserves out by Sept. 1. and according to it I should be in the states by August 20, and out of the Navy by Sept 1. So I guess those are the plans I'll have to work on.

Had a letter from Mrs. W.B. Winchell the other day which informed me all about their home. It sounds like a grand place and she is very much looking forward to your coming visit. Hardly seems possible that Julia is a senior at CC.

Tis a pleasant Sunday morning here. Have Completed my OD, made Ward rounds, and then to Mass. Am now listening to the radio and looking forward to a quiet, pleasant day.

Am just sitting here thinking about home so had best close as have run out of news.

Till Later,

Lots and lots of love, Bill

*   *   *

4/18/46

Dear Mother & Dad,

Didn't get my letter written to you yesterday. Hope this isn't delayed very long in reaching you.

I've got a little fungus? infection on the back of my neck which is far from incapacitating, but is surely annoying. I've been fairly free from such trouble. Did have a little heat rash but it hasn't bothered after I got a little more tanned. One has to keep up his fluids and eat a little more salt than usual.

Recently I've been accompanied to the movies by Capt. Reed's boy who is about 10 yrs. I go practically every night as it helps to pass the time and get your mind off things. He is quite a brat, and his folks let him do about as he pleases.

I am wondering about little Linda. You should have been an M.D. Mother; for I think you can still diagnose more cases than I.

Tomorrow is Good Friday. I bet Tom comes down for Easter. Would surely like to be there with you all—

Really not much excitement these days around here. Had best close for now. Unil Later,

Lots and lots of love, Bill

*   *   *

4/21/46

Dear Mother & Dad,

Today is Easter Sunday and is really a beautiful day on Saipan. Have been to Mass at Charan Kanoa. They had Mass out in the open by the school. We had to sit in the sun and now we know why the Chamaurros always go to 5:00 AM Mass. The heat here is like the Missouri sultriness. The temperature rarely gets above 85. But it is lots hotter than La Junta at 110. The temperature at night goes to 75°.

Nichols, who came here with us will soon be leaving for the States for separation from the Service. He will be detached tomorrow from the hospital, and then leave on the first ship which will probably be by the end of the week. Rankin will leave in June and then I'll leave a little later. Would like to go back with Rankin but guess I'll have to stay a little longer.

Would surely like to be spending this day with you. Tom is probably home and all the family close around.

I remember Dr. McDonald. He gave us some of our lectures on pediatrics and As I recall he is a good doctor with both feet on the ground. I'm sure I'd not been as gruff as the fellow at Children's Hosp, to such gracious people as Justine & Aunt Betty.

I enjoy the letters of Tom's and thanks for sending them on.

Have been trying to improve my tennis game, but believe I've only produced Blisters on my feet.

Not much other news for the present. In about 5 weeks you'll be going to Atlantic City.

Lots and lots of Love, Bill

*   *   *

4/24/46

Dear Mother & Dad,

My roommates wife arrived today so he left me. Several other wives arrived today also—so it is getting to be quite a stateside place. Nichols will probably leave tomorrow on the ship on which they arrived. We now have as many officers at the hospital as we have enlisted men. We have the skipper, Rankin, myself, a hospital corps officer, and four nurses. We have 4 corpsmen and 4 other enlisted men. If it weren't for the native help they wouldn't be able to run this place.

Some of these natives are really very good. And some are quite attractive—How would you like to have a nice little brown daughter-in-law—There are several that would probably be pretty nice. Guess I've been here too long.

I received the notice of the subscription to Omnibook from you for 7 months. Thanks a million. However I hope I don't have to wait here to receive all of the issues.

One of the Tb. patients died today whom I've taken care of since I've been here. It was a little disheartening as he was one of the first pneumothoraxes and was only 18 yrs old.

Marie Hall should be very good help. You've surely been busy with all those abstracts.

Guess I've run out of News again Till Later

Lots and lots of Love, Bill

Enclosed are some pictures Mary sent me.

*   *   *

4/28/46

Dear Mother & Dad,

Today I received Dads letter telling of the big news of Tom's engagement. I can't say that I'm all together surprised as it has seemed that such an event has been developing all along. Tom warned me that I ought not delay my homecoming too long. I'm sure she is a fine girl to have a lug like T. propose to her. I'm surely anxious to get home to get acquainted with my future sister-in-law. Also, want to hear the details of Tom's proposal.

It was a year ago yesterday that we left Pearl Harbor for Okinawa.

This has been quite a busy weekend at the hospital—Not for me, but the other boys. They sent over a Jap boy with a fracture arm for our renowned expert medical attention. Also had a woman who didn't want to part with her placenta after delivery so had to remove it. A priest from Charan Kanoa got into a jeep accident and broke his Rt. humerus so at least had some excitement.

Now have the OD every other day, but it is not very difficult. I still have the Tb's and Charan Kanoa and also have pediatrics (5), and the Jap prisoners of war (7) so am not worked to death. It would be pretty difficult to overwork one Bill Sisson.

Am enclosing a picture from the Target showing Baker & wife who just arrived.

Till Later,

All my love, Bill

*   *   *

5/1/46

Dear Mother & Dad,

Today completes my 16 month since leaving the states. I've surely got them counted right down to the days. I still can't quite count the days. I hope I shall be home and out of the navy by August 20, but I'm afraid I can't count on it as I'll have to wait after Rankin as he has more points than I. I'll just have to wait and see how much time I can talk out of the skipper.

Diagnosed a case of Amebic dysentery today which you don't run across everyday. It was a POW and we can cure it. That's the way it goes—the people you want to help you can't and the people you don't care so much about you can cure.

I was quite upset to hear about Linda. I'm afraid I couldn't be of much help—especially here when I don't know anything about the signs and symptoms. You can't always say what will happen. The gracious Lord may bestow health again to her.

I find I hardly know anything about Margaret. From the clipping in the paper it appears that she is teaching school. As I recall she was just starting Denver University the last I knew—

Captain Reed the senior Medical officer of the island tried to get our skipper to trade Rankin or myself for one of the Medical officers at the Naval Base dispensary. It seems the Medical officers up there wasn't getting along with the Executive Officer. Our Skipper Said no.

I find the La Junta girl has arrived on Saipan. She was a roommate of Baker's Wife. I've not met her.

It surely sounded Good to hear you had brushed my. Clothes. I hope they will fit me. I don't think I've changed any. I may have put on a little weight.

I'm afraid I won't be able to find a little very soon for you mother, but perhaps within the next few years I can. I'm afraid I'm not very speedy in that business and you must give me as much time as Tom has.

Am glad you received the Easter Bouquet. won't be able to make it for your birthday on the 16h. I can never remember the Date of Dad's birth day—about Sept 7th—No? Anniversary—Aug 7th-28th this year.

Not Much other News

Lots & Lots of Love Bill

*   *   *

5/3/46

Dear Dad & Mother,

It's been some time since I've answered your letters. Perhaps within a few months I'll be able to call in person.

Before I forget it I am forwarding an important figure for you. My taxable income for the year of 1945 was $2199.44. I hope I sent on to you my taxable income for the year of 1944. Would you please ask Bud or find out how much money I owe the gov't. I've never made out an income tax return. If you would find out for me what I need to do to get square with Uncle Sam. I would surely appreciate it.

This afternoon we had a graduation exercise for 24 nurses whom we have trained since the hospital was established. It was quite an impressive ceremony. All the little Chaumorro girls looked very nice in their white uniforms.

I've never sent you my congratulations on being elected Pres. of the Rotary Club. They couldn't find a better man anywhere and in addition I know he is a real booster of Rotary.

It looks and is time that the Point system is over now and I didn't make it. However under the new system I should be out at about the same time. Not too soon for me.

You should be going to Colorado Springs tomorrow or the next day. Then shortly following Uncle Murray & Aunt Kitty will be in Colorado. Would surely like to have been in L.J. for that occasion.

Enjoyed the pamphlet boosting MacDonald for District Govenor.

Seems different to have brother Tom Engaged.—Well

Lots & Lots of Love, Bill

*   *   *

5/5/46

Dear Tom,

I got your good letter telling me all about your engagement. I'm really happy for you and send my Congratulations.

I was surely glad to get the invitation to be best man, since I had already accepted in my last letter. You know that I really want to be your best man since I didn't give you much of a chance to select anyone else.

I wish I could say for sure when I'll be home and out of the navy, for I think it would greatly help with your plans. I think I should be home and out of the navy by August 20. It's possible I might be home a little sooner, but just depends on how things work out.

Give ole Ty Woodruff my best regards. Would surely like to have seen ole Herb Hoover.

General Ike—Ishenhour (Sp ?) was here on Saipan the other day, but he evidently didn't get a chance to look me up.

I'm still looking after a few sick people in the mornings and sleeping in the afternoons. When Rankin leaves I guess I'll be standing the duty alone. Might as well for that's about all there is to do except see shows. I've seen so many shows that it'll be difficult to get me a theater again.

Sure am looking forward to your wedding. That is really something to be looking forward to—especially you.

Till Later,

Love, Bill

*   *   *

5/5/46

Dear Mother & Dad,

It is again Sunday and Starting out as a bright sunny day. I just finished the duty and have the whole day to loaf around.

Friday afternoon General Eisenhour (Sp?)Was on Saipan for a couple of hours, but I didn't even see the procession of cars and I understand he drove right by our place. He only stayed for a short time and went on about his business.

This mornings Target has a picture and clipping about the graduation we had for the nurses the other afternoon. I shall enclose it in this letter.

I received a letter from Aunt Fan and From Tom yesterday. Surely enjoyed them Tom told me all about his engagement, and invited me to be best man. I had already written and accepted the invitation.

You will be leaving for New York soon, and before you leave have a favor to ask of you. I'll be separated in or about San

Francisco, and have no dress clothes. So I would like for you to send my blues to Virginia where I can pick them up. Please include a white cap cover, and a few white shirts. I'll drop Ginnie a line to be expecting them.

I was surprised to hear that Dud had given up his place. I had thought everything was going along very well with him.

Don't believe I have much more news for the present.

Until Later

Lots & Lots of Love

Bill

*   *   *

5/8/46

Dear Mother & Dad,

This coming Sunday I understand is Mother's Day. I've sent you no flowers or Greetings or anything to let you know I'll be thinking of you. A week from today is your Birthday Mother. Happy Birthday from Saipan

Got the Clipping about the big parking area they built in San Francisco. That was built before I went to San Francisco. It is quite a place all right. Such a thing in Denver would be a good Idea. Also the letter from the Ø4. Hope they have better luck than when I was their.

The Murray Sissons are Probably in L.J. Now. It won't be long till you are on your way back East. Everything will work out fine for us; For you will be back settled at home before I arrive. Surely looking forward to it!

Lots & Lots of Love, Bill

*   *   *

5/12/46

Dear Mother & Dad,

Today is Mother's Day and Thursday is your Birthday. I've surely been thinking about you today, and hoping soon I can give you a great big kiss.

On this side of the Pacific we are just waiting till we can get to the other side.

Yesterday afternoon they had a big ceremony at Chalan (I have been misspelling it all the time) Kanoa, honoring the officers' wifes. They had the school choir sing and the Kanaka's do their native dances. It was really very good and very interesting. The Kanakas enjoy doing their native customs and putting on the native costumes. There was a picture in the paper—which I'll enclose. This is really getting to be a regular army & navy place with the wives here. They have set the big line between the officers & enlisted men's wifes. Following the ceremony they had a fancy buffet supper for the officers and their wifes here at our mess—then a dance later. I had supper, but didn't attend the dance. This place is not for me. At least the army & navy part of it.

Yesterday afternoon Mrs. Baker brought the little La Junta girl down to swim, and I met her. She seems to be a very nice girl. We enjoyed relating our news about the home town. When introduced and I told her I was from L.J.—"Oh, you're Tommy—I of course regretted to deny it after the manner in which she said it, but I had to inform her I was his brother.

I get most of your letters, but I usually get the whole weeks in one day, and then others go without. I've not seen any Green Tea.

The Ringworm or whatever I had has cleared completely.

Believe I've brought you up to Date on Saipan.

When you get this letter you'll be getting ready for your trip back east—Have a good time.

Lots and lots of Love, Bill

* * *

5/16/46

Dear Mother & Dad,

Received your letters from Colo. Sprs. By now the Sissons have come and soon will be gone. Was glad to Hear that Mac. got the district Governorship. You will have a great time in Atlantic City together.

Missed wrighting to you last night. I went out for the evening for a change. The Bakers had a little get together. A couple from La Junta was there. They are very nice kids and I enjoyed exchanging bits of information.

There is a big rumor going around now that we'll leave the island by 6/15/46 which is a good rumor if it is true but I am taking it with a grain of salt.

The medicine angle is still very interesting. We haven't seen any typhoid fever which is rather strange until the last week. Two young boys died from some obscure cause and Dr. Rankin's post mortem showed that it is no doubt typhoid. I just wonder if I'll ever amount to a darn—I should have diagnosed one case. Sometimes—I get a little afraid of myself. I just get lazy and don't use my head.

Have covered the high spots. Till Later,

Lots & lots of love, Bill

*   *   *

5/19/46

Dear Mother & Dad,

The sun is just coming up on Saipan and I'm up only because they called me for a delivery. It's a little late to be going back to bed, and a little early to eat breakfast so shall write you a letter.

Friday night had a big time. A doctor from the Army hospital had a date with a navy nurse at the naval hospital and needed another man for her friend. We went to an army dance and since the date I had was a very good dancer I had a fine time.

They got a message yesterday from the commander of the Mariannas that all the doctors in the Mariannas would be held until the last batch of the reserves were shipped home, so it looks like it will be later than June 15 Probably July 15—Aug 1. before I'll be on a ship heading for the good ole States.

Sounds like you had a very enjoyable time in Colo Sprs and then a good visit with the M. Sissons. This has really been quite a spring for you. You will be about ready to get on the train, when this reaches you, for Atlantic City. I'll surely be anxious to hear all about the big time back there. Is Tom going to work this summer in L.J. and finish school this fall as he once proposed.

Enjoyed Lil Abner very much—also enjoy your letters very much. Till Later,

Lots & Lots of love, Bill

*   *   *

5/22/46

Dear Mother & Dad,

Received the letter following the receipt of mine asking you to send my uniform to San Francisco. I'm afraid that it built up your hopes prematurely. I was afraid it might and didn't stress the fact that I have no inside information about a quick departure. As a matter of fact things now don't look so good as all medical officers will have to wait till the last quota to go. Under it however we should be in the States by Aug 20 at the latest.

You may have left L.J. by the time it reached Colo. I'll drop you a note at Winchells.

Was sorry to hear that Ginny was having some difficulties with her job. She is a grand girl and has had several disappointments, but always takes them in stride. She surely won't have any difficulty getting what she wants and needn't put up with an unpleasant situation.

Sunday the Staff—Rankin, Trainer (our hospital corps off), the skipper, and myself and our four nurses went on a picnic to the other side of the island. Had a good time. We have another medical officer now so now only have the duty every third day. His name is Bradsher. He is a jg like Rankin and I. He finished med. school in the class behind me.

Rankin has a bright idea to buy a jeep out here cheap, take it back with us, and then we will be able to drive home. At first it appealed to me, but am beginning to wonder—that long a jeep ride would be—unbearable and besides I want to get home the quickest way possible after I hit the west coast.

Think I have covered the high spots.

Lots & lots of love,

Going home is such a pleasant way to occupy ones mind that we have already begun planning on it. Bill

*   *   *

5/26/46

Dear Mother & Dad,

I presume that the Santa Fe is striking along with the other railroads, so shall write this letter home. However I hope that it is in time for you to make your trip East.

Today has been a busy day. We immunized the whole village of Chalon Kanoa today against tetanus and typhoid fever. It was quite a job and took us 8 hours. I've just about got blisters on my fingers from giving shots. Everything went along all right however.

Yesterday afternoon Rankin and I went to a cocktail party a dentist friend of Ranks had for his wife. Saw lots of people we knew there and had a good time. The night before I was invited over to the McComas'—The Bakers were there and had a right good time.

I see I've surely misinformed you or created at least a wrong impression as to when I might be coming home. I think by now I realize and hope you do too the only thing I can expect is to be in the States by Aug. 20. I'll be home for Watermelon day, I hope.

Hope the trip comes out O.K.

Till Later all My Love, Bill

*   *   *

5/28/46

Dear Mother & Dad,

I wrote Sunday to you to La Junta, and not knowing the result of the railroad strike I didn't know whether you would get to go on your trip. I was surely glad to hear that it was quickly over. I'll sent this note to Atlantic City and hope it reaches you before you leave.

The mail has picked up lately and the other day I received a letter in 6 days. It surely makes home seem not to far away when they come quickly.

I was sorry I built up your hopes for my return to the states in June. It was surely unintentional and without basis. It surely is good to have some family close to you that eagerly await my return. All I know now is that I'm supposed to be in the States by Aug 20. I wouldn't have expected you to come to the west coast and miss your trip East. In fact it will probably be a lot easier for you, if I just speed by the west coast and meet you at home. When I land I'll give you a ring and we'll decide. Would surely like to be home for the return trip of the Sissons to Missouri, but it looks doubtful.

Today received the registration card for the boy scouts. I think I am really a little old to be a Boy Scout, but surely was really nice to know ole Buck remembers me.

They have fixed up a building to be a Tb. sanitarium here and it is really going to be quite nice. They may move the patients over this Friday. I'm beginning to see the results of some of our treatment and it is quite satisfying to see that not all of them die.

Believe I've run out of news.

Lots & Lots of love, Bill

*   *   *

5/30/46

Dear Tom,

Surely enjoyed hearing from you. When you get this you will be back in La Junta and finished with spring quarter. I'll bet you did all right with your exams and came out with good grades.

You are probably about right about my return to the States— about July 30. or perhaps after. The sooner the better—as far as I'm concerned.

Tom I wrote a letter to Harvard Med. School about a course there they are offering to doctors and told them they could write to me at home. If a letter comes from them to me would you open it, keep the letter, and tell me what it says.

Not much other news for the present; so shall Close

Love, Bill

Enclosed is a cartoon from Esquire. We got a kick out of.

*   *   *

5-30/46

Dear Mother & Dad,

Didn't get a letter off to you yesterday. I had a slight cold and when to bed early and am much improved today.

Today is Memorial Day as well as Ascension Thursday and I went to Mass, but didn't go to the memorial day services as I was

O.D. Did have some fun this afternoon as Rankin and I took out an appendix. The first in a long time.

When you receive this letter you will have completed the convention in Atlantic City. Hope you had a good time. I'll bet you had a grand time and are having a grand time with the Winchells. Especially with Bill off to show you the sights.

My status on coming home remains the same—No prospects very soon. Had a letter from Walsh and he is all settled in Philadelphia with a residency in medicine. I wonder what I'll do. I'll just have to wait and see what I can get after I get home. I think I'll just relax at home for a nice long time.

Also had a letter from Tom. He'll be home next week and will be able to help out at the office, for which Dad will be happy. Tom knows these military outfits pretty well as he doesn't expect me home until July 30th, and that is probably more nearly right.

Surely have enjoyed the Lil Abner clippings and will miss them while you are back East.

Believe I've given you the latest news of Saipan.

Lots & Lots of love, Bill

*Memorial Day was always on May 30, until they decided to make it and some of our other holidays on a Monday to give people 3-day weekends.

*   *   *

6/2/46

Dear Mother & Dad,

Today I start on month #18 and hope don't have to count more than one or two more. One year ago tomorrow we landed on Okinawa. We slept in the mud—That was quite a day.

A big fear came over us yesterday that we might be kept out here until we had completed 2 years service in the navy which would mean 5 more months for me. However Rankin and I read this order today and don't believe we are included in it.—Just those V-12 Med Students who went on active duty on or after 1 March 1946. We are still planning on being home and out of the Navy by Aug 20.

Am surely anxious to hear about your trip. I'll bet your having a grand time. Tell the Winchells hello for me.

This morning we gave shots to some of the natives again, and only a few and were finished in 1 1/2 hr. I have the duty today, but there isn't very much happening. As a matter of fact went to the show. Very little happening these days.

Till later

Lots & Lots of love, Bill

*   *   *

6/5/46

Dear Aunt Fan,

Now is a good time to let you keep up on my welfare, and at the same time answer your good letter of over a month ago. I'm not very speed-o at this writting letters.

At the present time there is not much news of interest on Saipan. We are all just hoping that by some hook or crook we'll be able to leave this tropical isle. There isn't much immediate hope for that however.

Surely enjoyed hearing the latest news about the ranch. Would surely like to get home and ride a little and see the cows.

We—Rankin & I have been working on the Tuberculosis problem a little bit. He reads the X-ray films and I see about getting the people in for the X-rays and take care of the cases of tuberculosis. We have X-rayed all of the school children—then the X-ray machine broke down. After considerable trouble we got it fixed and then started on the village proper. They have the village divided into five districts and as soon as we finished the first village district the machine broke down again, which brings us up to date. I don't know when we will get it fixed again and still have 3-4 more mo. work to do to finish the village and maybe more. I hope we won't have to see it's completion. They have also built a really good or rather remodeled other quonset huts into a very satisfactory sanitarium. I think we shall move into it soon.

During the Japanese time and the first year of our occupation no strict Isolation was done,for these people and as a result when we first came here we saw an awful lot of deaths due to tuberculosis, especially in children. We have isolated all the cases we know about and think we really have done some good. If the survey is completed and all cases are isolated, I'll bet Tb. will be less than half the problem in five years that it is now, (here on Saipan).

Sort of a dull subject, but just to let you know I am just not lolling in the sun all the time.

Love, Bill

*   *   *

6/5/46

Dear Mother & Dad,

Hows the New York atmosphere? I was surely glad to get the letter following the strike and telling that you had the go—ahead for your trip for now I know you got to make your trip all right.

Had some disappointing news the other day—the Captain—the senior med. off. of the Island interrupts the dispatch on the V-12 boys so as to include us in it. If that's the and that's the way it is until someone higher tells the Captain different, we will have to stay in the navy 2 years altogether after internship. I've got 19 mo. He also says the rotation plan for Med. off. if 20 mo. now—So we are all befuddled about it. No one knows and you just can't tell what is going to happen.

Another party tonight at the golf course, but I'm stuck with the duty again. Oh well a show—a little reading, and that's my evening anyway.

Have a grand time. Hope to see you soon. Not much news on this end.

Till later

Lots & Lots of love, Bill

*   *   *

6/9/46

Dear Mother & Dad,

I shall send this letter home as it might not reach you in N. York, and will therefore avoid a delay in your receiving it.

I surely wish I were home now and the family would be together again for a wonderful summer. Perhaps I'll get home before School starts this fall and then we'll be together for awhile.

I am receiving the Omnibook and have enjoyed several stories in it all ready. Also received a box from you the other day. I think it a good idea not to send any more however for it will be 2 months before they would get here.

This morning we again gave shots and think now we'll rest for a few Sundays. Only have one more day of shots to go and we'll probably do that in about two weeks.

The nurses here got their orders. At least one new one will come to take their place. That will be the third batch of nurses we've seen. I've had five skippers since I've been here. As a matter of fact Rankin and I are the old guard here now. We just keep hoping.

Rankin and I play a big game of tennis this afternoon, but we only finished one set 9-7.

Am about out of news—Till later

Lots & Lots of love, Bill

*   *   *

6/12/46

Dear Mother & Dad,

Tis another day in Saipan and have just returned from a rather entertaining movie. We just got back in time as it is now raining a little shower. The rain here is much like that on Hawaii— suddenly clouds up rains & then quits. Sometimes it rains fairly hard.

We moved the Tb. patients into the Tb. sanitarium Monday. It was once the orphanage when the Japs were here. The Japs never looked after their orphans and thus had quite a few. The Chaumorros always take care of their orphans. There are three wards—One for men & one for women—and the other is not in use yet. There are about 30 patients all together-

Last night went up to the Bakers for a little get together for the #202 staff and really had a fine time.

You are at the present time having a big time at the Winchells. Have been receiving the clippings that JoAnn has sent and surely enjoyed them. Received two books from you today and am looking forward to reading them.

Had a letter from Joe Cowgill & Woody Brown who are looking forward to separation from the Navy, but don't know what they'll do after that—neither do I.

Believe I've covered the highlights of the news. Till later,

Lots & Lots of love, Bill

*   *   *

6/16/46

Dear Mother & Dad,

This letter will find you home again after your trip. I've received the letter written on the train and one from Atlantic

City. Am glad that my letter reached—you there. I was afraid that it might miss.

This morning Rankin had planned sort of a picnic for some of the native nurses and myself, but the higher-ups didn't approve. I don't mind at all, for I got some extra sleep in fact slept past my appointment for Mass with one of our Navy nurses. It's the first time I've missed taking her. I then went to a later mass at the Army hospital.

Ole Rankin the son of a gun is now a Lieutenant. He just made it and I miss by a month and 5 days. I hope I'm not in the navy long enough to make it. It'll probably be at least 2 and probably 3 months before the next AlNav.

Ole Rankin is really lucky there is a good chance that he may leave Saipan the end of this week. Maybe with luck I'll get away the middle of July. That's only a month away. But don't count on it as you know the navy.

Little Jo Ann has surely been getting the clippings out to me.

I guess it's summer in Saipan for my prickly heat has come back a little. "Prickly" is surely a good word for it.

Till later, Lots & Lots of love, Bill

*   *   *

6/19/46

Dear Dad & Mother,

Perhaps the mailman will reach you first, at anyrate Mother will call if he reaches her first.

This is a big day for me as tomorrow I board a ship for the beginning of my trip home. I got my orders this morning, though I knew they could send me if they would for the last 4-5 days.

I don't see how they can hold me now by any means except a hurricane.

The trip is apt to be a long one, but won't seems long since I'll be going East and getting more nearly the same time as you. Will try to write, If not—See you in the good ole USA.

Lots & Lots of Love, Bill

*   *   *

6/19/46

Dear Mother & Dad,

I know you will be as happy to receive this letter as I am in writting it. Tomorrow at 1:00 PM we muster to board the SS Samuel Chase on the start of the trip home. It may come as somewhat of a surprise to you as it has to me.

About 5 days ago orders came through to send back all of the remaining reserves, but Capt Reed of the navy base requested to hold all his Doctors. Our Skipper fortunately for us just requested more help, but he wouldn't tell me whether I would get to go until this morning. Rankin had the ok several days ago and is all set.

I've been packing and saying good bye and getting my orders straightened out all day. It all has come so sort of as if it would just be another dream that it just doesn't quite seem as if we are really going.

It looks like it is going to be sort of a long trip. The Chase first goes to Guam and then from there to the Panama Canal and the East Coast. We may change in Guam and wait for a ship to the West Coast—I don't know.

Still have lots of packing to do—so perhaps I'll get a chance to write before I get home, if not maybe the next you hear from me will be by phone.

Lots and lots of love, Bill

*   *   *

6/23/46

Dear Mother & Dad,

Have completed the first lap of the long journey home and although it was only 150 mi, we are at least getting into the traffic. We didn't leave the 20th as the ship was late. We left the afternoon of 21st and arrived in Guam yesterday where we left the ship to catch another here bound for the West Coast. No telling how long we'll have to wait—at least a week probably.

Got ahold of Willie Grant last night and we went to the Com. Mariannos Club for a couple of drinks. Rankin and I were pretty tired so we left early. Today Grant is going to take us to his place for dinner and then the beach for a little sun & water. Grant is still attached here in Guam, but is going to try to get released to go back with us. He would be here only 2-3 weeks anyway.

It was really sort of sad for me to leave Saipan. The natives really made me feel as if they were sorry to see me go. All those in the dispensary gave me little gifts as did many of the Tb. patients and native girls. It was really enjoyable working with them. The navy nurses had a party for us on Friday including 2 nurses who are also leaving soon. They had some flower leis made for us and they were really beautiful.

After we left, there is only one Medical Officer at the hosp. the skipper. He is really a good egg—especially for letting us go. He made me kind of busy, but I think one man can handle the job if he lets the natives do most of the work. The Skipper is about 32 yrs old and is a commander in the regular navy. He is smart enough, but just lacks a little self confidence, which seems peculiar in his case as he is quite an athlete. This experience of being alone should really do him a lot of good. Hope we don't have to wait too long here for a ship.

Till later

Lots & lots of love, Bill

*   *   *

San Francisco—August, 1946
Maddie Wright, Bill Sisson, Margaret Mae Floyd,
Johnny Moore, Virginia Sisk, Clair Rankin